PYTHON FOR EXPERIMENTAL PSYCHOLOGISTS

Edwin S. Dalmaijer

Routledge
Taylor & Francis Group

LONDON AND NEW YORK

First published 2017
by Routledge
2 Park Square, Milton Park, Abingdon, Oxon, OX14 4RN

and by Routledge
711 Third Avenue, New York, NY 10017

Routledge is an imprint of the Taylor & Francis Group, an informa business

British Library Cataloguing in Publication Data
A catalogue record for this book is available from the British Library

Library of Congress Cataloging-in-Publication Data
Names: Dalmaijer, Edwin S., 1990- author.
Title: Python for experimental psychologists / Edwin S. Dalmaijer.
Description: Abingdon, Oxon ; New York, NY : Routledge, 2017. | Includes bibliographical references and index.
Identifiers: LCCN 2016019564| ISBN 9781138671560 (hardback : alk. paper) | ISBN 9781138671577 (pbk. : alk. paper) | ISBN 9781315616933 (ebook)
Subjects: LCSH: Psychology, Experimental – Data processing. | Psychology, Experimental – Research – Computer programs. | Python (Computer program language)
Classification: LCC BF39.5 .D35 2017 | DDC 150.285/5133-dc23
LC record available at https://lccn.loc.gov/2016019564

ISBN: 978-1-138-67156-0 (hbk)
ISBN: 978-1-138-67157-7 (pbk)
ISBN: 978-1-315-61693-3 (ebk)

Typeset in Bembo
by HWA Text and Data Management, London

Visit the companion website: www.routledge.com/cw/dalmaijer

Printed and bound by CPI Group (UK) Ltd, Croydon, CR0 4YY

PYTHON FOR EXPERIMENTAL PSYCHOLOGISTS

UNIVERSITY OF
WINCHESTER

Martial Rose Library
Tel: 01962 827306

Programming   ience,
and Python i   uitive
variable man   imple
arithmetic to
  Python for   ıming
experience w   alyses
in Python. T   ; how
to get input f   g. eye
trackers); hov   basic
principles of   liques
required to a
  Written in   ython
that are rele   s also
accompanied   gures,
along with e   ion of
Python.

Edwin S. D   nental
Psychology,   dalone
software pac

To be returned on or before the day marked above, subject to recall.

CONTENTS

TABLES AND FIGURES

Tables

Figures

ABOUT THIS BOOK

This work is targeted at researchers in experimental psychology and cognitive neuroscience, who have no previous experience with Python or programming. It is suitable for students and staff, and aims to provide a basic working proficiency in Python. After working your way through this book, you will have the knowledge and skills required to script experiments and analyses.

A major problem in psychology education is that students have very little exposure to programming, even though most academic jobs require that one knows how to script experiments and data analyses. It is hard to believe how much manual labour some researchers (or their assistants) go through to process their data. They spend countless hours selecting, sorting, and moving data from one spreadsheet to another, only because no one ever bothered to teach them how to code. That's a waste of time, and of human intelligence. If you want to work in experimental psychology, but do not know how to do programming (yet), this book might just save a few years of your life.

Please do note that truly mastering a complete programming language is a long process that is unlikely to ever end. This book is *not* a complete overview of every detail in the Python language. Rather, it teaches you what you need to know as a scientist in the fields of experimental psychology and cognitive neuroscience. The things you learn from this book will help you understand more advanced programming. This is important if you want to develop yourself further. You need the basic knowledge from this book in order to know what to ask on programming forums, and to understand the answers that some nerds will give you there.

About Python

Python is an amazing programming language, originally developed by Guido van Rossum (who remains Python's benevolent-dictator-for-life). It sports an easily readable syntax, a very large user base, and extensive functionality. It can be used for almost anything, including basic calculations, flying drones, live-streaming your cat to the internet, plotting world domination, and much more. Python is at the optimum of usability and functionality, which means that you can learn how to do actually useful stuff relatively quickly.

About the author

Edwin Dalmaijer studied psychology (BSc) and neuroscience and cognition (MSc) at Utrecht University in the Netherlands. He is currently reading for a PhD in experimental psychology at the University of Oxford, where he is an Early Stage Research Fellow funded by a grant from the European Commission's Marie Sklodowska-Curie programme.

Edwin's profoundly lazy nature inspired him to learn how to automate menial data-handling. He got hooked on programming, and spent his nights exploring Python. Ever since, Edwin has been exploiting his programming skills to steal the jobs of more talented researchers who have less coding experience. He authored several Python toolboxes, standalone software packages, and teaching materials.

ACKNOWLEDGEMENTS

This book would have never been here, if it wasn't for the support of colleagues, friends, and family. I won't explicitly name everyone here, for space reasons, but I'm grateful to all of you.

My eternal gratitude goes out to Ignace Hooge, who introduced me to programming in Matlab, and to Sebastiaan Mathôt, whose code and help allowed me to find my way in Python. I'm also grateful to the people behind PyGame and PsychoPy, for providing excellent documentation, and to lots of anonymous (aspiring) programmers, for asking and answering tons of questions on the Stack Overflow programming forums.

In addition, I should thank all the people at Utrecht University who had the courage to hire me for programming tasks. A special mention for Chris Paffen and Stefan van der Stigchel, who were the first to employ me there.

As for actually writing this book, I am indebted to Masud Husain, my PhD supervisor. Even though he's always reminding me that I should stay focused on my research and my thesis, he was incredibly supportive when he found out that I was writing this incredible distraction. I also owe the late Glyn Humphreys, our former and beloved head-of-department. He allowed me to organise the Python course that this book is based on, and brought me in contact with the publisher (additional thanks to Eli Fulcini, for encouraging and facilitating that). I'm also grateful to the participants of that course, for their enthusiasm, and for their suggestions and corrections.

Huge thanks go to my colleagues at the University of Oxford, my labmates in the groups of Masud Husain and Mark Stokes, my friends, and especially to my partner Kiki. All of you managed to cope with my continuous nagging and obsessing over this book, and you provided me with the support I needed to pull through. Bonus points for Laura Grima and Sean Fallon, who inquired about (or were involuntarily bothered with) my progress almost every day in the final weeks before the deadline.

I feel the people at Routledge deserve a mention here too, especially the copy editors who had to deal with my submission. It was a bit of a mess due to a variety of incompatibilities between my open-source software, file formats, and fonts on the one hand, and the proprietary versions my work had to be converted into on the other. Thanks so much for your patience! I'm also grateful to Michael Strang, who handled the project until the book passed reviews and was commissioned, and to Julie Toich and Elizabeth Rankin, who handled it until publishing.

Finally, I would like to thank my parents, for doing me the massive favour of making and raising me. Mum, Dad, I owe you guys.

1

PYTHON

Python is a programming language. Not just any programming language: it's currently one of the most popular in the world. Whichever type of ranking you use, Python usually ends up in or just under the top five. It even seems to be the most discussed language on Reddit's programming forum (www.reddit.com/r/programming/).

Why is this important? There are two main reasons why you should care. The first is that a more popular language has a larger user base. If you run into an issue, there is a better chance that someone else has run into the same problem, and they might have already solved it. Almost the best thing about the internet is that it's full of programming resources. Simply search for your problem (or error message) and you are very likely to find the solution on Stack Overflow (http://stackoverflow.com) or a similar programming forum.

The second reason you should care about how widespread your programming language is, is that it could inform you how beneficial it is to learn it. If you learn a very obscure language, such as E-basic (from E-Prime) or PCL (from Presentation), you will be perfectly able to do most of what you want in your academic research. However, you might find it hard to find any other employers that will be interested in your obscure skill. If you care about your CV, it would be better to learn a language that other labs or companies are familiar with. For example, in academia you will have better chances of being hired if you know Matlab or Python. Outside academia, more web-oriented languages are usually preferred, such as Java, PHP, and Python. Therefore, knowing Python could be good for your career.

One of the reasons Python is so popular is that it is very versatile. You can use it to make computer games, do PC-to-PC communication, or to run websites. As an experimental psychologist, this versatility means that you will be able to use it to not only create your own experiment scripts, but also to do an automated analysis of your data. In addition, you could use Python scripting and a webcam to spy on co-workers (*Stop stealing my cookies, Nancy!*), or to do exciting computer vision projects.

Another reason for Python's popularity is that it is easy to use. Python scripts are readable. Very readable. So readable, in fact, that some compare it to reading English. While that is definitely an exaggeration, script readability is one of Python's strong points. It appeals to new users, like you, who should be able to pick up the language relatively quickly.

Obviously, there are also downsides to using Python. Experienced programmers will point out that it is a relatively slow language – and they are right. Python is sluggish, especially compared with 'proper' programming languages (like C and C++). Fortunately, there will be very few times when this will be an issue, because Python will still work faster than you need. Even when you run into speed issues, some clever soul will have found a way to solve them. The NumPy library, which you will get to know later, is an example of how you can do quick calculations in Python (its underlying source is not native Python, which is irrelevant to users, but makes it quicker). Despite its appeal, some people will move on to more basic languages after learning Python. Yet, even for them, Python was a good first language to learn the core concepts of programming.

In sum, Python is good for beginners, and for those who like a versatile and user-friendly programming language.

If you're a fan of xkcd comics, you might be pleased to know that there is a Python module for creating plots in xkcd style: http://jakevdp.github.io/blog/2013/07/10/XKCD-plots-in-matplotlib/. Cool!

Installation

Python can be installed on a lot of different operating systems. These include Windows, OS X, and almost every version of Linux. You can find installers at http://python.org, and most Linux systems will likely have it pre-installed. But before you start downloading stuff, read on to know what to install.

Versions

There are a few different version of Python. Although they are similar, it does matter which one you install. The two most relevant versions are Python 2.7, and Python 3.4. You might be inclined to think 3.4 is the newest version, and you would be right. However, 2.7 still receives updates. Although Python 3 is the future, Python 2 is still actively maintained to support people who haven't upgraded yet.

Why don't we all upgrade to Python 3, you ask? Well, Python is not just the basic programming language. It has been extended by third parties (mostly volunteers), in the form of external packages or *libraries*. These are collections of code that are useful for specific things, like programming cognitive experiments. Libraries that were developed for Python 2 do not always play nice with Python 3. Not all libraries have been updated for Python 3 yet, partly because Python 2 is still available. Another issue is that most of the external packages are maintained by enthusiasts who could have stopped maintenance, or could be too busy to perform a time-consuming upgrade. Remember that these people are volunteers: they have work to do, partners to please, children to raise, friends to see, and lives to live. These are widely regarded as more important than upgrading a Python library.

The same is true for a different distinction between versions. 'Recently' most operating systems have received a major upgrade, they went from 32-bit to 64-bit. This is because computers became increasingly powerful, and were built with increasingly more working memory. A 32-bit system can work with up to 4 gigabytes of memory at a time. Usually, tasks do not require a computer to address more than that in one go. However, some tasks do require more. For these, a 64-bit system is ideal.

Virtually all modern computers sport a 64-bit processor. However, there is a difference between processors and the operating systems (OS) that they run. If your processor is 64-bit, you can still run a 32-bit OS, or even 32-bit applications within a 64-bit OS. The other way around is not possible, so you can forget about running a 64-bit OS or 64-bit applications on a 32-bit processor.

So what's the connection with Python? As you might have anticipated, there are 32- and 64-bit versions of Python. As with versions 2 and 3, not all Python applications can run on 64-bit yet. This means that you will be safer off installing a 32-bit version.

Bottom line: you should probably install Python 2.7, 32-bit. (But check out the Anaconda and WinPython sections before you do!)

Dependencies

You just read about external packages that add extra functionality to Python. Some of these external packages run without any further ado. You install them, and they are ready to use. Others, however, require other external packages to be installed.

When one package requires another, this is a *dependency* for that package. In this book, we will use the external packages listed in Table 1.1:

TABLE 1.1 Python libraries used in this book

Name	Website	Description
SciPy	http://scipy.org	A collection of libraries with all you need to do science. Useful for statistics and distributions.
NumPy	http://numpy.org	Does fast calculations on multi-dimensional arrays.
Matplotlib	http://matplotlib.org	High-level, very elaborate plotting library.
PyGaze	http://pygaze.org	Toolbox for eye-tracking experiments, with an easy syntax. Depends on PyGame and/or PsychoPy.
PyGame	http://pygame.org	Amazing package for game development. Perfect for experimenters, who basically make boring games.
PsychoPy	http://psychopy.org	Designed for psychophysics experiments; has impeccable timing and great functionality. Depends on pyglet and/or PyGame, and on PIL and NumPy.
PIL	http://pythonware.com	The Python Imaging Library (PIL) can be used for basic computer vision, and to handle most image formats.
pyglet	http://pyglet.org	Package for OpenGL multimedia. Required by PsychoPy, which in turn is required for PyGaze.

If you are building your own installation, be sure to get matching packages (for example, versions for 32-bit Python 2.7). Better yet, install Anaconda (see Chapter 2), which already includes half of the listed dependencies. Even better, install a modified version of WinPython (see the WinPython section), which includes all of the above packages.

Anaconda

Instead of installing Python, and then installing all required external packages separately, you could opt for installing Anaconda. You can download it from the Continuum website: http://store.continuum.io/cshop/anaconda/. Despite being produced by a company, Anaconda is free. It comes pre-loaded with a lot of cool stuff; but you will still need to download PyGaze, PyGame, PsychoPy, and pyglet.

WinPython

WinPython (http://winpython.github.io/) is a Windows-only solution that saves you from having to bother with dependencies. This beautiful piece of work includes a lot of the packages required in this book, and has the bonus advantage of being portable. That means it will run from anywhere: You can copy it to a USB or external hard drive, and it will run from there. This is a great feature if you are a student, suffer from a restrictive IT department, or do not want to install Python on all computers you use. Anywhere, anytime you need to do programming: simply bring this portable version.

Another amazing WinPython feature, is that there is a modified version that comes with all the dependencies you need for this book. You can download it from the companion website:www.routledge.com/cw/dalmaijer

FIGURE 1.1 This is an example of an anaconda you should not download
Source: Wagner Meier, via Wikimedia Commons under the licence https://creativecommons.org/licenses/by-sa/3.0/legalcode.

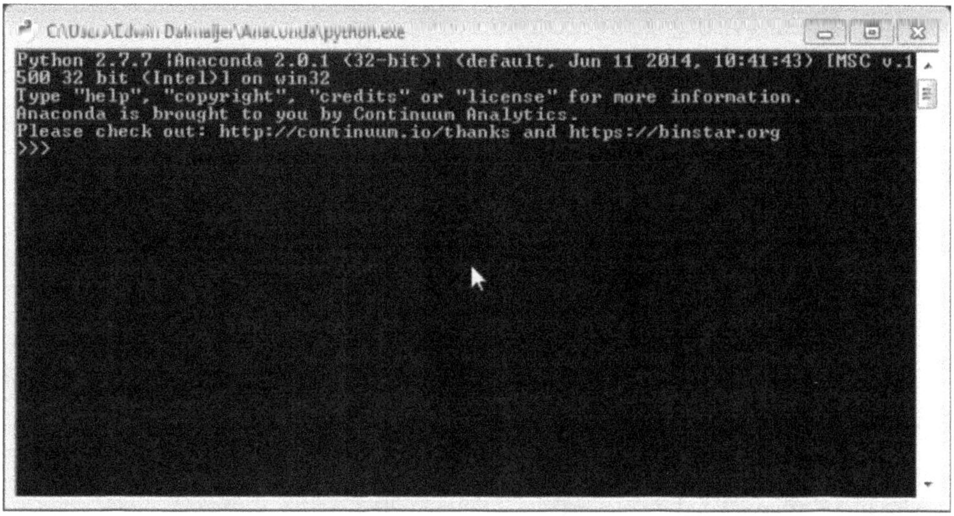

FIGURE 1.2   This is a Python Interpreter

Interpreter

Even now that you have an installation up-and-running, you might still have no clue where to start. Time to get hands-on!

You can speak to Python (and it can speak to you) via an *interpreter*. The most basic of interpreters is python.exe on Windows. To open it, go to where you installed Python (usually under C:\python27\python.exe, or C:\Anaconda\python.exe). If you are using WinPython, simply open the WinPython folder and open WinPython Interpreter.exe.

If you are using OS X or Linux, open a terminal and type `python`, then press Enter.

In the first sections of this book, you will primarily use the interpreter. It's a great tool to get to know the basic concepts. Once you get to the point of writing actual scripts, the book will switch to using a script editor.

Editor

A *script editor* is a bit like Open/Libre Office Writer or Microsoft Word. It allows you to write text, and will often have a few features that make this easier (such as syntax highlighting). Code editors can be very simple. In fact, you could write scripts using NotePad on Windows (or equivalent simple text editors on other platforms).

Of course, you will likely want something more helpful. If you installed Python from its website, you will have automatically installed IDLE (Integrated DeveLopment Environment). This is a simple editor, but works just fine. A rather exceptional code editor is Spyder. It works on all platforms, and is actually included with both Anaconda and WinPython. So if you have installed either of those, you already have it.

Spyder has some very useful options. Firstly, it sports a familiar interface for people with experience in Matlab, R, with the NetBeans IDE (for Java, PHP, C, and C++), or

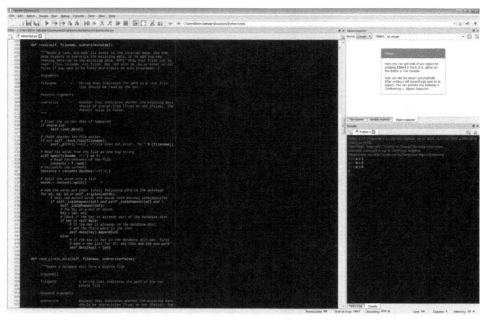

FIGURE 1.3 This is the Spyder code editor in a white-on-black, greyscale colour scheme. +10 old-fashioned nerd points!

with the Java Editor. That is also an advantage for novice programmers, who will later be able to switch to other editors more comfortably. Another advantage is that Spyder has its own built-in interpreters (called *consoles*). If you run a script in Spyder, you will have the option of running it in a standard interpreter, an IPython interpreter (which is more advanced), or an external system terminal. You might not realise it yet, but this versatility is nice, and these are useful options. Finally, Spyder is highly customisable. This means you can set the colouring of nearly everything (background of windows, different kinds of code, etc.). Set your backgrounds to a dark colour for extra nerd credibility!

The most important reason for using Spyder, though, is its brilliant code introspection. While you type, Spyder checks your code for errors. It will also automatically provide documentation for the functions you are typing.

The PyGaze version of WinPython and the Spyder editor are highly recommended.

2

VARIABLE TYPES

Variables are very important in programming. Before learning about what they are and how to use them, perhaps it would be good to get some intuitive feeling for them. In the following sections, you will play around with all sorts of variable types to get a hang of things.

Numbers

Numbers can be represented in different ways. The most notable difference is between integers and floating points. An *integer* is a number without a fractional part, for example 10, 0, or –5. A floating point, or *float*, is a number with a fractional part, such as 1.23, –99.9, or 1.0.

Intuitively, it would seem floats can be used to be more precise. However, never say this when you are at a mathematician's house party! Fractions can be represented precisely by writing them as an integer division, whereas floating point numbers are only approximations of an actual number. For example, if one third of all mathematicians are overly anal party-poopers, you could precisely represent this number as 1 / 3. Alternatively, you can only approximate the precise number by using 0.333. This is close, but will never represent the *actual* number of mathematicians that ruin parties by being overly anal about stuff like this.

Fortunately, in soft sciences like psychology, people never really care about this. We do observations that can vary from the amount of milligrams of a certain substance in the blood of a participant, to the number of participants that answer 'yes' to a questionnaire item (e.g. 'Have you ever been at a party that was ruined by a mathematician who was being overly anal?'). By definition, an observation can never be of absolute precision. It can, however, be precise enough. What precise enough is, and how precise your observation can actually be, depends on what you investigate and how you do your measurements. For more information on how many decimal numbers to use in a specific case, search the internet for 'significant figures'. I highly recommend reading at least the Wikipedia entry (http://en.wikipedia.org/wiki/Significant_figures). In this book, we will ignore the notion of significant figures completely, but that doesn't mean you should.

Now that you are confused about the preceding information, let's get back to the point: Python can deal with integers and floats, and you still don't have a clue when to use which. Here's a rule of thumb: *always use floats, unless integers make more sense*. When do floats make more sense? If you want to do some arithmetic on your data, when you use proportions, or when you're confused about what type of number would make the most sense. When do integers make more sense? If you are dealing with an indivisible unit, for example the size of an image in pixels. You simply cannot use 199.5 pixels, so your image will have to be either 199 or 200.

Integers

Let's start actually using these concepts. Fire up a Python interpreter, and start typing:

```
2 + 2
```

Expected result, right? 2 + 2 = 4. In your face, Radiohead! Now let's try subtraction:

```
5 - 3
3 - 5
```

This should also be an expected result to you. Five minus three does indeed equal two. And three minus five equals minus two. Let's move on quickly:

```
3 * 2
```

Brilliant, Python can do multiplication. Would it be able to do exponentiation as well? Let's try 3^2 (the square of three, or three to the power of two):

```
3 ** 2
```

The syntax might seem a bit weird, with the double asterisk. You might be used to exponentiating with a caret or circumflex (^), e.g. in spreadsheet editors (LibreOffice Calc or Microsoft Excel) or Matlab. In Python, the caret is used as a different operator (you will learn about it later on), so don't use it for exponentiation!

All right, now let's check out division:

```
5 / 3
```

Wait, what? 5 / 3 = 1? Is Python joking? Not quite, as you have asked for an *integer division* of five by three. In fact, five divided by three is one, with a remainder of two. When you divide two integers, Python only reports the result and not the remainder. To report the remainder, use the % operator:

```
5 % 3
```

So 5 / 3 = 1, and 5 % 3 = 2. This actually makes sense! However, you were probably looking for an answer like 5 / 3 = 1.6666666666666667. For this, we need to turn to floats.

Floats

We want to calculate how much 5/3 is, but we would like the answer to be an approximation rather than an absolutely precise answer (because we are not an overly anal mathematician). For this, we are going to use floats. You can use floats by writing numbers as a fraction:

```
5.0 / 3.0
```

Boom! 5.0 / 3.0 = 1.6666666666666667. The cool thing about floats is that they are contagious. If you use only one in your calculation, the answer will automatically be a float. Example:

```
5 / 3.0
```

However, you should be careful with this logic: although using a float in a calculation will result in a float answer, it will not force numbers in intermittent calculations to be floats! Example:

```
(5 / 3) * 2.0
```

The answer might seem wrong, but: 5 / 3 = 1, and 1 * 2.0 = 2.0, so (5 / 3) * 2.0 = 2.0. Now try the alternative:

```
(5 / 3.0) * 2
```

5 / 3.0 = 1.6666666666666667, and 1.6666666666666667 * 2 = 3.3333333333333335, so (5 / 3.0) * 2 = 3.3333333333333335.

Now that you understand what a float is, you can use them in exponentiation. Aside from being a good exercise, float exponentiation can also be useful. Let's take the square of three (3^2) as an example. In Python, you write this as 3**2, and the result should be 9. The inverse of this calculation, is taking the square root of 9, which is 3. Now, in mathematics, the square root of a number can also be expressed as an exponentiation. In this example, the square root of 9 is the same as $9^{1/2}$. In Python, you can write this as 9**0.5. Try the following in an Interpreter to see for yourself:

```
3.0 ** 2
9 ** 0.5
```

Did that blow your mind? The square root of a number can be written in exponent notation! This is SO exciting!

Remember the Pythagorean theorem? In a right triangle, the square of the hypotenuse (that's the side opposite the right angle) is equal to the summed squares of the other two sides. You can write this as $a^2 + b^2 = c^2$. The square root of c^2 will give you the length of the hypotenuse, so you can write $c = \sqrt{a^2 + b^2}$. Let's say $a = 3.0$ and $b = 4.0$, and try this in Python!

```
(3.0**2 + 4.0**2) ** 0.5
```

BOOM! You got this number thing down!

Assigning variables

Variables are a key concept in programming. In fact, variables form the building blocks of all your future scripts. They act like pointers, allowing you to access data via labels that you assign yourself. Variable names can contain letters (upper and lower case), some characters (such as underscores), and numbers; but they must always start with a letter. For example, you can make a variable with name `test` to refer to the number 5, like so:

```
test = 5
```

You can now use this variable to do all sorts of freaky stuff. You could, for example, use it in calculations:

```
test - 3
test + 5
test + test
```

As you can see, using it in calculations does not actually change the variable. If you would want to reassign it a different value, simply overwrite it:

```
test = 4
```

If you want to know the current value of a variable, simply type its name in the interpreter and press Enter.

```
test
```

You can also change variables by referencing themselves:

```
a = 2
a = a + 1
```

You can even create new variables based on the values of others!

```
a = 2
b = 3
c = a + b
```

You can make it even more confusing, and define one variable by using another:

```
a = 2
b = a
```

Be wary that both variables (`a` and `b`) point to the very same data (2). So Python only keeps 2 in memory, and knows that variable names `a` and `b` are associated with this number. This may seem like an unimportant sidenote now, but it will prove to be important when you learn about lists.

Booleans

Booleans are named after the logician George Boole, who approached logic as though it was a type of algebra. He formalised logical operations, which we now know as AND, OR, and NOT. Logic operations can produce one of two results: True or False, which can also be denoted as 1 and 0.

These operations are built into practically all electronic circuits, and are an essential part of programming. It is imperative that you learn how to implement them, and that you sacrifice a goat to George Boole to honour his legacy. (*Note: don't actually sacrifice a goat. Goats are amazing animals, and should be left alive. If you feel like sacrificing something, please sacrifice some lettuce to a goat. In Boole's honour, of course.*)

Before you go on to start your own lettuce-sacrificing Boole fan club, you should probably find out how Booleans work. Type the following into an interpreter:

```
a = 1
b = 1
a == b
```

The result should be True, indicating that both variables point to the same number. Note that while '=' (one equals sign) means *'assign this value to this variable name'*, '==' (two equal signs) means *'equals'*. This is different from what you are used to, because normally '=' means *'equals'*, and '==' does not quite mean anything. It is important to remember this difference, because you will at some point write 'a = b' where you intended to write 'a == b', and that mistake will likely crash your script. Let's move on:

```
a = 1
b = 2
a == b
```

The result is now False. We could also ask Python whether a *'does not equal'* b:

```
a != b
```

This is True, because a and b do not point to the same value. You can also directly use True or False in your code:

```
a = True
b = False
c = True
```

This allows you to use logic operators, such as AND (&) and OR (|):

```
a & b
a | b
```

The first will test whether both variables are True, and will return True if they are. The second will test if either variable is True, and will return True if one or both are. There is another operator, the exclusive or (XOR, ^), which tests whether two Booleans are the same, and returns True only if they are different:

```
a = True
b = False
c = True
```

```
a ^ b
a ^ c
```

The XOR operation is True for the first test (a ^ b), but not for the second (a ^ c). Contrast this with the OR, which is True in both cases:

```
a | b
a | c
```

Note that Booleans can be used with normal mathematical operators, but then the values True and False will be interpreted as 1 and 0.

```
True + True
True - True
True + False
3 * True
```

Whether or not this makes any sense, depends on the context in which you use these operations. Normally, multiplying True by three does not make it any more True. (*Except to politicians, who seem to think their drivel becomes more True by repeating it.*)

Finally, another cool thing about Python is that you can use English words to do the same things as the symbolic operators. You can check if variables are equal:

```
a = 1
b = 2

a is b
a is not b
```

You can also use written logical operators:

```
a = True
b = False

a and b
a or b
not a
```

Letters

In some situations, you will need to use some text; for example when you want to present instructions to participants. In Python, a text is referred to as a *string*. These are defined by using either single or double quotation marks. Python provides a number of built-in functions to easily manipulate strings to do cool stuff, as you will see real soon!

Strings

Time to define your first string. Type the following into an interpreter:

```
a = "Hello World!"
```

```
b = 'Hello World!'
```

Although you have used two different kinds of quotation marks, the resulting strings are identical:

```
a == b
```

The advantage of being able to use more than one type of quotation mark, is that you can use the other within the string:

```
a = "Programming is 'fun'..."
```

There are more characters that you can use within strings. Some of these are useful for formatting:

```
a = "I love newlines.\nI wish I could marry them.\n\nSigh..."
b = "TABS\tARE\tAWESOME\t!"
```

As you might have seen, \n produces a return (or a 'newline'), and \t a tab (a bit of whitespace).

You can use mathematical operators to combine strings:

```
a = "spo"
b = "on"
a + b
```

Or to multiply them:

```
a = "lala"
10 * a
```

But not to subtract or divide them, because that would not make any sense.

String functions

Functions have not been explained yet, but you will get to know them quite intimately later on. A function is a collection of code that will make your computer do something specific. Some functions are standalone things; you can *call* them at any time without having to do anything more than typing their name. One such function is print, which will simply show a value in the interpreter:

```
print("Hello world!")
```

This may not look very useful to you now, but you will learn to appreciate it later on.

Some functions are not independent, like print, but are associated with a certain type of variable. Strings, for example, have a few of these built-in functions. Programmers usually refer to these built-ins as *methods*. A few examples:

```
a = "I love you!"
b = "get away from me, crazy person."
a.lower()
```

```
a.upper()
b.capitalize()
```

The `lower` method will make all letters in a string lower case, whereas the `upper` method will make them all upper case. This is great if you want to emphasise things, or if you are speaking to a foreigner that does not understand English. The `capitalize` method will make only the first letter upper case.

Some other funky string stuff:

```
a = 'test'
a.center(10)
a.count('t')
a.replace('s', 'x')
```

As you could see, the `center` method adds spaces to the front and back of your string (the amount of added spaces was 10 in this example), centring the original string. The `count` method counts the number of occurrences of `'t'`, or anything else you would like to count. The `replace` method can be used to replace one part of the string by another. This could be very useful if you want to convert files, and need to change file names:

```
a = 'example.jpg'
b = a.replace('.jpg', '.png')
print(b)
```

Wildcards

One thing you might have tried, is combining a string with a number:

```
a = "I'm number "
b = 1
a + b
```

You will have faced a TypeError, because you can't combine strings and integers in this way. There are other ways to make this work, though. You could use the `str` function, to turn your number into a string:

```
a + str(b)
```

This works, but will turn into a hassle once things get complicated:

```
a = 'Every '
b = ' days, I brush my '
c = '. I like this.'
a + str(30) + b + 'finger' + c
```

A better alternative is to use wildcards. Wildcards are special characters, that you can choose to fill out with other values. To replace the previous example:

```
a = 'Every %d days, I brush my %s. I like this.'
print(a)
```

You can recognise the wildcards by the % sign. The letters directly after the % sign indicate what kind of value the wildcard is for. `%d` is a place holder for a *d*ecimal number, and `%s` is a place holder for a *s*tring. Let's try filling them out:

```
a % (30, 'finger')
```

The % sign after the string indicates that you will fill the places that are held by wildcards with actual values. The values are provided between round brackets. Let's try another, using the `%f` wildcard for *f*ractional numbers:

```
'%.0f percent of British people are female.' % (50.7)
'%.1f percent of British people are female.' % (50.7)
'%.2f percent of British people are female.' % (50.7)
```

The `%.Xf` wildcard will round your number to X decimals. Pretty neat, huh?

Sets

Up until now, you have only seen single values (although strings can be seen as a collection of individual characters). Sometimes it can be useful, or even necessary, to combine multiple values together in a single set.

Think about a reaction-time experiment: a researcher collects one response time in every trial. If you want to calculate the median response time, it could be very useful to collect all individual response times in one variable, rather than having one variable for each individual response time. This allows for easier access and calculations.

Now imagine the researcher was also using an eye tracker. This device allows you, amongst other things, to measure pupil size. It will produce lots of data; sometimes over 1000 data points per second! If you want to store all these in a manageable fashion, you simply cannot use a single variable per data point. It would be more efficient to store all data points from one trial in a set. Of course, with a lot of trials, it would be very inefficient to use a single variable per trial. So you will want to store the data sets of every trial into another set. You then end up with a set (of all trials) that contains more sets (each of a single trial), each of which contain a lot of data points (each data point being the pupil size sometime during a trial).

You can easily see this escalate, for example if the researcher decides to add electroencephalography (EEG) recordings. With over 64 electrodes, thousands of data points per trial, and hundreds of trials, you will end up with sets of sets of sets of data! This 'big data' might seem overwhelming now, but you will get a grip on it later on. First you will need to learn about the basic building blocks of Big Data: variables that can hold multiple values.

Lists

Although some terms in programming might seem a bit weird, the name of the list variable is quite self-explanatory. A list is simply a list of other values. Remember how a variable is a reference to a value? A list is a reference to a bunch of values. These values can be integers, floats, strings, or any other variable type. Let's see this in practice:

```
a = ['one', 'two', 'three']
```

The variable a is now a list (you can recognise it by the square brackets) that contains the values 'one', 'two', and 'three'. If you want to use one of the values, you will have to use its *index*. The index of a value is its position in the list. That sounds simple enough, but Python has a little quirk that could throw you off a bit at first: it starts counting at 0. So the index number of the first value is 0. The index of the second value is 1, the index of the third is 2, etc. To refer to a particular index, use the variable name and the index between square brackets:

```
print(a)
print(a[0])
print(a[1])
print(a[2])
```

Simple enough, right? So why would Python start counting at 0? Well, it makes sense on multiple levels. One of the reasons is that it allows you to index by counting backwards. Lets see what happens if we use –1 as an index number:

```
print(a[-1])
```

It accesses the last value! So counting backwards from 0 allows you to index from the end of the list rather than from the beginning. There are situations in which this can be very useful! (For instance when you want to impress n00bs with your 1337 haxx0r skillz.)

Apart from accessing one index at a time, you can also index a whole *slice*. You can do so by using the index of the first value you want to access, a colon, and the index of the value *after* the last value you want to access. For example, a[0:3] means 'the values in variable a from index 0 to index 3 (not inclusive!)':

```
a = [4, 5, 6, 7, 8, 9]
print(a[0:3])
```

Something you will see a lot later on, is the concept of *nested* lists first. A nested list is a list that is contained by another list:

```
a = [ [10, 20, 30] ]
```

The first index of this list contains the value of the nested list: [10, 20, 30]. This nested list can also be indexed:

```
print(a[0])
print(a[0][0])
print(a[0][1])
print(a[0][2])
```

Nesting can go on ad infinitum, but it is highly unlikely that you would want to do that. An example of where nested lists are useful, is in the numeric representation of an image. You could represent the colour of each pixel by a list of three values: one for red, one for green, and one for blue. You could represent every horizontal line in the image as a list of nested [R, G, B] lists (one for each pixel). You could put all these line-lists in a single list, which would then be a good representation of the entire image.

The following is an example of a 3 × 3 pixels image of a white (255, 255, 255) plus sign ('+') on a grey (128, 128, 128) background:

```
[[ [128,128,128],  [255,255,255],  [128,128,128] ],
 [ [255,255,255],  [255,255,255],  [255,255,255] ],
 [ [128,128,128],  [255,255,255],  [128,128,128] ]]
```

One could refer to such a construction as a *matrix*. You will learn about how to create and use these a bit later on.

Lists, like strings, have a few built-in functions that can be used to manipulate them. For example, the `index` method can find the index of a value in a list:

```
a = ['a', 'b', 'c']
a.index('b')
```

There is also a method to reverse the order of a list:

```
a.reverse()
print(a)
```

If you want to remove values from a list, there are two methods to choose from. The `remove` method allows you to choose a value of which the first occurrence should be removed. The `pop` method allows you to choose an index, of which the value will be removed.

```
a = [10, 20, 30, 40]
a.remove(20)
print(a)
a.pop(0)
print(a)
```

Of course, there are methods to add values to a list as well. The first of these is the `append` method, which allows you to add values to a list:

```
a = [10, 20, 30]
a.append(40)
print(a)
```

Another list-expanding method is the `extend` method. This is intended for joining two lists together:

```
a = [10, 20, 30]
b = [40, 50, 60]
a.extend(b)
print a
```

If you think append and extend seem to do the same thing, and are interchangeable, you would be wrong. Have a look at the following example:

```
a = [10, 20, 30]
b = [10, 20, 30]
c = [40, 50, 60]
a.append(c)
b.extend(c)
print(a)
print(b)
```

As you can see, the append method nested the second (c) list within first list (a), whereas the extend method combined two lists (b and c) into a single one.

At this point, it would be good to remember what was explained about the nature of Python variables (see the section on assigning variables): they are merely pointers to values. Let's look at the following example:

```
a = [1, 2, 3]
b = a
print(a)
print(b)
```

Both variables point to the exact same value. Neither of them contains a unique copy of [1, 2, 3]. Now look at what happens if you change one:

```
a.append(4)
a.extend([5,6])
print(a)
print(b)
```

Both a and b changed! Ahh! Usually, this is not the kind of behaviour you would like to see. In programming, we say that lists are mutable. This means that you can change them if you want to. This also means that they can be accidentally changed, so be careful.

There are ways to get around this issue. For example, you could use a mathematical operator to extend a list:

```
a = [1, 2, 3]
b = a
a = a + [4, 5, 6]
print(a)
print(b)
```

Another alternative is to use the copy function, which we have to import from the copy module (more on importing will follow later, just go with it at this point). This will force Python to make a copy of the underlying value, instead of having both variables point towards the same underlying value:

```
from copy import copy
a = [1, 2, 3]
b = copy(a)
a.append(4)
```

```
print(a)
print(b)
```

Tuples

Lists are great, but you have seen some of the risks of using them on the previous page: they are susceptible to accidental mutation. Although you now know ways to prevent accidental changing, they do require you to pay attention. If only there was some kind of list that cannot be changed, to prevent you from accidentally changing it altogether … Well, it must be your lucky day! Look no further, because here is the immutable list-like variable: the *tuple*.

```
a = ('one', 'two', 'three')
print(a)
```

Although it looks like a list, smells like a list, and actually feels like a list, it definitely is *not* a list! Just try appending something:

```
a.append('four')
```

Oh no, an error! Maybe you could change one of its values?

```
a[0] = 'zero'
```

HA! You puny mortal cannot touch it! However, you can completely overwrite it:

```
a = ('zero', 'two', 'three')
```

As you might have guessed, the take-home message here is that lists can be changed, but tuples cannot. However, all variables can be overwritten by simply redefining them. There are further similarities between tuples and lists, namely in the `count` and `index` methods:

```
a = [1, 1, 2, 3]
b = (1, 1, 2, 3)

a.count(1)
b.count(1)

a.index(2)
b.index(2)
```

So, when should you use tuples, and when lists? It is mostly up to personal preference. In general, people use tuples when they know the values they contain should remain *constant*. For example, the resolution of a computer display should probably be the same throughout an experiment. And maybe the size of a particular stimulus too.

Vectors

All right, so now that you can make a list of values, let's do some calculations with them! Try adding one to a list of numbers:

```
a = [5, 6, 7]
a + 1
```

Too bad, lists do not work like that! If you want to add one to each value in your list, you are going to have to do it value by value:

```
a[0] = a[0] + 1
a[1] = a[1] + 1
a[2] += 1
print(a)
```

Two points to note here. The first is that "a[0] = a[0] + 1" is the same thing as "a[0] += 1". The other point is that manually adding one to each value is a hassle. It seems like little work if you only have three values in your list, but imagine doing this for an entire EEG dataset! Programming is supposed to make your life easier, not to enable you to do manual labour in a cooler way.

Computations that involve a whole line of numbers are called *vector calculations*, and they can make your life very easy. To do them in Python, you need to get acquainted with NumPy (Oliphant, 2007).

NumPy is an *external package* or *library*. It is not included with the basic installation of Python, and is created and maintained by volunteers. Everyone can make external packages, and a lot of useful ones are available. Think of them as apps on your phone: they were not there when you first got it, but you can download them to add functionality. This is both the beauty and the Achilles' heel of Python, as external packages can be really useful, but they can also be hard to find, and some are an absolute pain to install.

Fortunately, some brilliant minds have put together Python installations that contain all of the main scientific libraries. They are called Anaconda and WinPython, and a modified version of the latter comes with this book. The instructions in the first chapter of this book should have helped you download it. If you are using these installations, please do read on. If not, make sure you install NumPy before you go on to the next section!

NumPy arrays

All right, time to create your first *vector*. In NumPy, a vector is called an *array*, and they can contain any type of value you would like. They are very similar to lists in that sense. Keep in mind, though, that you can only do calculations with NumPy arrays that contain numbers, or that contain nested NumPy arrays that contain numbers. You can easily make a NumPy array out of a list:

```
import numpy
a = [1, 2, 3]
```

```
b = numpy.array(a)
```

```
b + 1
```

You can index NumPy arrays in the same way that you index lists:

```
b[0] += 1
b[1:3] += 10
print (b)
```

Great! Now see what happens when you try other mathematical operations:

```
a = numpy.array([1, 2, 3, 4])
a - 2
a * 3
a / 2.0
```

You can even do this using two (or more) arrays:

```
a = numpy.array([1, 2, 3])
b = numpy.array([2, 4, 6])

a + b
b - a
a * b
b / a
```

One very important thing to note here is that the way these calculations are performed is *per point*: a*b is equivalent to a[0]*b[0]; a[1]*b[1]; a[2]*b[2]. This is not a matrix multiplication, and that can be confusing to some people. For example, users of Matlab (a different programming language to which NumPy is very similar in a lot of ways) will expect a*b to reflect a matrix multiplication, which is the default in that language. Discussing which is better for what (and why) is beyond the scope of this book.

There are tons of other very cool things that you can do with NumPy, and you will have a chance to play with it a little later on.

Dictionaries

The final set you should learn about is called a **dictionary**, but is better know by the abbreviation **dict**. A dict is somewhat like a list, in the sense that it is a variable that can hold more than one value at a time. However, the way you index these values is quite different! Take a look at this:

```
a = {0:1, 1:2, 2:3}
b = [1, 2, 3]

print(a[0], b[0])
print(a[1], b[1])
print(a[2], b[2])
```

Currently, variable a (a dict, recognise it by the curly brackets) seems like a more elaborate version of variable b (a list). However, there is one big difference: in a list you can access values by using their index number, whereas in a dict this index is called a **key**. And keys can be any number or string you would like them to be! Next example:

```
a = {'banana':1, 'horse':2, 19:1, 3:'cookie'}

print(a['banana'])
print(a['horse'])
print(a[3])
print(a[19])
```

Cool, right? You can also add new entries to your dict after creating it:

```
a['answer'] = 42
print(a)
```

Using dicts can be very useful, for example if you want to store all data from one participant into the same variable. You could create a dict with keys 'RT' for the response times, and 'accuracy' to indicate whether a response was correct. Or you could create a dict for all data, with keys for every participant. Each of these keys could point to the aforementioned dicts for single participants, which had keys for all your measures:

```
data = {}
data['subject-1'] = {'RT':[300, 256, 115], 'acc':[1, 1, 0]}
data['subject-2'] = {'RT':[400, 512, 268], 'acc':[1, 0, 1]}
```

Dicts can contain any kind of value, including other (nested) dicts.

Classes

Before we go on to the good stuff, there is one more type of variable that you need to know. This is a very important one, and a fundamental part of the Python language.

Take a step back from programming for a second. If there is a window, take a look outside. If not, try to find better accommodation, because working without windows is awful. Can you see a car? And maybe another? If you can't, just imagine two different cars (but don't make them too different!). The two cars are obviously similar: they both have four wheels, a steering wheel, a motor, windows etcetera. However, they are also obviously different: they might have different colours, different types of wheels, different motors, and so on.

You could think of the cars as two **instances** of the same **class**. They were built by using the same general blueprint that dictates wheels go on the bottom, lights on the front and the back, and that the steering wheel should be inside (preferably at the front). However, the cars were realised using different types of wheels, different shapes of lights, and different types of steering wheels (one could be leather, and the other plastic). The blueprint is a car's definition, whereas a car is a specific realisation of the blueprint.

If you understand this example, you understand the basic principle of **object oriented programming**. In this style of programming, we would refer to the blueprint as a class, and to a specific car as an instance. Instances can also be referred to as objects, hence the name 'object-oriented'.

In programming, objects can have **properties** and **methods**. Properties are internal variables, which define an individual instance's settings (think of a car's colour). Methods are internal functions that determine what each instance of a class can do (think of a car's ability to drive).

In Python all variable types are essentially objects. That is a bit of trivia you will not likely use when programming, but it comes in handy when you want to impress people at a dinner party:

Nerd 1:   I am *such* a programmer, I am *acing* Java.
Nerd 2:   Screw Java, I'm learning Go – did you know *Google* made that?
Nerd 3:   I learned C++ in just *21 days*!
You: Pfft, C++ is just a silly way to make C object-oriented. Did you know Python was *designed* to be object-oriented? All variable types are really just objects.

(Be careful not to do this when *real* programmers are around. They *will* destroy you. Escape by pointing somewhere, asking "Is that R2D2?", and then making a run for it.)

Python and most external packages offer really useful classes that can do just about anything. Displaying stuff on the screen? There's a class for that. Registering keyboard input? There's a class for that. Communicating to an eye tracker? There's a class for that. In the next sections, we will explore all of these.

Functions

Remember how you were promised that after learning about classes, you would get to do fun stuff? That was a lie. You need to learn about functions first. These aren't really a type of variable, but they are in a way. You don't have to worry about what they are precisely, but you should know that functions are a very important part of any programming language.

A **function** is nothing more than a collection of code that does a specific thing, or a few specific things. If you think that's a pretty vague definition, you're absolutely right. You can think about functions as descriptions of a task, such as building a bird house. Such a task requires input, like materials (wood, nails, and glue) and specifications (the house's dimensions). It also has an output: a bird house. The function itself would be a description of how to build the bird house.

A common example of a real-life function is a cooking recipe. A recipe tells you how to make a specific meal. Its inputs are ingredients, and its output is your dinner. Let's look at how the recipe for mashed potatoes is defined:

Make mash

Inputs:

5 potatoes, 1 clove of garlic, 6 teaspoons of oregano

Output:

mash

Procedure:

1) mince garlic

2) wash potatoes

3) peel potatoes

4) boil potatoes for 20 minutes

5) mash potatoes

6) add garlic and oregano to mash

7) stir mash

As you might have noticed, some of the individual steps could be defined as functions too. For example, the function "boil potatoes" has inputs (peeled potatoes, water, and a pan), outputs (boiled potatoes and hot water), and a procedure ("fill pan with water, put pan on stove, heat pan, wait for 20 minutes"). This can happen in programming too: some functions will call upon others to work.

As an exercise, let's see how you could define the function to make mash in Python:

```python
def make_mash(Npotatoes, Ngarlic=1, Noregano=6):

     potatoes = get_potatoes(Npotatoes)
     garlic = get_garlic(Ngarlic)
     oregano = get_oregano(Noregano)

     mincedgarlic = chop(garlic)
     potatoes = wash(potatoes)
     potatoes = peel(potatoes)
     potatoes = boil(potatoes, duration=20)
     mash = smash(potatoes)

     mash = stir(mash, mincedgarlic, oregano)

     return mash
```

This might seem a bit weird to you, and it is. But there are a few things you should note. The first important thing is a general observation: the function `make_mash` calls on several other functions (e.g. `get_potatoes` and `stir`), which have not been defined and are not part of the basic Python language. For now, just assume that they are defined somewhere else.

Another important thing to note, is how a function is defined in Python. A function definition always begins with `def`, which is short for define. This is followed by the functions name, in this case `make_mash`. The function name is *always* followed by a set of round brackets. Within those brackets, inputs are defined. These inputs are called **arguments**, and you will get back to those later. The final part of the function definition is a colon, `:`.

All of the code that is part of a function, is **indented** You will learn more about indentation in the section on 'If statements'. For now, all you need to know is that Python recognises all code that is part of a function by its offset with regard to the function definition. The offset is four spaces (⎵⎵⎵⎵) in front of each line of code that is part of the function.

At the end of the code, the function **returns** a variable (`mash`). This is the output of a function, and it can be a single variable or a list of variables. Output variables can be numbers, strings, lists, tuples, classes, or even other functions.

Using a function is referred to as **calling** a function. The general syntax is like this:

```
output = function(input)
```

As an example, this is the syntax to call the `make_mash` function:

```
mash = make_mash(5, Ngarlic=1, Noregano=6)
```

This will call the `make_mash` function with as input five potatoes, one clove of garlic, and six teaspoons of oregano. The output will be stored in a variable named `mash`. You might have noticed how `Npotatoes` isn't directly referenced, but instead there is only a 5. This will be explained in the next section.

Arguments

Arguments are an important part of using functions, although they are not a requirement. In theory, you could define a function that has no input arguments. Arguments are variables whose names are defined within a function definition. In the `make_mash` function, there is one argument: `Npotatoes`. (We will get back to `Ngarlic` and `Noregano` in a bit.) `Npotatoes` was created in the following line:

```
def make_mash(Npotatoes, Ngarlic=1, Noregano=6):
```

You might wonder why there is no value associated with `Npotatoes`, like with `Ngarlic` and `Noregano`. This is because the value is only assigned when `make_mash` is called. If you want `Npotatoes` to be five, you call the `make_mash` function like this:

```
mash = make_mash(5, Ngarlic=1, Noregano=6)
```

If you are really hungry, and want to make mash with 10 potatoes, you call the `make_mash` function like this:

```
mash = make_mash(10, Ngarlic=1, Noregano=6)
```

The value of `Npotatoes` is only assigned when you call the `make_mash` function. This means it can be different every time. This is a crucial aspect of functions: they help you automate a task, but allow flexibility with arguments. You can use the same function to make very little or a whole lot of mash, only by changing the arguments' values.

In programming, providing values for arguments is often referred to as **passing** an argument. Importantly, **a call to a function will result in an error if you do not pass all arguments**.

Keyword arguments

Keyword arguments are basically the same thing as arguments, with one important exception: they have a default value. You can assign this default value in the function definition, as was done with `Ngarlic` and `Noregano` in the `make_mash` function:

```
def make_mash(Npotatoes, Ngarlic=1, Noregano=6):
```

The practical benefit of using keyword arguments, is that you don't have to assign their values when you call a function. For example, the following two calls to the `make_mash` function are equivalent:

```
mash = make_mash(5, Ngarlic=1, Noregano=6)
mash = make_mash(5)
```

As a result of having a default value, if you don't pass any keyword arguments, it will not cause an error. This is in contrast to arguments: if you don't specify an argument when calling a function, you do get an error.

It is useful to define sensible keyword arguments when you write function definition. This allows you to call the function without having to bother with specifying every little detail, but it does keep the option to bother with details open. In the `make_mash` example, this means that you could rely on the default amount of garlic (one clove), but if you really like it (and don't mind smelling of it), you could also throw in six cloves:

```
mash = make_mash(5, Ngarlic=6)
```

Of course, mash is a silly example, but you will encounter more practical examples of keyword arguments later in this book. When you do, think about what type of argument you would have used. In addition, you might want to think about whether you could *only* use keyword arguments. Is there a benefit of using arguments?

Local and global variables

Variables (including arguments and keyword arguments) are **local** to the function that they were created in. That means that the variable potatoes can be used throughout the entire `make_mash` function, but not outside of it. This might sound trivial, but it's not.

If you want a variable that was created within a function to be accessible from outside the function (i.e. in the rest of your script), you have to return it. This is why the definition of the `make_mash` function ends with `return mash`. If this last line was not there, the function would have no output. Consequently, you would not be able to use `mash`.

The reason that variables are local to a function, is that they would otherwise crowd your work space. Imagine a complicated function that would use 100 variables within. If you have a script in which you call this complicated function, you would have to make sure that *none* of your own variables share a name with those created within the complicated function. If one does, it will be overwritten, and your script might start behaving weirdly.

Another option to share variables between your script and the insides of functions, is to declare variables **global**. This means variables will be recognised in your script, and also within functions. This is not recommended, unless you have a good reason to do so. To declare a variable global, include the following line in your script:

```
global mash
```

And the following in your function definition (don't forget the indentation with four spaces):

```
    global mash
```

Create your first function

After learning about functions, it's time to define one yourself! This is an important moment in your personal programming history, so savour it. In the Interpreter, type the following line:

```
def hello_world():
```

After typing the line, hit Enter and type the following line (don't forget to start the next line with four spaces!):

```
    print('Hello World!')
```

Hit Enter twice, and maybe a few times more for good measure. Now call your own function by typing:

```
hello_world()
```

If you did everything correctly, 'Hello World!' should have appeared in the Interpreter. That was the result of your very first function! Congrats!

What you just did, is to define a function named hello_world, which takes no inputs, and produces no outputs. It simply prints 'Hello World!' to the Interpreter.

Create your second function

Let's make things more exciting. Let's create a function that does take an input! You could create a function that prints 'Hello World!' for a specified number of times. An argument within the function definition could be used to allow you to specify how many times the function should print 'Hello World!', like so:

```
def hello_world(N):
```

Where N is the amount of 'Hello World!'s. As you might remember from the section on strings, you can multiply a single string by an integer number to reproduce them. You can capitalise on this in your new function:

```
    print(N * 'Hello World! ')
```

Now hit Enter twice, and call the function!

```
hello_world(5)
```

You can also try to test the limits of your computer:

```
hello_world(10)
hello_world(100)
hello_world(100000)
```

Create your third function

As a final exercise in function definition, let's create a function that not only takes input, but also produces output! This function will move beyond the 'Hello World!' examples from before, and will actually do something useful: check if a value is equal to 42.

The function will be named is_this_the_answer, and the input argument will be named number. Type the following in the Interpreter and hit Enter:

```
def is_this_the_answer(number):
```

Now, the crucial part of the function is to check if the input is equal to 42. As you might remember from the section on Booleans, you can use a double is-equal sign to compare to variables. The result will be True if the variables are equal, or False when they are not.

```
    result = number == 42
```

The result is a Boolean that indicates whether number was equal to 42. The only thing left to do, is to return result.

```
    return result
```

Hit Enter twice, and test your function:

```
is_this_the_answer(7)
is_this_the_answer(3.50)
is_this_the_answer(42)
is_this_the_answer('kittens')
```

You can also assign the returned value to a new variable:

```
result = is_this_the_answer(42)
print(result)
```

Note that you do not have to use the same variable name that you used within the function. You can use any variable name you want! So the following code is equally valid:

```
a = is_this_the_answer(42)
print(a)
```

Pretty neat, huh?

MAKE SOME NOISE

After learning about all those variable types, it's time to do something cooler! In this random intermezzo, you will learn how to make visual noise.

Random numbers

In the previous sections, you learned how to use NumPy arrays. But there is more to NumPy than just vector calculations! There is a beautiful `random` module that allows you to generate random numbers:

```
import numpy

numpy.random.rand()
numpy.random.rand()
numpy.random.rand()
```

Just try it a few times, to make sure the numbers are actually random. If you do recognise a pattern, you might actually be right. A computer's random numbers are produced by an algorithm that depends on a fixed number, a **seed**. You can provide your own seed and see what happens:

```
numpy.random.seed(seed=14)
numpy.random.rand()
numpy.random.rand()
numpy.random.rand()
```

Seems to do the same, right? Now provide the exact same seed and do it again:

```
numpy.random.seed(seed=14)
numpy.random.rand()
numpy.random.rand()
numpy.random.rand()
```

The *exact* same 'random' numbers came out! Why is this relevant? Because it is important to realise that there is no such thing as truly random numbers in a computer. Officially, they are **pseudo-random**. Do not worry too much, though. For all our intents and purposes, these numbers are random enough.

Noise

Visual **noise** is the grey snow you see when an old television isn't set to a proper channel. It is the visual analogue of the feeling you have in your arm after sleeping on it. The individual snowflakes range from completely white to completely black. If we assign values to these colours, we could say white corresponds to 1, and black to 0. All values between 0 and 1 correspond to some shade of grey.

Using NumPy's `rand` function, we can actually create a field of random numbers. To do so, we only have to provide the width and height of this field. Let's try this with a field of 5 × 5 positions:

```
noise = numpy.random.rand(5, 5)
print(noise)
```

You can check the dimensions of a NumPy array by looking at its shape property:

```
noise.shape
```

Of course, grey noise is a little boring. Why not make it coloured? You might know that computers encode colours with three values: their red component, their green component, and their blue component. If we want to make a numerical representation of coloured noise, we will need to create three random numbers per pixel (a pixel is one coloured unit on your screen: a combination of three values in your field of numbers).

Although this may sound like a difficult problem, it's actually rather easy to make such a representation. You can simply add another dimension in NumPy's rand function:

```
rgb_noise = numpy.random.rand(5, 5, 3)
print(rgb_noise)
```

Matplotlib

Now you know how to make a numerical representation of visual noise, let's turn it into an image! To do this, we will use Matplotlib (Hunter, 2007). This is a library that can do very advanced plotting. For now, we will only use its `pyplot` module. This contains an `imshow` function, which can translate a field of numbers to an image.

To create the visual noise, you can use the same approach as before, but now with a bigger field. What about 500 × 500 pixels?

```
import numpy
from matplotlib import pyplot

noise = numpy.random.rand(500, 500, 3)
pyplot.imshow(noise)
pyplot.show()
```

The last function shows the figure you made in an interactive window. If you want, you can save it to your disk. Maybe show it to your grandmother.

"Look, granny, I can do programming!"

"That's nice, honey."

3

CREATING AND PRESENTING STIMULI

In this chapter, you will learn how to create some basic stimuli, and how to present these on a computer display. To do this, you will write scripts in which you will use classes from two external packages: PyGaze (Dalmaijer, Mathôt, & Van der Stigchel, 2014), and PsychoPy (Peirce, 2007, 2009).

These external packages can do pretty much anything you could need in a psychological experiment. This includes presenting stimuli on a monitor; producing sound; collecting responses from keyboards, computer mice, joysticks, and controllers; communicating with eye trackers; logging data; and accurately timing events. Which package you choose is entirely up to you (or your teacher, if you're using this book in a course module). You might want to play around with both PyGaze and PsychoPy, and choose whichever you like best.

Writing a book on programming is hard, because there are a lot of different ways in which you can explain it. The aim of this book is to provide you with an intuitive understanding of how to code psychological experiments. I (the author) feel that this process is aided by how PyGaze is designed, and by the user-friendly syntax it produces. That PyGaze fits my intuition of how experiments should be programmed is no coincidence: I was part of the team that developed it.

PsychoPy is a great package, and it is very popular among experimental psychologists and cognitive neuroscientists. Sometimes, it offers more advanced control over things that PyGaze might lack. Using the two packages together will allow you to do great things, in a relatively easy way.

Without delving too deep into software architecture, it is worth noting that PyGaze is built *on top* of a few other external packages (dependencies). This means that it requires a few other packages to do what it does. These include PyGame (www.pygame.org) and PsychoPy (one should suffice, but it's nice to be able to use both), NumPy, and libraries that are specific to different brands of eye trackers (you only need these if you actually use an eye tracker). Do not worry, though: the modified WinPython package described in Chapter 1 of this book contains all of the required packages.

Scripts

Unlike in previous chapters, where you punched some lines into an interpreter, in this chapter you are going to create **scripts** to do your bidding. A script is nothing more than a collection of lines, which will be executed one-by-one.

Programming languages that run scripts per line are called *interpreted languages*. These differ from *compiled languages*, which pre-translate the entire script before actually running it. Generally speaking, compiled languages are quicker to run, but interpreted languages have some other things going for them. For example, because scripts are not compiled up front but on-the-go, scripts written in an interpreted language can *rewrite themselves while running*. Let that sink in, and maybe read Stephen Hawking's artificial intelligence warning (www.bbc.co.uk/news/technology/-30290540).

Nowadays, most programming languages can be implemented both as interpreted or compiled, so it's not a language feature any longer. Also, you could probably think of a way in which compiled languages rewrite themselves to kill the human race. So do not worry about the distinction too much. All you really need to know at this point, is that Python will run your scripts line by line.

experiment.py

The key script in your experiment is going to be **experiment.py**. If you want, you can also name it differently (bubbles.py, for example). The extension .py indicates that this is a Python script. The extension helps you and your operating system recognise the files. At some point, you will also encounter **.pyc** (and maybe .pyo) extensions. These are compiled Python files, which can be ignored for practical purposes.

If you are interested in further explanation on compiled file types, please read on. If you could not care less, please skip to the next paragraph. Both *.pyc* and *.pyo* files contain the translation of your script into *bytecode*. This is unreadable to humans, but useful to your computer. It is still a step away from *machine code*, though, which your computer eventually needs to make it do stuff. This is exactly why the lines between interpreted and compiled languages are quite blurry. There is a perfectly good reason for this pre-compilation: line-by-line compilation (=translation) of your script directly into machine code would be slow. Introducing an extra step makes Python run quicker. There are more advantages to this, but these are way beyond the scope of this book. Go look it up yourself, that's what the internet is for.

All right, back on track: an experiment usually consists of at least two scripts. There is one actual experiment script (containing lines of code that present stimuli, collect responses, log data, etc.), and another script with constants (explained in the next section). The best way of organising this is in a single folder for each experiment. *Each experiment folder should contain its own experiment.py and constants.py.*

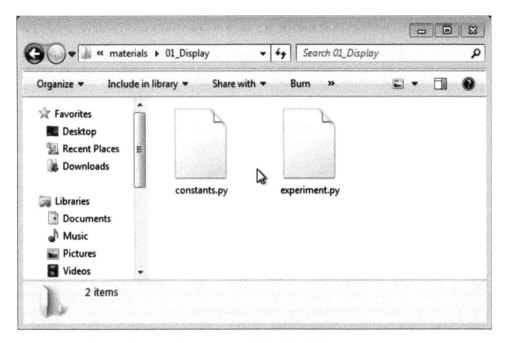

FIGURE 3.1   This is what a simple experiment folder looks like

constants.py

The constants script will contain all the variables that do not change in your experiment. These include the display resolution, the experimental conditions, and the number of trials in each condition.

The idea behind having a separate file to store your experiment's parameters, is that its separates the settings from the experimental procedure. The experiment script (`experiment.py`) is usually quite long, and relatively complicated. If you want to change something relatively simple (e.g. the inter-trial interval's duration, or the size of a stimulus), it would be a pain to have to go through the entire experiment script and change every relevant bit. If you collect all parameters in a separate file (constants.py), it will produce a concise overview. Changing parameters here is very easy, because they're all in one place.

If you are a little lost at this point, that is normal. You have only read theory about scripts, and no actual scripts yet. Once you start programming, things will start to make sense.

The display

It is time. You will now write your very first script. Open an editor. Spyder would be good, if you have it (it is explained in the 'Editor' section of Chapter 1 of this book). Now create two new scripts, and save them both in the same folder. Name one **constants.py** and the other **experiment.py**.

Find out what resolution your display is. If you are on Windows, you can do this by right-clicking on your desktop and selecting 'Screen Resolution'. If you have more than one display (good for you!), you need the resolution of your main display. In constants.py, type the following:

PyGaze code
```
DISPTYPE = 'pygame'
DISPSIZE = (1920, 1080)
```

PsychoPy code
```
DISPSIZE = (1920, 1080)
```

Where 1920 should be your own screen width, and 1080 should be your own screen height. The `DISPTYPE` refers to what library will be used by PyGaze to do the visuals (and the response collection). You can choose between 'pygame' and 'psychopy'. This will not change *what* PyGaze does, but *how* it does it. The developers give you this option, because both libraries come with their own advantages. PsychoPy generally has a better timing accuracy, whereas PyGame is usually more stable.

If you're using PsychoPy, you don't have to specify this option. PsychoPy does have two back-ends, but we will go with the default. Usually, there is little reason to choose otherwise.

We can define some other stuff in the constants as well, for example the default foreground and background colours. These are labelled `FGC` and `BGC`, respectively. They are coded as RGB triplets, which are three values between 0 and 255. The first value codes the amount of red, the second the amount of green, and the third the amount of blue. A value of 0 means no colour, whereas 255 means full colour. So (255, 0, 0) would be bright red, (0, 255, 0) would be bright green, and (255, 105, 180) would be hot pink.

Please note that PsychoPy codes colours in the same way (as RGB triplets), but with different values. In PsychoPy, the minimal colour value is –1, and the maximum is 1. So the PyGaze colour (255, 0, 0) corresponds with PsychoPy colour (1, –1, –1); both are the same red. This is explained in the next section, 'Units and colours in PsychoPy Windows'.

Let's make your foreground black, (0, 0, 0), and the background grey, (128, 128, 128). The foreground is the default colour of lines and text. The background colour is really just that: the colour in the background of the display. Write in constants.py:

PyGaze code
```
FGC = (0, 0, 0)
BGC = (128, 128, 128)
```

PsychoPy code
```
FGC = (-1, -1, -1)
BGC = (0, 0, 0)
```

Ok, this will get things sorted. Now open experiment.py, and type the following:

PyGaze code
```
from pygaze.display import Display
```

PsychoPy code
```
from psychopy.visual import Window
```

For PyGaze, this will turn to the `display` module, which is part of `pygaze`. Out of that, it will import the `Display` class. For PsychoPy, it will turn to the `visual` module, and import the `Window` class.

Often, you need to import specific functions or classes before you can use them. Remember how a class is basically a blueprint, e.g. for a car? The Display and Window classes are the blueprints for objects that you can use to show things on the computer monitor. A car blueprint will not drive you to work; for that you need an actual car. The same is true for a Display or Window: tt won't drive you to work. Also, you will need to actually build one out of the blueprint. The code for that is rather easy:

PyGaze code
```
disp = Display()
```

PsychoPy code
```
disp = Window(units='pix', fullscr=True)
```

Be sure *not* to run your script yet, because you haven't scripted the closing of your display yet. If you run the display now, it will simply stay on FOR EVER! To prevent that, add the following line:

PyGaze code
```
disp.close()
```

PsychoPy code
```
disp.close()
```

This code *calls* the Display or Window class's `close` method. `disp` is an **instance** of the Display or Window blueprint, which describes close it. After displaying everything you wanted with `disp`, use the `close` method to shut down the Display instance.

A useful thing about PyGaze, is that it recognises files that are called '*constants.py*', as long as they are placed in the same folder as the experiment script. PyGaze will understand that the file contains your settings, and will use them to overwrite the default values. You won't even have to explicitly run constants.py for this to work!

If you use PsychoPy, you will have to actively import variables from constants.py. You can do this by adding the following line at the very start of your script:

```
from constants import DISPSIZE
```

Alternatively, you can choose to import everything at once (the asterisk means 'all'):

```
from constants import *
```

Now, change the line where you define `disp` to make sure the Window will use the correct resolution:

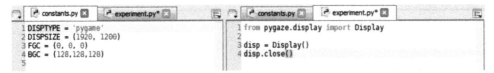

FIGURE 3.2   If you're using PyGaze, this is how your code should look at this moment

```
disp = Window(size=DISPSIZE, units='pix', fullscr=True)
```

Save your files, and turn to the next chapter to learn how to run your experiment!

Units and colours in Psychopy Windows

As you might have noticed, the Window class requires you to specify units. In this case, we set it to 'pix', which stands for 'pixels'. This is a straightforward mapping, as pixels are a unit that your computer and monitor are familiar with.

PsychoPy also offers different units of measurement for distances on your monitor. These include centimetres and degrees of visual angle. However, these units require PsychoPy to know exactly how many pixels can fit into a centimetre on your monitor, and how far a participant is sitting from the monitor.

In addition, PsychoPy offers normalised units. These range between –1 and 1, and represent relative distances. On a monitor with a resolution of 1920 × 1080 pixels, a horizontal distance of –1 (left edge of the monitor) to 0 (monitor centre) will correspond to 960 pixels. On a monitor with a resolution of 1024 × 768, the same horizontal distance will correspond to 512 pixels.

In this book, I will always use pixels. The upside is that this is the most conventional and straightforward unit of distance on a computer monitor. The downside is that pixels are specific to your monitor: a stimulus with a size of 200 pixels will have a different size in centimetres on two different monitors, because pixel sizes differ between monitors. Fortunately, you can measure how wide your monitor is, and calculate the amount of pixels per centimetre. From that, you can calculate a stimulus' size in centimetres and in visual angle.

Even though you can use pixels in both PyGaze and PsychoPy, the two libraries differ in how they define their coordinate systems. In PyGaze, the top-left corner of the screen is (0, 0), and the values increase as you go down and to the right. For example, on a 1920 × 1080 monitor, the top-right corner would be (1920, 0), and the bottom right corner would be (1920, 1080). The monitor's centre would be at (960, 540). In PsychoPy, things are a bit different. The monitor's centre is defined as (0, 0), and the values increase as you go up and to the right. For example, on a 1920 × 1080 monitor, the bottom-left corner would be (–960, –540), the bottom-right corner would be (960, –540), and the top-right corner would be (960, 540).

PyGaze represents colours in values for red, green, and blue that range from 0 to 255. In PsychoPy, colours can also be defined as values for red, green, and blue. However, these values range between –1 and 1. The logic behind this, is that colours can be represented as deviations from grey, which is defined as (0, 0, 0). Some additional examples: (–1, –1, –1) is black, (1, 1, 1) is white, (–1, 0, 0) is red, and (1.0, –0.18, 0.41) is hot pink.

PsychoPy also offers alternative colour spaces: colours can be defined as a combination of their hue, saturation, and value (HSV); or in a colour space that speaks to the specifics of human colour perception. If you want to know more, please read www.psychopy.org/general/colours.html.

In this book, you will use the default colour space: RGB triplets with values between –1 and 1.

As usual, if you find yourself confused about these things, just go with it. Although colour spaces are a fascinating topic to elaborate on, they are beyond the scope of this book.

Running scripts

To make this book compatible with every code editor, it will teach you the general way of running a Python script. Most editors will also have the option to run scripts. Sometimes this works beautifully, and sometimes this causes weird interactions between the script and the editor running it.

The following approaches should always work. They all come down to using the **command line** to order Python to execute your script.

Windows: run using batch files

On Windows, the easiest way of running a Python script, is by creating a **batch file**. This file type is native to Windows, and can hold some really basic commands. On running (by double-clicking) the batch file, Windows will execute these commands.

The first step in creating a batch file, is to find where your python.exe is located. If you have installed Python using an installer from the Python website, you will likely find it in C:\python27\python.exe, or in C:\Users\YourName\python27.exe. If you installed Anaconda, it will likely be C:\Anaconda\python.exe or C:\Users\YourName\Anaconda\python.exe. If you use WinPython, it will be in a folder called 'python-2.7.X' (with the last X being the version number), which is included in the WinPython package.

The next step is to create a new text file. Go to the folder in which you keep `constants.py` and experiment.py. Right-click, and select 'Create new file', and 'Create empty text file'. Name the file 'RUNME'.

Open the newly created text file, and copy in the location (=path) of python.exe. Next, put double quotes around the path. The first line of your text file should be something like this example:

```
"C:\Anaconda\python.exe"
```

This is the first part of the command. In English, it reads "Make Python run ...". Add the name of your experiment script to finish the command:

```
"C:\Anaconda\python.exe" "experiment.py"
```

The line reads 'Make Python run experiment.py', which is exactly what you want. There is just one further thing to add: a command that makes Windows pause after running the script. This will allow you to see any potential warning or error messages that occur while running the script (if you do not include the pause, Windows will close the command prompt immediately after running your script). The command to make Windows pause is `pause`. Who would have guessed?

```
"C:\Anaconda\python.exe" "experiment.py"
pause
```

Now there is just one more step: you need to convert the text file into a batch file. First close the text editor. Next, right-click on RUNME.txt (the file you just created), select 'Rename', and change '.txt' into '.bat'. Windows will ask you whether you really want to change the file's extension, and warn you that it could potentially change the files function. This is exactly what you want, so click 'Yes'.

Important: If you do not see the '.txt' extension when changing the file name, your file explorer is set to hide known file extensions. This is really annoying, and can be turned off. In the file explorer, press Alt, then press 'Tools' and 'Folder options...'. Now untick 'Hide extensions for known filetypes' in the 'View' tab, and click 'OK'. You should now be able to see (and change!) the extensions of your files.

Linux and OS X: run using terminals

If you are using Linux (yay!) or OS X (boo!), the process of running your Python scripts is a bit easier than on Windows. Simply copy the location to the folder that holds your experiment script (for example, '/home/YourName/Documents/my_experiment'). Now open a Terminal (simply type 'Terminal' in a search, if you do not know how). Type the following command (but with your own path instead of the example!):

```
cd '/home/YourName/Documents/my_experiment'
```

This means 'Change the current folder to /home/YourName/Documents/my_experiment'. The command `cd` is to change directories. Directory is another word for folder.

Now that the terminal knows where it should be looking for your experiment, issue the command to run it:

```
python "experiment.py"
```

This will make (the default installation of) Python run your experiment.py script.

Running your script

After reading the preceding section, you know how to run the script you wrote in the 'Display' section earlier in this chapter. Please run experiment.py now!

That's not doing very much, is it? It is not because you made an error (if you followed the instructions correctly, that is), but because the script really does nothing more than opening and directly closing a Display. This will probably manifest itself like a brief black flash on your monitor. More will be added to your script in the next chapters, until you have a proper experiment!

Killing your script

~~Sometimes~~ Very often, a script will not run as you intended, and crash. If you run script according to the procedures above, a crash should kill the active Display in most cases. However, sometimes (due to silly programming mistakes) the Display will remain visible and stuck. In these cases, you can kill it via three easy steps:

1 DON'T PANIC!
2 Press the **Alt** and **Tab** keys at the same time (only once!). This will cause the Terminal (=Command Prompt in Windows) to become active in the background. You will not see this, because the Display is still in the way.
3 Press the **Ctrl** and **C** keys at the same time. This will make the terminal kill your Python script, and save the day!

Timing

To make the Display appear longer, you could add a pause between its initialisation (the moment you create `disp`) and its closing (the moment you call `disp.close`). PyGaze and PsychoPy have simple functions to make an experiment pause for a bit. In PyGaze, this function is called `pause` (again, very convenient naming), and it is part of the `libtime` module. In PsychoPy, the function is called `wait`, and it's part of the `core` module. To import it, add the following line at the start of the experiment.py script you created in section 'The display':

PyGaze code
```
import pygaze.libtime as timer
```

PsychoPy code
```
from psychopy.core import wait
```

A part of these lines is new to you: `as timer` indicates that Python should import the `libtime` module, but that we will refer to it as `timer` in the rest of the script, rather than as `pygaze.libtime`. There is no functional benefit, but it is convenient because `timer` is shorter to type.

Now call the `pause` function between creating and closing the Display. PyGaze requires you to put in the amount of milliseconds you would like to wait, whereas PsychoPy requires you to use seconds. To wait 2 seconds, *pass* 2000 to the `pause` function, or 2 to the `wait` function. Your entire experiment.py script should now be:

PyGaze code
```
from pygaze.display import Display
import pygaze.libtime as timer
```

```
disp = Display()
timer.pause(2000)
disp.close()
```

PsychoPy code

```
from constants import DISPSIZE
from psychopy.visual import Window
from psychopy.core import wait

disp = Window(size=DISPSIZE, units='pix', fullscr=True)
wait(2)
disp.close()
```

Now run the script. If you did everything correctly, you should see a black screen that stays on for two seconds, and then closes. You might recall setting the background colour to grey. So why was the screen black? (Note: this does not always happen; sometimes the Display starts out grey, for various reasons.)

If you create a Display, you open up the possibility of presenting on the monitor. But you will need to call the Display's show method to explicitly make something appear. In PsychoPy, this function is called flip. It is important to be aware of this one-way process: you fill the Display object with whatever you want (in this case only the background, but you will learn about more complex drawing in the next chapter), then you call the Display object's show method to push the Display object's content to the actual monitor.

To complete your current script, add the following line between disp = Display() and timer.pause(2000):

```
disp.show()
```

Now run experiment.py again, and marvel at the satisfying greyness of your monitor.

Screens

Because a grey screen is a bit boring, this section will teach you how to show more interesting stuff on a Display. To do this, you need to get acquainted with the concept of Screens. These are blank canvases that you can use to draw lines, shapes, images, and other stimuli.

While only one Display can be active at a time, you can create all the Screens you want. Screens exist 'in the background': they are not visible on your monitor until you explicitly fill the Display with one. That means that, if you want to display a stimulus, you will have to create a Screen first, then draw the stimulus on, then fill a Display with your Screen, and then call the Display's show method.

Seems like an awful lot of effort; why not draw on the Display directly? Well, every drawing operation takes time. A computer monitor is refreshed at a rate of 60 times per second (or even higher!). This allows very little time for actual drawing (about 17 milliseconds per monitor refresh). If you have a large image, drawing it directly to the display might well take up more than a single monitor refresh.

Whether this is a problem, depends on your experiment. If the image is an illustration to a questionnaire, you are probably not concerned with millisecond-accurate timing. But if you are trying to present the image for precisely 50 milliseconds (three monitor refreshes), accidentally adding or losing one monitor refresh can really mess up your timing.

So how do Screens solve this problem? If you draw an image on a Screen, it will still take a bit of time. However, the Screen is not displayed directly. You can prepare your stimulus during phases of your experiment where timing is not critical (during a short break between trials, for example). After drawing the Screen, all you need to do during the timing-critical phase of your experiment, is to fill the Display with it. You then call the Display's show method, and call it again after three monitor refreshes have passed (so that your image was presented for exactly 50 milliseconds).

There is more to millisecond-accurate timing, but we will come back to this later. For now, it is important to understand that it is best to divide your experiment (or single trials within your experiment) into a preparation phase where stimuli can be drawn on Screens, and a run phase where the Display can be filled with the prepared Screens.

In PsychoPy, things are slightly different. Where PyGaze uses collections of stimuli, PsychoPy uses individual stimuli. The same principles apply, though: you want to create the stimuli during a phase of the experiment where timing is not critical. Then, when timing is critical, you can quickly draw the prepared stimuli on the display.

This method has been used by experimental psychologists even before computers. Slide shows for overhead projectors were prepared in advance by manually drawing on slides, and no drawing was done while the participant was present (obviously!). Nowadays, it is implemented in high-quality experimental software (e.g. OpenSesame – Mathôt, Schreij, & Theeuwes, 2012), and by you in your digital experiments!

That was all the boring (but important!) theory. On the next page, you finally get to draw on Screens!

draw_fixation

Psychological experiments are full of fixation marks. They are usually a plus symbol ('fixation cross'), but can also be an 'X' or a dot. They signal that the participant is supposed to look at the mark, and keep their eyes as still as possible. This is called a fixation, hence the term 'fixation mark'.

PyGaze Screens have a special method for drawing fixation marks: draw_fixation. You can pass multiple **keyword arguments** to determine what kind of mark you want, and where. A keyword argument is simply a value that you pass to the method, marked by a special word. It's a bit like defining a variable, but one with a special name that is only valid within the method. An example:

PyGaze code

```
from pygaze.screen import Screen

fixscreen = Screen()
fixscreen.draw_fixation(fixtype='dot')
```

You see that `fixtype='dot'` looks a bit like defining a new variable, but in a weird location: between the round brackets that contain the values passed to a method. This is because `fixtype` is a keyword argument. It does not *have* to be specified, but it *can* be. If you do not specify it, it will fall back to a default option (which would be 'cross' here).

There are other keyword arguments you can pass to `draw_fixation`: colour (for which the default is the foreground colour from constants.py), `pos` (for which the default is the Screen centre), `pw` (the width of the line, for which the default is 1 pixel), and `diameter` (the diameter of the fixation mark, for which the default is 12 pixels). Because you have not specified these in the example above, they will fall back to their default values.

In PsychoPy, there is no specific function to draw a fixation mark. However, there is a class for drawing circles. The code for that requires you to import the `Circle` class, which is part of the `visual` module (the backslash at the end of the third line means it continues on the next line).

PyschoPy code
```
from psychopy.visual import Window, Circle

disp = Window(units='pix')
fixmark = Circle(disp, radius=6, edges=64, \
      lineColor=(0,0,0), fillColor=(0,0,0))
```

The keyword argument `radius` allows you to set the radius (half of the diameter) of the circle. The `edges` keyword is a bit of a funny one: it determines the quality of your circle. The number should be a power of two (2, 4, 16, 32, 64, 128, 256, etc.). The higher it is, the nicer (rounder) your circle will look, but the more time it will take to draw.

Let's see fixation marks in practice. Open your experiment.py from the 'Timing' section, and add the code from above in there. In PyGaze, you will also need to fill the Display with fixscreen, by using the Display's `fill` method. In PsychoPy, you will need to call the Circle class's `draw` method to make it appear. The correct code is below:

PyGaze code
```
from pygaze.display import Display
from pygaze.screen import Screen
import pygaze.libtime as timer

disp = Display()
fixscreen = Screen()
fixscreen.draw_fixation(fixtype='dot')

disp.fill(fixscreen)
disp.show()
timer.pause(2000)

disp.close()
```

PsychoPy code
```
from constants import DISPSIZE, FGC
from psychopy.visual import Window, Circle
```

```
from psychopy.core import wait
disp = Window(size=DISPSIZE, units='pix', fullscr=True)
fixmark = Circle(disp, radius=6, edges=64, \
     lineColor=FGC, fillColor=FGC)
fixmark.draw()
disp.flip()
wait(2)
disp.close()
```

Now run experiment.py and see what happens!

draw_image

If all went well, you should have seen a black dot in the centre of the monitor. If the dot was not there, check if your code matches the code given in the last section. If it was a different colour, check what foreground colour (FGC) you defined in constants.py. If the dot was in a different position, check if the DISPSIZE in constants.py matches your actual resolution.

A single fixation dot is a bit boring. Let's succeed it with an image. Being able to draw images is a good skill to have, because they appear in all sorts of experimental paradigms. Download the image from the companion website www.routledge.com/cw/dalmaijer and put it in the same folder as experiment.py. To make it appear on a Screen, you can use PyGaze's draw_image method, or PsychoPy's ImageStim class.

PyGaze code
```
imgscreen = Screen()
imgscreen.draw_image('example.png')
```

PsychoPy code
```
from psychopy.visual import ImageStim

disp = Window(units='pix')
img = ImageStim(disp, image='example.png')
```

Now let's include this in experiment.py. Because of timing precision, you want to create both fixscreen and imgscreen before actually showing them. After this, you want to present the fixation dot for one second (1000 milliseconds), present the image for two seconds (2000 milliseconds), and then close the Display.

PyGaze code
```
from pygaze.display import Display
from pygaze.screen import Screen
import pygaze.libtime as timer
disp = Display()
fixscreen = Screen()
```

```
fixscreen.draw_fixation(fixtype='dot')
imgscreen = Screen()
imgscreen.draw_image('example.png')

disp.fill(fixscreen)
disp.show()
timer.pause(1000)

disp.fill(imgscreen)
disp.show()
timer.pause(2000)

disp.close()
```

PsychoPy code

```
from constants import DISPSIZE, FGC
from psychopy.visual import Window, Circle, ImageStim
from psychopy.core import wait

disp = Window(size=DISPSIZE, units='pix', fullscr=True)
fixmark = Circle(disp, radius=6, edges=64, \
        lineColor=FGC, fillColor=FGC)
img = ImageStim(disp, image='example.png')

fixmark.draw()
disp.flip()
wait(1)

img.draw()
disp.flip()
wait(2)

disp.close()
```

The name of the image was passed as a regular argument (without passing it, the draw_image method would not work) to the Screen's draw_image method. Further optional keywords are pos (indication the position of the image's centre on the Screen, which defaults to the Screen centre), and scale (indicating the scale factor, a value by which the image's size should be multiplied, for which the default is 1.0).

PsychoPy's ImageStim also has an optional pos keyword, which works in the same way as draw_image's. To change the image's size in PsychoPy, you can use ImageStim's size keyword; if you pass size=(500,400), the image will be resized to 500 × 400 pixels.

Now run experiment.py and enjoy!

Advanced: creating patches

This section is an advanced one. You will learn something about the inner workings of PyGaze, and you will learn how to exploit these. Essentially, you will be hacking the package a bit. If you want to score nerd points, do go on. If you can't be bothered, skip over the next few pages (you won't miss too many essential bits).

Stimuli that are often used in psychological experiments are Gabor and noise patches. A **Gabor patch** is a sinusoidal black-to-white-and-back pattern viewed through a Gaussian filter (clear in the centre, fades out towards the extremities). A **noise patch** is visual snow (a random mixture of pixels in different shades of grey), optionally viewed though a Gaussian filter.

Gabor patches are very popular in psychophysics, because they are a strong stimulator of early visual areas in the brain. Furthermore, it is relatively easy to make them move (when you change the phase of the sinusoidal pattern, a Gabor appears to be 'flowing'), and their stripy pattern gives them a clear (and adjustable) orientation. In addition to being a good stimulus, Gabors simply look cool. Enough reasons to include them in your experiments!

Noise can be used to *mask* other stimuli. If you want your participants to be exposed to a certain stimulus for a very brief time (for example to investigate the effect of presentation time on the quality of perception) you cannot simply present said stimulus for a short time. If you show an image and replace it by a neutral screen, an *afterimage* will remain. Even though the image is no longer visible, the participant will see it fade away slowly in their mind's eye. To prevent this, you can 'overwrite' the afterimage with a new stimulus. Noise patches are great for that.

PsychoPy has a brilliant built-in patch generator. Because PyGaze is written on top of PsychoPy (using its functions and classes internally), you can use PsychoPy's classes directly. You can only do this if you set `DISPSIZE='psychopy'` in constants.py, though!

Create a new folder, and two new (empty) script files: constants.py and experiment. py. In constants.py, write the following (make sure DISPSIZE matches your resolution):

```
DISPSIZE = (1920, 1080)
```

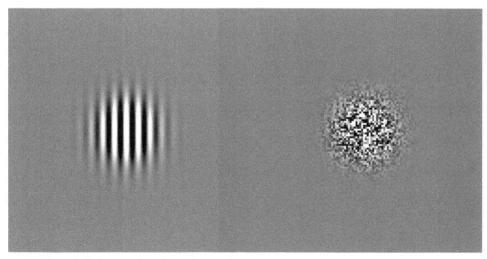

FIGURE 3.3   A Gabor patch and a noise patch

```
DISPTYPE = 'psychopy'
```

Gabor patches

Although Gabor patches seem complicated to make, doing so is actually very easy with PsychoPy. You can use the GratingStim class for PsychoPy's visual module:

```
from psychopy.visual import GratingStim

gabor = GratingStim(window, tex='sin', mask='gauss', \
      sf=0.05, size=200)
```

Let's break that last line down. `window` is an instance of PsychoPy's Window class, which you have seen before. `tex` is short for texture; it's set to 'sin', which is short for 'sinusoidal'. `mask` is the filter through which the stimulus will be visible, and 'gauss' is short for Gaussian. `sf` is the **s**patial **f**requency, which in this case is the number of cycles per pixel for the sinusoidal grating. It is set to 0.05 cycles per pixel, or 1 cycle per 20 pixels (1 cycle / 0.05 pixels per cycle = 20 pixels). `size` is the width and height of the stimulus in pixels. It is set to 200 pixels; together with the sf this makes a Gabor with 10 cycles (200 pixels / 20 pixels per cycle = 10 cycles).

If `DISPTYPE='psychopy'`, PyGaze creates a PsychoPy Window. You do not normally have to access this directly. However, you do need it for custom PsychoPy stimuli. The Window is called `expdisplay`, and is part of the PyGaze module. You can access it like this:

PyGaze code

```
import pygaze

gabor = GratingStim(pygaze.expdisplay, tex='sin', \
      mask='gauss', sf=0.05, size=200)
```

Another thing that only works when `DISPTYPE='psychopy'`, is accessing a Screen's internal list of stimuli. Each Screen object has a property called `screen`. When you use PsychoPy as your Display type, the `screen` property is a list of PsychoPy stimuli. You can simply add your Gabor to it. This bypasses all of the Screen's drawing functions (and thus is a bit of a hack!), but it works nicely. To add a value to a list, use its `append` method:

PyGaze code

```
gaborscreen = Screen()
gaborscreen.screen.append(gabor)
```

Now add everything together in one experiment.py script, and run it. The pure PsychoPy example code is also listed in the following code:

PyGaze code

```
import pygaze
from pygaze.display import Display
from pygaze.screen import Screen
import pygaze.libtime as timer
```

```
from psychopy.visual import GratingStim

disp = Display()
gabor = GratingStim(pygaze.expdisplay, tex='sin', \
      mask='gauss', sf=0.05, size=200)
gaborscreen = Screen()
gaborscreen.screen.append(gabor)

disp.fill(gaborscreen)
disp.show()
timer.pause(1000)
disp.close()
```

PsychoPy code

```
from constants import DISPSIZE
from psychopy.visual import Window, GratingStim
from psychopy.core import wait

disp = Window(size=DISPSIZE, units='pix', fullscr=True)
gabor = GratingStim(disp, tex='sin', mask='gauss', \
      sf=0.05, size=200)

gabor.draw()
disp.flip()
wait(1)
disp.close()
```

Noise

You have encountered visual noise before, in the first 'Make some noise' section. In that section, you created random numbers with the NumPy library and visualised them with the Matplotlib library. In this section, you will use PsychoPy to do the visualisation. You will still use NumPy to create the random numbers:

```
import numpy
noise = numpy.random.rand(64, 64)
```

This creates a field of 64 × 64 pixels. This seems like an odd number, but PsychoPy requires it to be a power of two ($2^1=2$, $2^2=4$, $2^3=8$, $2^4=16$, $2^5=32$, $2^6=64$, $2^7=128$, etc.). The higher this number is, the finer the noise grating is going to be. There is one problem: PsychoPy does not define colours between 0 and 1, which is the range of the current random values. Instead, PsychoPy uses a range of –1 (black) to 1 (white). This means you have to convert the current values!

The difference between the range 0 to 1 and the range –1 to 1, is that the latter is twice as wide. So the first part of the conversion is to multiply all random numbers by two:

```
noise = numpy.random.rand(64, 64) * 2
```

However, this leaves you with random numbers on a range of 0 to 2. This is one up from the range we want, –1 to 1. Therefore we simply subtract 1 from all the random numbers. If you think about it, it makes sense: 0 – 1 = –1, and 2 – 1 = 1. In code:

```
noise = (numpy.random.rand(64, 64) * 2) - 1
```

To visualise the noise, all you have to do is use it as the texture to a GratingStim:

PyGaze code

```
import pygaze

from psychopy.visual import GratingStim
noisepatch = GratingStim(pygaze.expdisplay, tex=noise, \
     mask='gauss', size=200)
```

PsychoPy code

```
from constants import DISPSIZE
from psychopy.visual import Window, GratingStim

disp = Window(size=DISPSIZE, units='pix', fullscr=True)
noisepatch = GratingStim(disp, tex=noise, mask='gauss', \
     size=200)
```

You can add this patch to a Screen in the same way you added the Gabor stimulus. In experiment.py, create an extra Screen object. Then add noisepatch to the Screen's stimulus list (see code below). For PsychoPy, all you have to do is call the noisepatch's draw method.

PyGaze code

```
from pygaze.screen import Screen
noisescreen = Screen()
noisescreen.screen.append(noisepatch)
```

If you combine what you learned on the previous page with the experiment.py script from the Gabor patches chapter, you end up with the following experiment.py script:

PyGaze code

```
import pygaze
from pygaze.display import Display
from pygaze.screen import Screen
import pygaze.libtime as timer
import numpy
from psychopy.visual import GratingStim

disp = Display()
gabor = GratingStim(pygaze.expdisplay, tex='sin', \
     mask='gauss', sf=0.05, size=200)
gaborscreen = Screen()
gaborscreen.screen.append(gabor)
```

```
noise = (numpy.random.rand(64, 64) * 2) - 1
noisepatch = GratingStim(pygaze.expdisplay, tex=noise, \
    mask='gauss', size=200)
noisescreen = Screen()
noisescreen.screen.append(noisepatch)

disp.fill(gaborscreen)
disp.show()
timer.pause(1000)

disp.fill(noisescreen)
disp.show()
timer.pause(2000)

disp.close()
```

PsychoPy code

```
from constants import DISPSIZE
import numpy
from psychopy.visual import Window, GratingStim
from psychopy.core import wait

disp = Window(size=DISPSIZE, units='pix', fullscr=True)
gabor = GratingStim(disp, tex='sin', mask='gauss', \
    sf=0.05, size=200)
noise = (numpy.random.rand(64, 64) * 2) -1
noisepatch = GratingStim(disp, tex=noise, mask='gauss', \
    size=200)

gabor.draw()
disp.flip()
wait(1)

noisepatch.draw()
disp.flip()
wait(2)

disp.close()
```

Does it work if you run it?

Comments

Your scripts are gradually becoming longer and more complicated, so this would be a good time to learn about **comments**. A comment is one or more lines that are ignored by Python. You can add them as little notes to yourself, or to other people (who might be using your scripts at one point).

While programming, you might think you will remember what you did and why. **But you will not.** Even though the code is right there, you will find yourself staring at your screen, wondering what the bleep you did.

This will be a very frustrating experience, because of three reasons:

1 You have code that works, and you want to change it slightly. This should be easy, and should not take too much time. But without comments, you have no clue what the code does. You now need to spend ages on figuring it out. AGAIN!

2 Because you cannot quite figure out what *exactly* you did, you go by assumptions about what you did to adjust or extend your script. This makes you more prone to making mistakes, leaving you with broken scripts and/or lots of debugging effort.

3 You realise that your past self implemented something in a very clever way, which you now struggle to comprehend. You realise your cognitive skills are declining. Also, because the uncommented code you are looking at is only two weeks old, you realise the decline is very rapid. In addition, you realise that you can't even recall what you did two weeks ago, so your memory must also be failing. You're getting old.

By not commenting your code, you are faced with frustration, potentially flawed scripts, and an unpleasant insight into your own mortality.

The following code is the code we just seen, but with added comments. Comments are preceded by a number sign (also known as 'pound sign' in US English, or as 'hashtag' to Twitter geeks). For clarity, it's this character: **#**

Please do use comments from now on. It makes you look like a professional coder. (And please avoid saying 'hashtag' to the '#' in code comments. People will not take you seriously if you do.)

```
import pygaze
from pygaze.display import Display
from pygaze.screen import Screen
import pygaze.libtime as timer
import numpy
from psychopy.visual import GratingStim

# Initialise a new Display instance (specifications are in
# constants.py).
disp = Display()

# Create a new GratingStim. The sinusoidal texture and the
# Gaussian mask will make it into a Gabor. The spatial
# frequency of 0.05 cycles per pixel will make it have
# 1 cycle every 20 pixels.
gabor = GratingStim(pygaze.expdisplay, tex='sin', \
     mask='gauss', sf=0.05, size=200)

# Initialise a new Screen instance for the Gabor.
gaborscreen = Screen()
```

```
# Add the GratingStim to the gaborscreen's screen property
# (a list of all PsychoPy stimuli in the Screen).
gaborscreen.screen.append(gabor)

# Create random numbers between 0 and 1 (numpy.random.
# rand), converted to numbers between 0 and 2 (*2), and
# then converted to numbers between -1 and 1 (-1). The size
# must be a power of 2!
noise = (numpy.random.rand(64, 64) * 2) - 1

# Create a new GratingStim. Using the noise array as
# texture will result in visual snow. The mask is Gaussian
# (to match the Gabor).
noisepatch = GratingStim(pygaze.expdisplay, tex=noise, \
        mask='gauss', size=200)

# Initialise a new Screen instance for the noise.
noisescreen = Screen()

# Add the GratingStim to the Screen's screen property (as
# with Gabor).
noisescreen.screen.append(noisepatch)

# Fill the Display with the Gabor Screen that was prepared
# earlier.
disp.fill(gaborscreen)

# Present the Display (Gabor will now be on the monitor).
disp.show()

# Wait for 1000 milliseconds (Gabor is still on the
# monitor).
timer.pause(1000)

# Fill the Display with the noise Screen that was prepared
# earlier.
disp.fill(noisescreen)

# Present the Display (noise is now on the monitor).
disp.show()

# Wait 2000 milliseconds (noise is still on the monitor).
timer.pause(2000)

# Close the Display (this will end the experiment).
disp.close()
```

The script is now almost twice as long, even though there is absolutely no extra functionality. However, you will be able to understand it two weeks, months, or years from now. That will be a *huge* time-saver! (Well worth all the effort of typing comments!)

4

PROCESSING RESPONSES

Almost every computer-based experiment in psychology and cognitive neuroscience requires participants to respond in one way or another. The most common instrument to collect these responses is the computer keyboard. In the following sections, you will learn how to collect and process key presses.

Are peripherals accurate enough?

Some researchers claim that keyboards are too slow for their purposes, as they require 'millisecond accuracy'. Because it is important to know your tools, this chapter will investigate this claim.

In most operating systems, **peripherals** (keyboards, mice, joysticks, game controllers, etc.) are **polled** at a certain rate. Polling a device means checking its state: are any of the keys or buttons pressed, or is there movement along any of the axes? The polling rate determines how often an operating system checks for new input. If the polling rate is 60 Hz, the keyboard will be checked roughly every 17 milliseconds. If a key is pressed 2 milliseconds after the last 'poll', it will take another 15 milliseconds for it to be picked up.

Traditionally, the polling rate of keyboards and mice was 60 Hz, matching the standard display refresh rate. This makes sense: if the display is updated only once every 17 milliseconds, why should you check for input more than that? The input is used to update the display, so polling devices twice every display refresh will result in one redundant poll.

An example: imagine your mouse is at screen coordinate (10, 10) at time 0 ms (this coincides with the latest screen refresh). Now you move your mouse, which it is polled at a rate of 120 Hz. The mouse was registered to be at point (15, 15) at time 8 ms, and at (20, 20) at time 17 ms. The display is updated to show the mouse cursor at coordinate (20, 20) at time 17 ms. The data from time 8 ms is disregarded for the updating of the monitor, because it's old data. This means that polling the mouse at a higher rate than the monitor refresh is effectively useless.

Clearly, the engineers who thought this up were efficient, but not psychophysicists. If you are very interested in human ergonomics, and would like to see a high-resolution mouse trajectory, can you still use standard computer peripherals?

Most modern peripherals are connected via USB. Most operating systems poll the USB port at a rate of 125 Hz (every 8 milliseconds). This means you will have an average timing error of 4 milliseconds. Some extra inaccuracy is added on by further delays, e.g. in the signal from your input device having to travel to the computer, and within the computer's processes that make sure the input reaches your software.

This can be improved by using software (**drivers**) that polls the USB port more often, and with specialised instruments that can handle this. These are available, and can boost the polling rate to (over) 1000 Hz. That's one data point every millisecond! Such devices are popular among gamers, who think they might avoid getting shot in their virtual heads if their keyboard registers their key-bashing a millisecond or two quicker.

There are researchers who argue that with timing imprecisions of several milliseconds, one cannot investigate mental processes that sometimes occur only during a few milliseconds. Therefore, they buy expensive devices (often connected in more intricate ways then USB) with extremely high polling rates to achieve 'millisecond accuracy'.

So are they right? Yes, but only if the participants they were testing were free from timing imprecision. As all cognitive scientists know, people are not so consistent in their response times. In fact, people are so inconsistent that we need a lot of trials to accurately measure the distribution of their response times. This human timing inaccuracy is way higher than the timing inaccuracy of computer peripherals. The bottom line is that *using keyboards is perfectly fine in most experimental designs*. For a more in-depth discussion, please read Damian (2010).

Keyboard input

Now that you know you can use the keyboard in experiments, it is time to explore how to actually do it. Get started with a new, empty experiment: create a new folder and create two Python scripts, constants.py and experiment.py.

In constants.py, type the following:

PyGaze code

```
# display resolution (should match monitor settings!)
DISPSIZE = (1920, 1080)

# display type (either 'pygame' or 'psychopy')
DISPTYPE = 'psychopy'

# foreground and background
FGC = (0, 0, 0)
BGC = (128, 128, 128)
```

PsychoPy code

```
# display resolution (should match monitor settings!)
DISPSIZE = (1920, 1080)

# foreground and background
FGC = (-1, -1, -1)
BGC = (0, 0, 0)
```

Now, open experiment.py and type the following:

PyGaze code
```
import random
from pygaze.display import Display
from pygaze.screen import Screen
from pygaze.keyboard import Keyboard

# create a new Display instance (to interact with the
# monitor)
disp = Display()

# create a new Screen (to use as a canvas to draw on)
scr = Screen()
```

PsychoPy code
```
import random
from constants import *
from psychopy.visual import Window, TextStim
from psychopy.event import waitKeys

# create a new Display instance (to interact with the
# monitor)
disp = Window(size=DISPSIZE, units='pix', fullscr=True)
```

These are the basics for your new script. In this script, you will present a vowel on the monitor, and ask people to press the corresponding key. To do so, we need at least two things: a list of vowels, and a **Keyboard** instance (or PsychoPy's waitKeys function).

You can use PyGaze's Keyboard class or PsychoPy's waitKeys function to check if any keys are pressed during a certain period. PyGaze's Keyboard can take two keyword arguments; keylist dictates which keys can be pressed (you pass a list of all key names that you want to allow); timeout dictates how long the Keyboard instance will wait for input before giving up. Note that by setting these things when creating the Keyboard instance, you are setting its defaults. When using the method to check for key presses, you can specify other values for the allowed keys and the timeout.

PyGaze code
```
# a list of vowels
vowels = ['a', 'e', 'i', 'o', 'u', 'y']

# create a new Keyboard instance, to monitor key presses
kb = Keyboard(keylist=vowels, timeout=None)
```

PsychoPy code
```
# a list of vowels
vowels = ['a', 'e', 'i', 'o', 'u', 'y']
```

Keys have specific names, and some can be quite unexpected. However, the letter keys are named after their letters. Very easy. The same goes for the numbers, by the way (but not for those on the number pad!). So when you make a list of the vowels, this is also a list of the associated key names.

For the timeout, you can pass any number of milliseconds. You can also pass None, which means precisely what it says: no timeout (the Keyboard will wait for a key press forever). None (with a capital N!) is special in Python; it means 'this has a value of nothing'.

In PsychoPy, you don't have to create a Keyboard instance. Later on, you can use the waitKeys function to achieve the same functionality. An explanation of this function will follow later.

The next bit of the experiment script is to randomly select a vowel from the list, and present that on the monitor. Start with randomly choosing a vowel from the list:

PyGaze code
```
# randomly choose one vowel
letter = random.choice(vowels)
```

PsychoPy code
```
# randomly choose one vowel
letter = random.choice(vowels)
```

Easy, right? The random module has a choice function that randomly picks one value out of a list. To present this on the monitor, you must draw it on your Screen instance in PyGaze, or create a TextStim instance in PsychoPy.

PyGaze code
```
# draw the vowel on a Screen
scr.draw_text(text=letter, fontsize=128)
```

PsychoPy code
```
# create a TextStim for the vowel
vowelstim = TextStim(disp, text=letter, height=128)
```

PyGaze Screen's draw_text method and PsychoPy's TextStim class can take several keyword arguments shown in Table 4.1.

After drawing your text on a Screen, you need to pass that Screen to the Display. Then you need to update the monitor by showing the Display (PyGaze). If you're using PsychoPy instead, you have to draw the TextStim, and then flip the Window.

PyGaze code
```
# fill the Display with a Screen and update the monitor
disp.fill(scr)
disp.show()
```

PsychoPy code
```
# draw the text stimulus
vowelstim.draw()

# update the monitor
disp.flip()
```

TABLE 4.1 draw_text and TextStim keywords

draw_text keyword	TextStim keyword	Purpose
text	text	A string with the text that should be presented on the Screen. You can include newlines ('\n') in this string, to include continue your text on another line.
colour	color	The colour of the text, as a (red, green, blue) tuple with values between 0 (no colour) and 255 (full colour) in PyGaze, or values between –1 (no colour) and 1 (full colour) in PsychoPy.
pos	pos	The position of the text's centre (or top left) on the Screen, as a (x, y) coordinate. The values should be in pixels, between 0 and the Screen width/height. In PyGaze, (0, 0) is the top left. In PsychoPy, (0, 0) is the screen's centre. The top left of a monitor with a resolution of 1024 × 768 pixels would be (–512, –384), and the bottom right would be (512, 384).
center	N/A	Boolean (True or False) that indicates whether the text should be centred. (Please don't ask why 'colour' is in British spelling and 'center' is in American ...) This keyword is not applicable in PsychoPy, which will automatically centre your text.
font	font	The type of font to be used. The default should be fine in most cases, but you can add true type font files (.ttf) to the resources directory of your PyGaze installation. Pass the name of these files (without the extention) to use them (e.g. font='ubuntu'). You should also be able to use the names of most of the locally installed fonts.
fontsize	height	The height of the font in pixels (an integer value!). Note that not all letters in your text will be this high: individual letters' sizes depend on the font. The size here is the box that surrounds the letter, including some empty space at the top and the bottom.
antialias	antialias	A Boolean (True or False) that determines whether the font is anti-aliased. If you don't know what that is, read en.wikipedia.org/wiki/Spatial_anti-aliasing. If you don't care, just ignore this keyword.

As it currently is, your script will display one randomly selected vowel. The only two things left to do, are to catch a participant's response (which is them striking the key that matches the vowel), and to neatly close the Display afterwards. To catch a key press, use the Keyboard's get_key method (and close the Display with the familiar close method):

PyGaze code

```
# wait for a response
key, presstime = kb.get_key()

# close the Display
disp.close()
```

PsychoPy code

```
# wait for a response
resplist = waitKeys(maxWait=float('inf'), keylist=vowels, \
⎵⎵⎵⎵    timeStamped=True)

# select the first response from the list
key, presstime = resplist[0]

# close the Display
disp.close()
```

As you might be able to read from the script, the `get_key` method **returns** two values: the name of the key that was pressed (or None when no key was pressed!), and the time of the keypress (or the time of the timeout, when no key was pressed). The code above catches both of those values in two separate variables, that are separated by a comma: `key` and `presstime`. You can also catch them in a single variable, by using `result = kb.get_key()`. The resulting variable would then be a list, with the pressed key's name (or None) at its first index, and the time of the keypress (or timeout) at its second index.

The `waitKeys` method does a very similar thing, but its output is slightly different: It will return a list of events rather than a single event. So if you pressed the 'A' key at time 5000, the output of PyGaze's `kb.get_key()` will be `['a', 5000]`. The output of PsychoPy's `waitKeys` will be `[('a',5.0)]`. This is the reason for the extra step in the PsychoPy code, where the first item in the response list (at index number 0) is selected.

If you run your current experiment.py, you should see a vowel on the monitor, and you should see it disappear after pressing a vowel on the keyboard. What you do not see, is feedback on whether you pressed the correct vowel. In the next section, you will learn how to give participants feedback based on their responses.

If statements

You have reached an important section. It will teach you about the **if statement**, an important building block of almost all software. People use if statements to run code that is specific to a certain occasion. For example, to turn on the heating in a room when the temperature is low (e.g. below 15°C), or turn off the heating when the temperature is comfortable (e.g. above 20°C). You could even incorporate a third option: to turn on the air conditioning when the temperature is too high (e.g. above 25°C).

In experimental psychology, you can use if statements when you want your experiment to do one thing when a participant's response is correct, but something else if it is not. To see this first-hand, open (a copy of) the script that you wrote in the last section. After the line where you define the key variable, add the following:

Same code for PyGaze and PsychoPy

```
# check if the pressed key matches the displayed letter
if key == letter:
⎵⎵⎵⎵correct = 1
else:
```

```
     correct = 0
```

You should recognise the double 'is equal to' sign (==) from the chapter on Booleans. It makes what programmers call a **conditional statement**, which always results in a Boolean. In other words: the outcome can either be True or False, but nothing else. So 'if key==letter': means '*if the variable "key" has the same value as the variable "letter", then execute the code in the following lines.*' What code is in the following lines, is determined by **indentation**: the amount of whitespace before each line of code.

Indentation

In Python, indentation is an integral part of your code. Without it, if statements and other functionality will not work. One indent can be a tab, two spaces, or four spaces. Which you use, depends on your code editor's settings. Although indentation is considered a matter of personal preference, there are some guidelines that you should take into account. The first is to never mix indentation types. Always use either tabs or spaces, and obviously never mix two or four spaces as one indent.

If you do mix indentation types up, you deserve to receive an electric shock from a cattle prod, according to Python Enhancement Proposal 666 (www.python.org/dev/peps/pep-0666/). Another guideline is provided in Python Enhancement Proposal 8 (PEP 8, www.python.org/dev/peps/pep-0008/#tabs-or-spaces), where *the creator of Python argues in favour of using four spaces*.

Python reads code that is on different indentations as separate blocks. With every indent you include before a line, you effectively nest it within earlier lines. Try to predict what the next code will print:

```
a = 1
b = 2
c = 3
if a == 1:
    if b == 2:
        if c == 3:
            print('strawberry')
        else:
            print('raspberry')
    else:
        print('blueberry')
else:
    print('banana')
```

In the current state, it would print strawberry. However, if c was not 3, it would print raspberry. If b was not 2, the value of c would not matter at all (because c is only evaluated when b==2!), so blueberry would be printed. If a was not 1, none of the other lines would be run, and banana would be printed.

See how nesting works with indentation? Only if code at a lower indentation gives the go-ahead, then code on the next line (at a higher indentation) is run. It is a hierarchical process that could go on ad infinitum (that's Latin for "FOR EVER!!1!"). As a last exercise, compare the next two *snippets* of code, and try to predict what would be printed in both. Are they equivalent? Why not?

```
a = 1
b = 2
if a == 1:
     if b == 2:
          print('cow')
     else:
          print('chicken')
else:
     print('pig')
```

```
a = 1
b = 2
if a == 1 and b == 2:
     print('cow')
else:
     print('pig')
```

Providing feedback

Now that you know about if statements and indentation, it's time to get back to your programming. Open the experiment.py you created in the section on 'keyboard input', and that you modified in the section on if statements. Now add the following after the correct = 0 line:

PyGaze code

```
# on a correct response...
if correct:

     # ...provide nice feedback
     feedback = "Well done!"

     # (0,255,0) is green
     fbcolour = (0, 255, 0)
# on an incorrect response...
else:

     # ...provide nasty feedback
     feedback = "You're wrong!"

     # (255,0, 0) is red
     fbcolour = (255, 0, 0)
```

PsychoPy code:

```
# on a correct response...
if correct:
     # ...provide nice feedback
     feedback = "Well done!"
     # (-1, 1, -1) is green
```

```
      fbcolour = (-1, 1, -1)
# on an incorrect response...
else:
      # ...provide nasty feedback
      feedback = "You're wrong!"
      # (1, -1, -1) is red
      fbcolour = (1, -1, -1)
```

This defines the feedback string and the feedback's colour, but does not show the participant anything yet. For that, you need to update the Screen and Display in PyGaze, or the Window in PsychoPy:

PyGaze code

```
# first clear the Screen of its current content
scr.clear()

# then draw the feedback text
scr.draw_text(text=feedback, colour=fbcolour, fontsize=24)

# show the Screen with feedback
disp.fill(scr)
disp.show()
```

PsychoPy code

```
# create a stimulus for the feedback text
fbstim = TextStim(disp, text=feedback, color=fbcolour, \
      height=24)

# show the feedback
fbstim.draw()
disp.flip()
```

The Screen's `clear` method gets rid of all the current content (in this case, the vowel that was drawn on it before). If you do not call it, the vowel you drew previously will remain on the Screen, and the feedback text will be drawn over it. In PsychoPy, the Window is cleared after every call to the `flip` method, so there is no need to explicitly clear it.

As you might remember from earlier in this book, drawing on Screens (or creating new stimuli) immediately before showing them is not good for timing. That is ignored here, to keep the example simple. Keep in mind that this is not the optimal way of doing things!

If you run the current script, the feedback will only appear very briefly, and the script will close immediately after. It would be nice to have a self-paced ending, where the participant can end the experiment by pressing any key. For this end, use the `get_key` method or the `waitKeys` function without any restrictions on the allowed keys or the timeout. Add the following code directly after the `disp.show()` or `disp.flip()` line:

PyGaze code

```
# wait for any keypress
```

```
kb.get_key(keylist=None, timeout=None)
```

PsychoPy code
```
# wait for any keypress
waitKeys(maxWait=float('inf'), keylist=None)
```

Now run the script and see what happens!

Using wildcards in feedback

The current feedback is not very constructive. You could improve it by letting the participant know what went wrong (or right!). In the section on wildcards in Chapter 2, you learned how to insert values into strings by using %-notations. You might remember that wildcards can be for any kind of value: `%s` denotes a string, `%d` a decimal number, and `%1.2f` a fractional number with one number before and two after the full stop (e.g. 3.14).

Using what you know about wildcards, you can construct an additional feedback string. You should insert the following code directly after the `fbcolour = (255, 0, 0)` (PyGaze) or `fbcolour = (1, -1, -1)` (PsychoPy) lines. You should not indent the following line, because you want it to run in any situation:

Same code for PyGaze and PsychoPy
```
# construct an informative string by using variables
extrafb = 'The vowel was %s, and you typed %s.' \
␣␣␣␣ % (letter, key)
```

After `scr.draw_text(text=feedback, colour=fbcolour, fontsize=24)` or after `fbstim = TextStim(disp, text=feedback, color=fbcolour, height=24)`, add extra lines to draw the extra feedback:

PyGaze code
```
# determine the position of the extra feedback

# (at half the screen width, and 60% of the screen height)
extrafbpos = (int(DISPSIZE[0]*0.5), int(DISPSIZE[1]*0.6))

# draw the extra feedback
scr.draw_text(text=extrafb, pos=extrafbpos, fontsize=24)
```

PsychoPy code
```
# determine the position of the extra feedback

# (at half the screen width, and 60% of the screen height)
extrafbpos = (0, int(DISPSIZE[1]*-0.1))

# create a stimulus for the extra feedback
extrafbstim = TextStim(disp, text=extrafb, pos=extrafbpos, \
␣␣␣␣ height=24)
```

```
# draw the extra feedback
extrafbstim.draw()
```

The int function turns floating point numbers into integers. You need integers, because the position is defined in pixels, which are indivisible units. This leaves you with one problem: DISPSIZE is defined in constants.py, but you just referenced it in experiment. py. That will not work … (Run the script to see for yourself!)

To mend this, you can directly import DISPSIZE from constant.py by adding the following line at the beginning of experiment.py:

Same code for PyGaze and PsychoPy

```
from constants import DISPSIZE
```

Alternatively, you can also import all variables from constants.py at once, by using the following notation (the asterisks means "everything"):

```
from constants import *
```

After adding the import you prefer, run the script again to see if it works. Does it provide you with better feedback? Does it satisfy your needs? ARE YOU NOT ENTERTAINED?!

Using sound for feedback

If you were not entertained by the informative feedback, you might be interested in learning how to give more obnoxious feedback. You could, for example, provide a burst of white noise ('KGGHRG!') when a participant makes an error. Or you could play a nice pure tone ('beeeeeeep!') when a response is correct. Even better: you can play a rewarding 'Ka-ching!' sound, loaded from a recording.

For this, you can turn to PyGaze's or PyshcoPy's Sound classes. You can use these classes to load a sound from a file, or to create one based on a few specifications. The files you can load need to be either raw .wav files, or .ogg files (an open-source audio format). Loading a sound file is as easy as passing a single keyword, soundfile or value, and the name of your file. Example:

PyGaze code

```
from pygaze.sound import Sound
kaching = Sound(soundfile='C:\ka-ching.wav')
```

PsychoPy code

```
from psychopy.sound import Sound
kaching = Sound(value='C:\ka-ching.wav')
```

You can also create your own sounds in PyGaze by specifying a few additional keywords. PsychoPy does not directly offer this functionality, but you will learn how to create your own sounds from scratch in the next 'Make some noise' section.

So you can create your own sound with PyGaze by using more keywords. The most important one is osc, which determines the type of oscillation for the sound. You can specify four different waves here:

1   sine will create a sinusoid: a pure tone;
2   saw will create a sawtooth wave: a pure tone and all its harmonics at the same intensity (quite a harsh sound);
3   square will produce a square wave: an oscillation that instantaneously jumps from minimum to maximum amplitude, instead of slowly approaching each like a sinusoid (resulting in another harsh sound);
4   the final option, whitenoise, randomly jumps to different amplitudes without any oscillatory pattern (this is similar to the sound you hear when a radio is not set to a channel).

To hear these oscillator types for yourself, open an Interpreter and type the following:

```
from pygaze.sound import Sound

sine = Sound(osc='sine')
saw = Sound(osc='saw')
square = Sound(osc='square')
noise = Sound(osc='whitenoise')
```

To play the sounds, you can use the Sound's play method. This takes one keyword argument, repeats, which determines the amount of times a single sound is repeated. A value of 0 will play the sound only once, a positive value of N will add on N repeats, and a negative value (e.g. –1) means 'repeat infinitely'. The default value is 0, so you don't have to bother with it for now. Run the following lines one by one:

```
sine.play()
saw.play()
square.play()
noise.play()
```

Pretty cool, eh? If you're in a computer lab, try to annoy your teacher by cranking up the volume, and playing the sound over the speakers of your computer!

Now that you know how to create Sounds, you can use them as feedback. As you might have noticed in the examples, the white noise sounds really annoying, whereas the sine wave is actually pretty kind on the ears. Let's reward correct responses with a 500 millisecond long sine wave, and punish errors with an equally long burst of noise. (Note: It's a bit harder to create noise in PsychoPy, so instead you can use a lower-frequency sine wave for feedback on errors.)

You can specify the duration of sounds in milliseconds by using the length keyword in PyGaze, or the secs keyword in PsychoPy:

PyGaze example
```
sine = Sound(osc='sine', length=500)
```

PsychoPy example
```
sine = Sound(secs=0.5)
```

You should also choose a frequency (or pitch) for your sound. This is the rate at which it oscillates: low frequencies produce 'low' sounds, whereas high frequencies produce 'high' sounds (is that why we refer to them as 'high' and 'low'?). Note that frequencies below 20 and over 20,000 cannot be heard by humans, and that the sounds at both ends of that spectrum need a high intensity to be perceived. Humans are tuned to optimally hear sounds around 4000 Hertz (1 Hertz = 1 vibration per second). That means you need a relatively low intensity to hear sounds with a frequency of around 4000 Hz, compared to sounds with a lower or higher frequency. Note that white noise, due to its inherent random variation, does not have a single frequency!

In PyGaze, you can specify the frequency by using the `freq` keyword and a value in Hertz. In PsychoPy, you can use the `value` keyword to achieve the same thing.

PyGaze example
```
sine = Sound(osc='sine', freq=4000, length=500)
```

PsychoPy example
```
sine = Sound(value=4000, secs=0.5)
```

Open (a copy of) the script you created in the previous section, and import the Sound class at the top of experiment.py:

PyGaze code
```
from pygaze.sound import Sound
```

PsychoPy code
```
from psychopy.sound import Sound
```

To create two Sound instances, add the following lines after the `scr = Screen()` line in the PyGaze code, or after the line where you define `disp` in the PsychoPy code:

PyGaze code
```
# Create two Sounds, one for nice and one for stern
# feedback
sine = Sound(osc='sine', freq=4000, length=500)
noise = Sound(osc='whitenoise', length=500)
```

PsychoPy code
```
# create two Sounds: one for nice and one for stern
# feedback
high = Sound(value=4000, secs=0.5)
low = Sound(value=400, secs=0.5)
```

The final step is to include an if statement between the `disp.show()` or `disp.flip()` line for the feedback, and the `kb.get_key(keylist=None, timeout=None)` or `waitKeys(maxWait=inf, keylist=None)` line to wait for a final keypress:

PyGaze code
```
# on a correct response...
if correct:
```

```
      # ...play the sine Sound
      sine.play()
# on an incorrect response...
else:
      # ...play the harsh Sound
      noise.play()
```

PsychoPy code

```
# on a correct response...
if correct:
      # ...play the high sine Sound
      high.play()
# on an incorrect response...
else:
      # ...play the low sine Sound
      low.play()
```

Now run experiment.py to see and hear what happens!

While loops

You know how to use a single keypress as a response, but what if you want people to type something? This provides you with two extra issues, both resulting from the fact that you will need to process more than just a single key.

The first issue is that your participants will have a multitude of options. People won't just be pressing letter keys, but also the Space bar or the backspace key. so you need more options in your if statement! Fortunately, this can be easily achieved by using **elif** (a combination of **el**se and **if**):

```
key, presstime = kb.get_key(keylist=None, timeout=None)

if key == 'c':
      print('chicken')
elif key == 'p':
      print('parsnip')
elif key == 't':
      print('tomato')
else:
      print('No soup for you!')
```

The second issue is that you will need to continuously check for new keyboard input, and include each new keypress into the response. This is going to be slightly harder, but not as hard as you might think.

One solution to continuous keyboard monitoring and display updating could be to copy and paste the code to collect, draw, and present a single keypress value:

```
# first keypress
key, presstime = kb.get_key(keylist=None, timeout=None)
scr.daw_text(text=key)
disp.fill(scr)
disp.show()

# second keypress
key, presstime = kb.get_key(keylist=None, timeout=None)
scr.daw_text(text=key)
disp.fill(scr)
disp.show()

# etc...

# N-th keypress
key, presstime = kb.get_key(keylist=None, timeout=None)
scr.daw_text(text=key)
disp.fill(scr)
disp.show()
```

But *repeating code is highly inefficient, ugly, and an absolute waste of time.*

A better solution is provided by the **while loop**: special functionality that is present in almost all programming languages. It allows you to cycle through the same lines of code until a conditional statement is met. While loops usually have a Boolean value (or a conditional statement) that could be considered a guard. When the guard says True, the loop will keep on looping. But when the guard says False, the loop will stop.

Let's look at a famous scene from Lord of the Rings, where Gandalf (our guard) decides that his friends can run across a bridge, but that a big flaming enemy SHALL NOT PASS! You could view this scene as a number of **iterations** (loops) through Gandalf's decision process. In this process, Gandalf first checks who passes by. Then he decides whether this passer-by is an enemy or a friend. If the passer-by is a friend, Gandalf does nothing, because he's cool with bridge-crossing friends. However, if the passer-by turns out to be an enemy, Gandalf decides to stop letting people through. After he decides to stop letting people through, he will destroy the bridge.

Gandalf's bridge-habits can be described by the following code snippet:

```
# pre-define the 'guard' value
gandalf_is_cool = True

# only continue if gandalf_is_cool is still True
while gandalf_is_cool:

      # check who crosses with this function
      passerby = check_who_goes_there()

      # if an enemy crosses, Gandalf loses his cool!
      if passerby == 'enemy':
            gandalf_is_cool = False
```

```
# destroy the bridge after the while loop
destroy_bridge()
```

Let's break this down. First, the value for gandalf_is_cool is preset to True. This will make the while loop run. Within the while loop, the function check_who_goes_there can return two values ('enemy' or 'friend'), which will be associated with the passerby variable. The if statement (within the while loop) checks whether the value of passerby is 'enemy'. If it is (and only if it is!), the variable gandalf_is_cool will be set to False.

It is important to realise that every single **iteration** (= loop) of the while loop will run the exact same code. First it checks whether gandalf_is_cool == True, and then it will run the code that is at one indent further than while gandalf_is_cool. If at some point gandalf_is_cool == False, the while loop will simply ignore all indented code, and skip to the next line at the same indent as while gandalf_is_cool. In the above example, that line is destroy_bridge() (comments don't count!).

If you understand this, you might see an important implication: if gandalf_is_cool never goes False, the while loop will keep going. For ever. This is what programmers call an **infinite loop**, and it can be a nasty bug that completely freezes your script.

While loop for responses

To make you remember and understand while loops a bit better, let's use one in a script. You could write a script that lets participants type a response, until they press Enter to confirm. Create a new folder, with new constants.py and experiment.py files.

In constants.py, define the constants that you always define:

PyGaze code

```
# the display size should match the monitor's resolution
DISPSIZE = (1920, 1080)

# the display type can be 'pygame' or 'psychopy'
DISPTYPE = 'pygame'

# the foreground and background colour are (red, green,
# blue) the values are 0 (no colour) to 255 (full colour)
FGC = (255, 255, 255)
BGC = (0, 0, 0)
```

PsychoPy code

```
# the display size should match the monitor's resolution
DISPSIZE = (1920, 1080)

# the foreground and background colour are (red, green, blue)
# the values are -1 (no colour) to 1 (full colour)
FGC = (1, 1, 1)
BGC = (-1, -1, -1)
```

In experiment.py, import the classes and constants that you need in the script:

PyGaze code
```
from constants import DISPSIZE
from pygaze.display import Display
from pygaze.screen import Screen
from pygaze.keyboard import Keyboard
```

PsychoPy code
```
from constants import DISPSIZE
from psychopy.visual import Window, TextStim
from psychopy.event import waitKeys
```

And create the instances of these classes that you will use later on:

PyGaze code
```
# create a Display to show things on the monitor
disp = Display()

# create a Screen for drawing operations
scr = Screen()

# create a Keyboard to collect keypresses
kb = Keyboard(keylist=None, timeout=None)
```

PsychoPy code
```
# create a Window to show things on the monitor
disp = Window(size=DISPSIZE, units='pix', fullscr=True)
```

In this script, you will present a single question on the top half of the monitor, and you will allow a participant to type a response in the monitor's centre. To achieve this, you could start by defining a question:

Same code for PyGaze and PsychoPy
```
# define a super-important question
question = 'What do you think of this question?'
```

After defining the question string, you could draw it on a Screen and present that Screen via the Display (PyGaze), or create and draw a text stimulus (PsychoPy). Of course, you should also think of a nice place on the Screen. How about horizontally centred, and placed at 20 per cent of the screen height? Make sure to turn the values for the position into integers, because pixels are indivisible!

PyGaze code
```
# define the question's position
qpos = (int(DISPSIZE[0]*0.5), int(DISPSIZE[1]*0.2))

# draw it on the Screen
scr.draw_text(text=question, pos=qpos, fontsize=24)
```

```
# fill the Display with the Screen
disp.fill(scr)

# present the current Display
disp.show()
```

PsychoPy code

```
# define the question's position
qpos = (0, int(DISPSIZE[1]*0.2))

# create a new text stimulus
qstim = TextStim(disp, text=question, pos=qpos, height=24)

# draw the question
qstim.draw()

# create an additional text stimulus for the response
# (this will be updated later)
respstim = TextStim(disp, text='', height=24)
```

Please note that `''` is an empty string: two single quotation marks. It is not one double quotation mark! This should all be familiar to you, and perhaps even a bit boring. Time to get on with the new stuff: a while loop that runs until the Enter key is pressed, and collects and presents keypresses while it is running.

Let's think about this for a second (always think before you start coding!). To be able to update a participant's response with each keypress, you need a variable that contains the response. This should start out as an empty string, and should be adjusted on each keypress.

How the text is adjusted, depends on the key that is pressed. If the key is the Space bar, a space should be inserted. If the pressed key is backspace, the last part of the response should be deleted. Of course, if the key is a character (letter, number, or interpunction), it should simply be appended to the response variable. To keep things simple, you could call this variable `response`, and it should be a string.

What else do we need in the while loop? A guard variable that starts out as True, but turns to False when Enter is pressed. To achieve this, you could define a variable called `done` that starts out as False. The while loop could use `not  done` as its conditional statement. If the Enter key is pressed, you set done to True to stop the loop.

Your current loop will look a bit like this (add it to experiment.py):

Same code for PyGaze and PsychoPy

```
# start with an empty response string
response = ''

# start undone
done = False

# loop until done == False
while not done:
```

```
      # do stuff
```

Note how `# do stuff` is undefined. Let's replace this by functioning lines, starting with the code to check for keypresses (add it to experiment.py):

PyGaze code

```
      # check for keypresses
      key, presstime = kb.get_key()
```

PsychoPy code

```
      # check for keypresses
      resplist = waitKeys(maxWait=float('inf'), \
           keyList=None, timeStamped=True)
      # use only the first in the returned list of
      # keypresses
      key, presstime = resplist[0]
```

Now add the code that evaluates the value of key. If the name of the pressed key is Space, add a space. An example (don't copy it into experiment.py just yet):

```
if key == 'space':
      response += ' '
```

If the key is a letter, a number, or interpunction, you should add it to the response. But how can you recognise the names of these keys? One thing they all have in common, is a very brief name: keys' letters, numbers (not number pad!), and interpunction are named after the character they represent. So if the name of the key has a length of one, you know it is going to be a character. You can check the length of strings (and lists, and tuples, and vectors) by using the `len` function. An example (don't copy it into experiment.py):

```
if len(key) == 1:
      response += key
```

What if the participant presses the backspace key? Then you want to keep everything in the current response, but not the last character. You could do this by indexing a slice of the response string. The slice should contain '*all characters in the string from the first index until the last index, but not including the last*'. If you remember the section on lists in Chapter 2, you know how to translate this into Python: `response[0:-1]`. Of course, if the string is still empty, you can't remove the last item. Trying to do so would even result in an error! So before trying to delete the last character of the response string, you should check if response's length is over 0. An example (don't copy it into experiment.py):

```
if key == 'backspace' and len(response) > 0:
      response = response[0:-1]
```

The final bit is checking whether the Enter key was pressed, and setting done to True when it is. Note that the Enter key is often labelled 'return'. An example (don't copy it into experiment.py):

```
if key == 'return':
     done = True
```

Now add it all together in experiment.py:

Same code for PyGaze and PsychoPy

```
     # check if the length of the key's name equals 1
     if len(key) == 1:

          # add the key to the response
          response += key

     # check if the key is the Space bar
     elif key == 'space':

          # add a space to the response
          response += ' '

     # check if the key's name was 'backspace' and
     # check if the response has at least 1 character
     elif key == 'backspace' and len(response) > 0:

          # remove the last character of the response
          response = response[0:-1]

     # if the key was none of the above, check if it
     # was the Enter key
     if key == 'return':

          # set done to True
          done = True
```

The final thing you should add to the while loop, is actually presenting the updated response. In PyGaze, first draw the response string on a Screen, then fill the Display with said Screen, and then show the Display. In PsychoPy, simply update the value of the text stimulus. Add the following lines to experiment.py:

PyGaze code

```
     # draw the current response on a Screen
     scr.draw_text(text=response, fontsize=24)

     # fill the Display with the response Screen
     disp.fill(scr)

     # show the Display on the monitor
     disp.show()
```

PsychoPy code

```
     # update the response stimulus
     respstim.setText(response)

     # draw the response stimulus
```

```
ⅬⅬⅬⅬ    respstim.draw()

ⅬⅬⅬⅬ    # update the monitor
ⅬⅬⅬⅬ    disp.flip()
```

As usual, end the experiment by closing the Display:

Same code for PyGaze and PsychoPy
```
# close the Display
disp.close()
```

If you run the current experiment.py, what happens? If you use PyGaze and have done everything according to this book, you should see the response turning into an unintelligible mess. This is not because the response variable turns into a mess, but because you keep drawing the updated response to the same Screen without ever removing the previous response!

In PyGaze, you have to reset the Screen before you draw an updated response on it. The Screen's `clear` method should come in handy here: it clears the Screen of whatever is on it. Unfortunately, it will also clear the question that you drew on the top of the Screen. This means that you will have to redraw that with every response update too.

With PsychoPy, there is a different issue: the question disappears after pressing the first key! This is because the `flip` method clears the entire monitor, and stimuli have to be actively re-drawn.

If you use PyGaze, replace the `scr.draw_text(text=response, fontsize=24)` line with the lines below. For PsychoPy, add the lines below after the `respstim.setText(response)` line.

PyGaze code

```
ⅬⅬⅬⅬ    # clear the current content of scr
ⅬⅬⅬⅬ    scr.clear()

ⅬⅬⅬⅬ    # redraw the question
ⅬⅬⅬⅬ    scr.draw_text(text=question, pos=qpos, fontsize=24)

ⅬⅬⅬⅬ    # draw the current response on a Screen
ⅬⅬⅬⅬ    scr.draw_text(text=response, fontsize=24)
```

PsychoPy code

```
ⅬⅬⅬⅬ    # re-draw the question stimulus
ⅬⅬⅬⅬ    qstim.draw()
```

If you run the script now (provided you did everything correctly), you should be able to type a response of letters, numbers, and interpunction. If your script is not running for some reason, the entire correct content of experiment.py is on the next page.

What was not possible in this example, is to use the Shift key to make letters into capitals, or numbers into weird characters. Implementing that is more complicated, and will not be covered in this book. Primarily because it is unlikely you will really need this in a serious experiment. (That's not to say questionnaires are not serious experiments, but they usually do not contain a whole lot of open questions, and there are better tools to collect a large amount of open answers.)

Important note on interpunction: In PyGaze, when DISPTYPE is set to 'pygame', interpunction keys will be named by their character, e.g. '.' or ';'. In PsychoPy or PyGaze with DISPTYPE = 'psychopy', they will be named by their character's official name, e.g. 'period' or 'semicolon'. This is why the above PsychoPy example didn't display interpunction. You can add additional elif statements to accommodate for this.

The following is the content of experiment.py as it should be at the end of this section. Comments have been removed to reduce the amount of lines. That does not mean it is OK for you to remove your comments!

PyGaze code

```
from constants import DISPSIZE
from pygaze.display import Display
from pygaze.screen import Screen
from pygaze.keyboard import Keyboard

disp = Display()
scr = Screen()
kb = Keyboard(keylist=None, timeout=None)

question = 'What do you think of this question?'
qpos = (int(DISPSIZE[0]*0.5), int(DISPSIZE[1]*0.2))
scr.draw_text(text=question, pos=qpos, fontsize=24)

disp.fill(scr)
disp.show()

response = ''
done = False

while not done:
    key, presstime = kb.get_key()

    if len(key) == 1:
        response += key
    elif key == 'space':
        response += ' '
    elif key == 'backspace' and len(response) > 0:
        response = response[0:-1]
    if key == 'return':
        done = True

    scr.clear()
    scr.draw_text(text=question, pos=qpos, fontsize=24)
    scr.draw_text(text=response, fontsize=24)
```

```
      disp.fill(scr)
      disp.show()
disp.close()
```

PsychoPy code

```
from constants import DISPSIZE
from psychopy.visual import Window, TextStim
from psychopy.event import waitKeys

disp = Window(size=DISPSIZE, units='pix', fullscr=True)

question = 'What do you think of this question?'
qpos = (0, int(DISPSIZE[1]*0.2))
qstim = TextStim(disp, text=question, pos=qpos, height=24)
qstim.draw()

respstim = TextStim(disp, text='', height=24)

response = ''
done = False

while not done:
      resplist = waitKeys(maxWait=float('inf'), \
            keyList=None, timeStamped=True)
      key, presstime = resplist[0]

      if len(key) == 1:
            response += key
      elif key == 'space':
            response += ' '
      elif key == 'backspace' and len(response) > 0:
            response = response[0:-1]
      if key == 'return':
            done = True

      respstim.setText(response)

      qstim.draw()
      respstim.draw()
      disp.flip()

disp.close()
```

MAKE SOME NOISE

Welcome to another random intermezzo! In this section, you will learn how to construct your own sounds, how to play them via PyGame, and how to save them to a file. There are two upsides to this. First, you can show the file you created to your loved ones, and they will be so proud of you! Second, you can make a lot of noise while making the file. Let's hope you are a student, working in a computer lab, and have access to working speakers.

What is sound?

Good question! Sound is nothing more than vibrating air (or water, or any other volume). The rate at which air vibrates determines what you hear. When something vibrates between 20 and 20,000 times per second, it produces a sound that humans can hear (and sometimes even feel!). The amount of vibrations per second is called the **frequency**.

That didn't quite answer the question of what sound is, it just redefined it as a 'vibration'. What is a vibration? In terms of air, it's like air molecules are doing the wave in a longitudinal fashion (they move forward and back again). In terms of your ear, it's very similar: the ear drum (tympanic membrane) moves back and forth in a regular motion.

With a bit of imagination, you can see how the ear drum's movement is like a swing: it moves forward a bit, then starts moving back, picks up speed, zips past the midline, slows down as it is being stretched the other way, stops entirely, and starts moving backwards. It will then pick up speed again, zip past the midline again, slow down again, stop, and start moving backwards again. The extent to which the drum is stretched (the furthest points in the swing) is called the **amplitude**.

So, in order to make sound, you need to be able to make a signal that goes up and down with a certain amplitude, at a frequency between 20 and 20,000 times per second.

Sinusoid and noise

You might remember such a signal from secondary school maths. If you don't, here's a spoiler: it's a **sinusoid**. You can create one using NumPy. To do so, you need a range of numbers between 0 and 2ϖ (that is two times the number pi, or roughly 6.3). You use 2ϖ, because it is the width of a single sine wave. NumPy's `sin` function can turn that range of numbers into an actual wave. Type the following code into an Interpreter:

```
import numpy

# create a range of numbers between 0 and 2pi
x = numpy.arange(0, 2*numpy.pi, 0.01)

# create a sine wave
sine = numpy.sin(x)
```

Now that you created a sine wave, you can visualise it by using Matplotlib:

```
from matplotlib import pyplot
```

```
# plot the sine wave
pyplot.plot(x, sine)
pyplot.show()
```

Looks cool, right? But not quite cool enough … Let's make some actual NOISE!

```
# create a bunch of random numbers
# (with the same length as the sine wave)
noise = numpy.random.rand(len(sine))

# compare the sinusoid and the noise
pyplot.plot(sine)
pyplot.plot(noise)
pyplot.show()
```

For the next bit, you will concentrate on the sine wave to learn about some digital sound basics. However, the same principles apply to noise, and you will get back to it shortly. If you look at the *y*-axis, you can see that the sine wave's maximum is 1 and its minimum is –1. That means its amplitude is 1. This is a little low for a sound, so you will need to adjust that a bit. Simply multiply the sine by 16383, which should be high enough:

```
sine = sine * 16383
pyplot.plot(x, sine)
pyplot.show()
```

The wave still looks the same, but the *y*-axis has changed: the wave's amplitude is a lot higher now! Now you have sorted that, turn your attention to the sound's frequency.

When you created the x variable, you used NumPy's arange function. This creates a range of numbers between a starting point (0) and an ending point (2*pi), with a certain step size. The higher the step size, the fewer points there will be in the wave. We call this number of points the amount of **samples**. Let's see what sampling does to a wave's shape:

```
high = numpy.arange(0, 2*numpy.pi, 0.01)
mid = numpy.arange(0, 2*numpy.pi, 0.5)
low = numpy.arange(0, 2*numpy.pi, 2)

pyplot.plot(high, numpy.sin(high))
pyplot.plot(mid, numpy.sin(mid))
pyplot.plot(low, numpy.sin(low))
pyplot.show()
```

As you can see, the higher the step size (thus the fewer samples), the poorer the representation of the sine wave becomes. Fortunately, computers have pretty decent computing power nowadays, so working with high numbers of samples shouldn't be a problem. We call the amount of samples the **sampling rate**, and it can go up to several millions of samples per second on very fancy systems! For this example, we will stick to 48,000, which is just about enough to cover all sounds that a human can actually hear.

Open a new file in a script editor, and call it **make_sound.py**. For this to work, you need to import some libraries. NumPy is one of them, but to do the sound production, you will need another two: PyGame and wave. PyGame is mostly used for game development, but we can use its `mixer` module. This allows you to make sounds out of the sound waves that you create with NumPy. `wave` is a Python module that allows you to create .wav files. We will come back to that later. For now, just put this at the beginning of your script:

```
import wave
import numpy
import pygame
```

First, you should define the constants that you just learned about:

```
# maximal sound amplitude and sampling rate
MAXAMP = 16383
SAMPLERATE = 48000
```

You will also need to set the amount of channels. Let's go for mono now, which is one channel. This will make the same sound come out of all speakers.

```
# mono
NCHANNELS = 1
```

Now you need to decide what your sound's length and frequency should be. Let's go for a three-second sound of 1000 vibrations per second (= 1000 Hertz):

```
# sound length (seconds) and frequency (Hertz)
SOUNDLEN = 3.0
SOUNDFREQ = 1000
```

Time for a few quick calculations: if your sound has a length of three seconds and a frequency of 1000 Hertz, that means your sound will contain 3 * 1000 = 3000 cycles:

```
# calculate the total amount of cycles
ncycles = SOUNDLEN * SOUNDFREQ
```

The sound will be sampled with 48,000 samples per second, so your entire sound will consist of 3 seconds * 48,000 samples = 144,000 samples. In every cycle, there will be 144,000 samples / 3000 cycles = 48 samples per cycle (spc).

```
# calculate the total amount of samples
nsamples = SOUNDLEN * SAMPLERATE

# calculate the number of samples per cycle
spc = nsamples / ncycles
```

Now that you know the amount of samples per second, you can calculate the step size for each cycle. Remember that a single vibration was made out of numbers between 0 and 2*pi, and that the step size determined the wave's representation? Let's make that range, and the associated sine wave:

```
# the stepsize is the distance between samples within a
# cycle (divide the range by the amount of samples per
# cycle)
```

```
stepsize = (2*numpy.pi) / spc

# create a range of numbers between 0 and 2*pi
x = numpy.arange(0, 2*numpy.pi, stepsize)

# make a sine wave out of the range
sine = numpy.sin(x)
```

The next step is to crank up the sine wave's amplitude:

```
# increase the sine wave's amplitude
sine = sine * MAXAMP
```

Now that you have created a single cycle (that's one vibration), you can simply repeat it to create a longer sound. After all, a sound is nothing more than a series of vibrations! To repeat the sound, you can use NumPy's `tile` function. This allows you to provide a vector (your sine wave), and the number of times you want it repeated (an integer):

```
# repeat the sine wave!
allsines = numpy.tile(sine, int(ncycles))
```

If you want to see if this works, simply plot it:

```
from matplotlib import pyplot
pyplot.plot(numpy.tile(sine, 4))
pyplot.plot(numpy.tile(sine, 2))
pyplot.plot(sine)
pyplot.show()
```

Numbers to sound

You currently have a series of 3000 cycles of a wave. The entire vector contains 144,000 numbers that represent a three-second long sound with a frequency of 1000 cycles per second. That's impressive. Time to make an actual sound out of that representation!

To make a sound, you can use PyGame's mixer module. This conveniently allows you to turn a NumPy array (such as the `allsines` vector that you just created) into a mixer. Sound instance. You will have to initialise the mixer module first, though:

```
# initialise the mixer module
# (it requires the sampling rate and the number of
# channels)
pygame.mixer.init(frequency=SAMPLERATE, channels=NCHANNELS)

# now create a sound out of the allsines vector
tone = pygame.mixer.Sound(allsines.astype('int16'))
```

You might be confused by the `allsines.astype('int16')` bit. It turns all numbers in `allsines` into 16-bit integers, which is the format that PyGame needs.

To play the sound, use its `play` method:

```
# play the sinusoid sound
tone.play()
```

Run the script (if you haven't yet) and enjoy your beautiful, self made, pure tone!

As promised, let's briefly return to noise. Noise is actually a bit easier to make. First, simply create an array of random numbers with the length of the amount of samples in your sound (using the same sound length, and the same sampling rate):

```
# create a series of random numbers
noise = numpy.random.rand(SOUNDLEN * SAMPLERATE)
```

The sine wave's values were between –1 and 1, whereas the noise's values are now between 0 and 1. To correct this, multiply all noise by 2 (so the values are between 0 and 2), and then subtract 1 (so the values are between –1 and 1):

```
# correct the value range (-1 to 1)
noise = (noise * 2) - 1
```

Now you can set the correct amplitude, as you did with the sine wave:

```
# increase the noise's amplitude
noise = noise * MAXAMP
```

And all that is left to do now, is to turn it into an actual sound!

```
# turn the noise vector into a sound
whitenoise = pygame.mixer.Sound(noise.astype('int16'))
# play the noise sound
whitenoise.play()
```

Pretty cool, eh? Maybe you should turn up your computer's volume, so that everyone around you can enjoy the sounds you just created.

Naturally, you want to share your work with your loved ones. Regrettably, PyGame's sounds are constructed in temporary memory, so you can't save them to a file directly. Because it would be such a shame for your family and friends to miss the opportunity to hear your beautiful noise, here's how to save your sound.

First, you need to open a new file. In this case, you need to open two: one for the sinusoid (the pure tone), and one for the noise. To do this, you can use the wave module's open function. This function requires a file name (a string, ending with '.wav'), and a letter indicating the opened file's mode (use 'w' for 'write').

```
# open new wave file objects
tonefile = wave.open('pure_tone.wav', 'w')
noisefile = wave.open('noise.wav', 'w')
```

Now you need to set some parameters. These are the frame rate, which is the sampling rate (you defined that earlier); the number of channels (also defined earlier); and the sample width (set this to 2, and don't think about it):

```
# set parameters for the pure tone
tonefile.setframerate(SAMPLERATE)
tonefile.setnchannels(NCHANNELS)
tonefile.setsampwidth(2)
```

```
# set the same parameters for the noise
noisefile.setframerate(SAMPLERATE)
noisefile.setnchannels(NCHANNELS)
noisefile.setsampwidth(2)
```

Now that the wave files know what kind of sound they are getting, you can write the sound to them. However, they require the sound to be in a specific format. This format is a raw buffer, which is basically a string of bytes (this means nothing to humans, but computers can read it). You can get the buffer from mixer.Sound objects, by using their get_buffer method. This buffer contains a byte representation of itself in its raw property. You should write precisely that to the files:

```
# get buffers
tonebuffer = tone.get_buffer()
noisebuffer = whitenoise.get_buffer()

# write raw buffer to the wave file
tonefile.writeframesraw(tonebuffer.raw)
noisefile.writeframesraw(noisebuffer.raw)
```

The only thing that's left to do now, is neatly close the two wave file objects, by using their close method.

```
# neatly close the wave file objects
tonefile.close()
noisefile.close()
```

If you run your script, you should now see two new files in the same folder that contains your script file (make_sound.py). They should be named 'pure_tone.wav' and 'noise.wav', and you should be able to play them with a media player.

This is still a relatively simple script, but it can be a good start for you to create more funky sounds. By simply changing SOUNDFREQ you can already change the frequency of the pure tone. Try to think of some more ways to mess with it! (For jokes, change numpy.sin into numpy.tan and enjoy.)

5

SCRIPTING AN EXPERIMENT

In this example, you will be creating your very own experiment. Unlike the earlier examples, this will be a complete experiment that includes everything from displaying stimuli to logging data. You will learn how to prepare stimuli up front, how to precisely control display timing, how to collect responses and calculate accuracy and reaction times, how to randomise trials, how to loop through a pre-defined list of trials, and how to store experimental data.

The vehicle for your learning trip will be a Posner-type, exogenous cueing task. This is a very influential paradigm that was originally conceived in 1980 by a Big Cheese in attention research, Michael I. Posner (Posner, 1980). Despite its age, variations of Posner's cueing paradigm are still used in contemporary research (for an example, see Mathot, Dalmaijer, Grainger, & Van der Stigchel, 2014).

The concept of exogenous cueing is relatively straightforward: a non-informative spatial cue attracts your covert attention. When a target appears on the location where your attention is attracted to (the cued side), you will be quicker and more precise with your response (relative to when a target appears on the non-cued side). This phenomenon is referred to as **attentional facilitation**. Curiously, this benefit is very short-lived: the time between the onset of the cue and the onset of the target should be under about 500 milliseconds. If the interval between cue and target is longer, some people will show an increased reaction time and decreased precision when responding to a target on the cued side. This is referred to as **inhibition of return**.

Other terminology associated with the Posner paradigm concerns the time between cue and target onsets. The difference between the two is called the **stimulus onset asynchrony**, or **SOA**. Another important term concerns the correspondence between the locations of the cue and the target. If both appear on the same location, the cue was **valid**: it correctly predicted the target. If the target appears on a different location than the cue, the cue was **invalid**. The rate at which the cue is valid, is referred to as the **validity**. A 50 per cent validity means that half of the cues accurately predict the target location, and the other half do not.

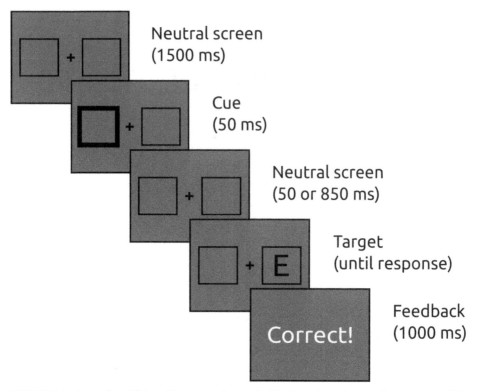

FIGURE 5.1 A single trial in a Posner cueing task. During the task, two boxes are visible on either side, while the participant keeps looking at the fixation cross in the centre. Very briefly (50 milliseconds), one of the boxes becomes a bit thicker than the other. This is a **cue** that draws the participant's covert attention: even though the participant is still looking at the centre, they are focusing their attention on the thicker box. After a short (100 milliseconds) or a long (900 milliseconds) interval, a letter **target** appears in one of the boxes. This can be an E or an F. In a valid trial, the cue and the target appear on the same side. In an invalid trial (shown here), the cue and the target appear on opposite sides. After the target appears, the participant has to indicate whether they see an E or an F. After pressing the E or the F key, the participant receives feedback

In experimental psychology, one would predict the results as follows: Ii the SOA is short (100 ms), there will be *lower* reaction times and *higher* precision for responses to a validly cued target (compared to an invalidly cued target). However, if the SOA is high (900 ms) there will be *higher* reaction times and *lower* precision for validly cued targets (compared to invalidly cued targets). In other words: a valid cue results in a brief period of facilitated attention for the cued location, followed by a period of inhibition of return of attention to the cued location.

Constants

Time to define some constants! Create a new folder, and open a new Python script: constants.py. Start by defining the constants that you should be familiar with by now:

PyGaze code

```
# the Display size should match the monitor resolution
DISPSIZE = (1920, 1080)

# the Display type should be set to 'psychopy' for this one
DISPTYPE = 'psychopy'

# foreground and background
FGC = (0, 0, 0)
BGC = (128,128,128)
```

PsychoPy code

```
# the Display size should match the monitor resolution
DISPSIZE = (1920, 1080)

# foreground and background
FGC = (-1, -1, -1)
BGC = (0,0,0)
```

You should also consider the **conditions** in this experiment. Or rather: all the things that will vary between trials. Both the cue and the target can appear on either the left or the right. There is also the SOA, which could be either 100 or 900 ms. And then there is the target, which could be an E or an F.

PyGaze code

```
# potential cue locations
CUELOCS = ['right', 'left']

# potential target locations
TARLOCS = ['right', 'left']

# potential SOAs
SOAS = [100, 900]

# potential targets
TARGETS = ['E', 'F']
```

PsychoPy code

```
# potential cue locations
CUELOCS = ['right', 'left']

# potential target locations
TARLOCS = ['right', 'left']

# potential SOAs
SOAS = [0.1, 0.9]

# potential targets
TARGETS = ['E', 'F']
```

TABLE 5.1 Screens used in each trial

Screen	Timing	Description
fixation	1500 ms	Gives participants time to prepare for the next trial.
cue	50 ms	Attracts attention to either the left or the right.
fixation	depends on SOA	A neutral screen between cue and target.
target	until response	Displays a target for participants to respond to.
feedback	1000 ms	Feedback to motivate the participant.

In addition, let's think about the timing of this experiment. Each trial will consist of five different screens shown in Table 5.1.

Before you go on to draw these screens, you could put their timing into the constants. Remember, in PyGaze times are in milliseconds, whereas in PsychoPy they are in seconds:

PyGaze code

```
# fixation time at the start of a trial
FIXTIME = 1500

# duration of the cue Screen
CUETIME = 50

# duration of the feedback Screen
FEEDBACKTIME = 1000
```

PsychoPy code

```
# fixation time at the start of a trial
FIXTIME = 1.5

# duration of the cue Screen
CUETIME = 0.05

# duration of the feedback Screen
FEEDBACKTIME = 1.0
```

You will return to the constants later on, but this is it for now.

Creating Screens

Open a new Python script file, experiment.py, and save it in the same folder as constants.py. In this experiment, you will create all of the experiment's different Screens up front. Preparing the Screens has a major advantage over creating them on the fly: it concentrates the time spent on drawing operations around the start of your experiment (where they cannot introduce timing imprecision), and it is more memory-efficient to create Screens beforehand than to create a new set of Screens on each trial.

Start the experiment.py script by importing all the libraries you need. Make sure to import everything from constants.py, as you will need most constants defined there:

PyGaze code

```
from constants import *
from pygaze.display import Display
from pygaze.screen import Screen
from pygaze.keyboard import Keyboard
import pygaze.libtime as timer
```

PsychoPy code

```
from constants import *
from psychopy.visual import Window, TextStim, Circle, Rect
from psychopy.event import waitKeys
from psychopy.core import wait
```

Next, create all the instances that you will need throughout the experiment: a Display for addressing the monitor, and a Keyboard to collect responses:

PyGaze code

```
# create a Display to deal with the monitor
disp = Display()
# create a Keyboard to collect responses
kb = Keyboard(keylist=None, timeout=None)
```

PsychoPy code

```
# create a Window to deal with the monitor
disp = Window(size=DISPSIZE, units='pix', \
       color=BGC, fullscr=True)
```

Instructions Screen

This is an easy one: create a new Screen and write some instructions on it (PyGaze), or create a new text stimulus (PsychoPy). You should know how from earlier chapters:

PyGaze code

```
# define the instructions
instructions = 'Welcome!\n\nIn this experiment, Es and Fs \
       will appear on either side of the screen. If you see \
       an E, press the E key. If you see an F, press F. \
       \n\nPlease try to be as fast and as accurate as \
       possible.\n\nGood luck!'

# create a new Screen
instscr = Screen()

# draw the instructions on the Screen
instscr.draw_text(text=instructions, fontsize=24)
```

PsychoPy code

```
# define the instructions
instructions = 'Welcome!\n\nIn this experiment, Es and Fs \
     will appear on either side of the screen. If you see \
     an E, press the E key. If you see an F, press F. \
     \n\nPlease try to be as fast and as accurate as \
     possible.\n\nGood luck!'

# create a new text stimulus
inststim = TextStim(disp, text=instructions, color=FGC, \
     height=24)
```

Fixation screen

A fixation screen is also something you have encountered before. You can use the Screen's `draw_fixation` method to draw a fixation mark of the type of your choice (a fixation cross, in this example), which will default to a central position (so you don't have to specify the `pos` keyword).

PyGaze code

```
# create a new Screen
fixscr = Screen()

# draw a fixation cross in the centre
fixscr.draw_fixation(fixtype='cross', diameter=12)
```

PsychoPy code

```
# create a Circle stimulus for fixation purposes
fixstim = Circle(disp, radius=6, edges=32, \
     lineColor=FGC, fillColor=FGC)
```

As in Figure 5.2, two boxes will be visible throughout the entire experiment: one to the left of the fixation cross, and one to the right. The locations of these boxes are not defined yet. Because you will use these locations often, it is a good idea to define them in the constants. This has the benefit that you can edit them in one place to change your entire experiment at once. Include the following in constants.py:

PyGaze code

```
# define the boxes' width and height (same number: they're
# square!)
BOXSIZE = 200

# define the boxes' centre coordinates
BOXCORS = {}
BOXCORS['left'] = (int(DISPSIZE[0]*0.25 - BOXSIZE*0.5),
     int(DISPSIZE[1]*0.5 - BOXSIZE*0.5))
BOXCORS['right'] = (int(DISPSIZE[0]*0.75 - BOXSIZE*0.5), \
     int(DISPSIZE[1]*0.5 - BOXSIZE*0.5))
```

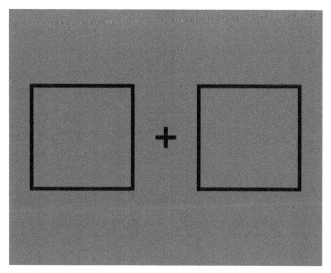

FIGURE 5.2   The fixation screen

PsychoPy code

```
# define the boxes' width and height (same number: they're
# square!)
BOXSIZE = 200

# define the boxes' centre coordinates
BOXCORS = {}
BOXCORS['left'] = (int(DISPSIZE[0]*-0.25), 0)
BOXCORS['right'] = (int(DISPSIZE[0]*0.25), 0)
```

If you remember the section on dictionaries in Chapter 2, you will recognise what kind of variable BOXCORS (short for 'box coordinates') is. It is a dictionary with two keys: 'left' and 'right'. The 'left' key unlocks the coordinate for the left box, and 'right' key points to the coordinate of the right box.

The coordinates are defined in a rather roundabout way, though. Let's take a closer look at the left one: it is defined as 25 per cent of the Display width and 50 per cent of the Display height. But from both of those values, half of the box size is subtracted. Why? Well, in PyGaze *rectangles are currently defined by their top left coordinate*. The centre of the left box is, in terms of Display width and height, (25 per cent, 50 per cent). The top-left corner is placed higher and more to the left of this coordinate. You need to *subtract half of the box height from the y-coordinate* (50 per cent of the Display height) to shift it upwards, and to *subtract half of the box width from the x-coordinate* (25 per cent of the Display width) to shift it leftward. What you end up with by subtracting half of the box width and height from the intended centre coordinate, is the intended top-left coordinate of the box.

In PsychoPy, you don't have to bother with the top-left corner, as it defines stimulus positions as the stimulus centre.

Now that you have defined their locations, it is time to draw the boxes on the fixation Screen. You can draw rectangles by using the Screen's `draw_rect` method in PyGaze. In PsychoPy, you can create two `Rect` stimuli for the left and right boxes. Add the following to experiment.py:

PyGaze code

```
# draw the left box
fixscr.draw_rect(x=BOXCORS['left'][0], y=BOXCORS['left'][1], \
     w=BOXSIZE, h=BOXSIZE, pw=3, fill=False)

# draw the right box
fixscr.draw_rect(x=BOXCORS['right'][0], y=BOXCORS['right'][1], \
     w=BOXSIZE, h=BOXSIZE, pw=3, fill=False)
```

PsychoPy code

```
# create the left box
lboxstim = Rect(disp, pos=BOXCORS['left'], \
     width=BOXSIZE, height=BOXSIZE, lineColor=FGC, \
     lineWidth=3)

# create the right box
rboxstim = Rect(disp, pos=BOXCORS['right'], \
     width=BOXSIZE, height=BOXSIZE, lineColor=FGC, \
     lineWidth=3)
```

PyGaze Screen's `draw_rect` method can take quite a few keyword arguments. The first are x and y, which specify the coordinate of the top-left point of the rectangle. Then there are w and h, which specify the width and height of the box (in pixels). These are equal in this case (both BOXSIZE), because you want squares. Another keyword is `colour`, to specify the colour of the box by using a (red, green, blue) tuple with values between 0 and 255. Finally, there are `pw` and `fill`. `pw` determines the **pen**width (or thickness) of the line that surrounds the box (in pixels). `fill` requires a Boolean that indicates whether the box should be a filled surface (on True), or should just be an outline (on False).

PsychoPy's Rect stimulus can also take quite a few keyword arguments. An important one is `pos`, which requires a list or a tuple that specifies the x- and y-coordinates of the rectangle's centre. There are also `width` and `height`, which allow you to specify the rectangle's width and height. You can adjust a rectangle's appearance by using the `lineColor` and `fillColor` keywords; the first is for the colour of a rectangle's lines, and the second for its body. The final keyword highlighted here is `ori`, which determines the rectangle's orientation in degrees.

Cue Screen

The cue screen will look almost exactly the same as the fixation Screen. The only difference is that one of the two boxes will have a thicker outline. Because the cue can appear on

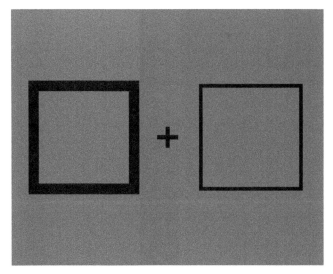

FIGURE 5.3   A cue screen with a cue on the left

either the left or the right side, you will have to prepare both! The most elegant way to do this, is by creating a **dict** to hold screens or stimuli for both options:

PyGaze code
```
# create a dict with two new Screens for the cues
cuescr = {}
cuescr['left'] = Screen()
cuescr['right'] = Screen()
```

PsychoPy code
```
# create an empty dict to hold both cue stimuli
cuestim = {}
```

As was mentioned before: the cue screens look almost exactly like the fixation screen. Fortunately, PyGaze allows you to copy one Screen onto another, by using the Screen class' copy method. After copying the fixation Screen to both cue Screens, all that is left to do is to draw the thicker outline for the cue (a penwidth of 8 instead of 3).

In PsychoPy, you can define the stimuli for the left and the right cue separately. You will have to re-draw all the basic stimuli (fixation mark, left box, and right box) between each Window flip, though.

PyGaze code
```
# copy the fixation Screen to both cue Screens
cuescr['left'].copy(fixscr)
cuescr['right'].copy(fixscr)

# draw the cue boxes with thicker penwidths
cuescr['left'].draw_rect(x=BOXCORS['left'][0], \
```

```
□□□□  y=BOXCORS['left'][1], w=BOXSIZE, h=BOXSIZE, pw=8, \
□□□□  fill=False)
cuescr['right'].draw_rect(x=BOXCORS['right'][0], \
□□□□  y=BOXCORS['right'][1], w=BOXSIZE, h=BOXSIZE, pw=8, \
□□□□  fill=False)
```

PsychoPy code

```
# create the left box
cuestim['left'] = Rect(disp, pos=BOXCORS['left'], \
□□□□  width=BOXSIZE, height=BOXSIZE, lineColor=FGC, \
□□□□  lineWidth=8)

# create the right box
cuestim['right'] = Rect(disp, pos=BOXCORS['right'], \
□□□□  width=BOXSIZE, height=BOXSIZE, lineColor=FGC, \
□□□□  lineWidth=8)
```

Target screen

The target Screens are slightly more complicated than the cue Screens. The same principles apply: you can create a dict that contains all target Screens, and you can copy the fixation Screen to copy in all basic stimuli. But then there are not only two different target locations (left and right), but also two different targets (E and F).

One way to solve this, would be to construct a dict for the target Screens with one key for each side ('left' and 'right', the same as with the cue Screens). However, instead of assigning two Screens to these keys, you assign two new dicts. These new dicts will

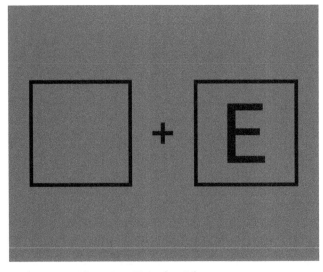

FIGURE 5.4 A target screen with a target E on the right

also have two keys each: 'E' and 'F' (one for each response), leaving you with four keys to assign Screens to. In other words: you create a dict with two nested dicts.

PyGaze code

```
# create a dict to contain further dicts to contain target
# Screens
tarscr = {}
tarscr['left'] = {}
tarscr['left']['E'] = Screen()
tarscr['left']['F'] = Screen()
tarscr['right'] = {}
tarscr['right']['E'] = Screen()
tarscr['right']['F'] = Screen()
```

PsychoPy code

```
# create a dict to contain further dicts to contain target
# stimuli
tarstim = {}
tarstim['left'] = {}
tarstim['right'] = {}
```

Now, copy the fixation Screen to each of the new target Screens (only applies to PyGaze):

PyGaze code

```
# copy the fixation Screen to each target Screen
tarscr['left']['E'].copy(fixscr)
tarscr['left']['F'].copy(fixscr)
tarscr['right']['E'].copy(fixscr)
tarscr['right']['F'].copy(fixscr)
```

In PyGaze, to draw each target, you must recalculate the boxes' top-left coordinates to their centre coordinates. You can do this so by simply re-adding half the boxes' size. (This isn't necessary for PsychoPy, as the box coordinates are already the centre coordinates.)

At this point, it might be clear that some things in this example are coded sub-optimally. Manually defining all Screens, or subtracting and re-adding values are not things you would normally do. Sorry about that! This was the clearest way of explaining the required concepts one-by-one. A bit later on, you will learn about for loops, which could have spared you a lot of this manual labour. Perhaps this is also a good lesson:

Programming a task does not make it more efficient per definition. A programming language provides you with better tools to be efficient, but you are still the one who has to implement the efficiency!

PyGaze code

```
# calculate the target positions
tarpos = {}
tarpos['left'] = (BOXCORS['left'][0] + BOXSIZE/2, \
       BOXCORS['left'][1] + BOXSIZE/2)
tarpos['right'] = (BOXCORS['right'][0] + BOXSIZE/2, \
```

```
␣␣␣␣   BOXCORS['right'][1] + BOXSIZE/2)
# draw all possible targets on the target Screens
tarscr['left']['E'].draw_text(text='E', pos=tarpos['left'], \
␣␣␣␣   fontsize=48)
tarscr['left']['F'].draw_text(text='F', pos=tarpos['left'], \
␣␣␣␣   fontsize=48)
tarscr['right']['E'].draw_text(text='E', \
␣␣␣␣   pos=tarpos['right'], fontsize=48)
tarscr['right']['F'].draw_text(text='F', \
␣␣␣␣   pos=tarpos['right'], fontsize=48)
```

PsychoPy code

```
# draw all possible target stimuli
tarstim['left']['E'] = TextStim(disp, text='E', \
␣␣␣␣   pos=BOXCORS['left'], height=48, color=FGC)
tarstim['left']['F'] = TextStim(disp, text='F', \
␣␣␣␣   pos=BOXCORS['left'], height=48, color=FGC)
tarstim['right']['E'] = TextStim(disp, text='E', \
␣␣␣␣   pos=BOXCORS['right'], height=48, color=FGC)
tarstim['right']['F'] = TextStim(disp, text='F', \
␣␣␣␣   pos=BOXCORS['right'],height=48, color=FGC)
```

That's it for the target Screens and stimuli, finally!

Feedback screen

There will be two possible feedback Screens: one for a correct response, and one for an incorrect response. You have implemented feedback before, so you know what to do. You have also seen the dict approach to Screens before (in the previous two sections). If you are wondering what the appropriate dict keys for the correct and incorrect Screen or stimuli are: why not try 1 and 0? (Tip: these are the values you will use later on to log correct and incorrect responses.)

PyGaze code

```
# create two new feedback Screens in a dict
fbscr = {}

# draw the incorrect feedback (evil red letters!)
fbscr[0] = Screen()
fbscr[0].draw_text(text='Incorrect!', colour=(255,0,0), \
␣␣␣␣   fontsize=24)

# draw the correct feedback (nice and green)
fbscr[1] = Screen()
fbscr[1].draw_text(text='Correct!', colour=(0,255,0), \
␣␣␣␣   fontsize=24)
```

FIGURE 5.5 A feedback screen with positive feedback

PsychoPy code
```
# draw the incorrect feedback (evil red letters!)
fbstim[0] = TextStim(disp, text='Incorrect!', height=24, \
     color=(1, -1, -1))
# draw the correct feedback (nice and green)
fbstim[1] = TextStim(disp, text='Correct!', height=24, \
     color=(-1, 1, -1))
```
BOOM, sorted!

A single trial

In this section, you will continue to work on experiment.py. You just created all the Screens or stimuli, and earlier you set the timing for each screen in constants.py, so now you should be ready to create a single trial and run through it.

Before the trials start, you will need to add the instructions (otherwise participants will not get what you want them to do). This is why you created the instructions screen:

PyGaze code
```
# present the instructions
disp.fill(instscr)
disp.show()

# wait for any old keypress
kb.get_key(keylist=None, timeout=None)
```

PsychoPy code
```
# present the instructions
inststim.draw()
disp.flip()
# wait for any old keypress
waitKeys(maxWait=float('inf'), keyList=None, timeStamped=True)
```

The keypress at the end is to make sure participants have time to read the instructions. They can press any key to start the experiment after they finish reading.

Each trial will begin with the fixation screen:

PyGaze code
```
# show the fixation Screen
disp.fill(fixscr)
fixonset = disp.show()
# wait for a bit
timer.pause(FIXTIME)
```

PsychoPy code
```
# draw the fixation mark, and the left and right boxes
fixstim.draw()
lboxstim.draw()
rboxstim.draw()
# update the monitor
fixonset = disp.flip()
# wait for a bit
wait(FIXTIME)
```

The PyGaze Display's show and the PsychoPy Window's flip methods return a timestamp of when it became visible. If you use PsychoPy, or set PyGaze's DISPTYPE to 'psychopy', you can be relatively sure that this timestamp is the time at which the monitor refresh started. More on this later! Let's continue with the cue:

PyGaze code
```
# show a cue Screen
disp.fill(cuescr['left'])
cueonset = disp.show()
# wait for a little bit
timer.pause(CUETIME)
```

PsychoPy code
```
# draw the fixation mark, and the left and right boxes
fixstim.draw()
lboxstim.draw()
rboxstim.draw()
# draw a cue
```

```
cuesstim['left'].draw()
# update the monitor
cueonset = disp.flip()
# wait for a little bit
wait(CUETIME)
```

This will show the cue on the left, and then wait for the very brief cue duration, before moving on to another fixation display:

PyGaze code
```
# show the fixation Screen again
disp.fill(fixscr)
cueoffset = disp.show()
# wait for the SOA minus the cue duration
timer.pause(100 - CUETIME)
```

PsychoPy code
```
# draw the fixation mark, and the left and right boxes
fixstim.draw()
lboxstim.draw()
rboxstim.draw()
# update the monitor
cueoffset = disp.flip()
# wait for the SOA minus the cue duration
wait(0.1 - CUETIME)
```

You subtract the cue duration from the SOA (100 milliseconds, in this example), because it concerns the stimulus **onset** asynchrony: the difference between the onsets of the cue and the target. Speaking of which:

PyGaze code
```
# show a target Screen
disp.fill(tarscr['right']['E'])
taronset = disp.show()
```

PsychoPy code
```
# draw the fixation mark, and the left and right boxes
fixstim.draw()
lboxstim.draw()
rboxstim.draw()
# draw a target stimulus
tarstim['right']['E'].draw()
# update the monitor
taronset = disp.flip()
```

Which brings you to collecting a response. The only allowed keys are 'e' and 'f'. Their names are lower-case letters, so they need to be converted to upper-case to be compared to the upper-cased targets:

PyGaze code

```
# wait for a response
response, presstime = kb.get_key(keylist=['e', 'f'], \
     timeout=None)

# turn the lowercase response into uppercase
response = response.upper()
```

PsychoPy code

```
# wait for a response
resplist = waitKeys(maxWait=float('inf'), keyList=['e','f'], \
     timeStamped=True)

# select the first response from the response list
response, presstime = resplist[0]

# turn the lowercase response into uppercase
response = response.upper()
```

After the response comes in, it's time to compare the response with the actual target ('E' in the current example). You can also calculate the reaction time: it is the difference between the onset of the target and the time of the key press:

Same code for PyGaze and PsychoPy

```
# check if the response was correct
if response == 'E':
     correct = 1
else:
     correct = 0
# calculate the reaction time
RT = presstime - taronset
```

The final part of a single trial, is to give the participant feedback. The feedback Screens and stimuli are coded 0 (incorrect) and 1 (correct). This coding corresponds with the value of your correct variable, so you can use that to select the appropriate feedback Screen or stimulus:

PyGaze code

```
# show the appropriate feedback Screen
disp.fill(fbscr[correct])
disp.show()

# wait for a bit to allow the participant to see the
# feedback
timer.pause(FEEDBACKTIME)
```

PsychoPy code

```
# show the appropriate feedback stimulus
fbstim[correct].draw()
disp.flip()

# wait for a bit to allow the participant to see the
# feedback
wait(FEEDBACKTIME)
```

And after all this, it is time to close the Display:

Same code for PyGaze and PsychoPy

```
# shut down the experiment
disp.close()
```

Even though this is only one trial, please run your current experiment.py. If an error pops up, make sure to double-check your code and fix it.

For loop

At this point, you have only created a single trial. If you want a whole experiment, you could copy-paste the single-trial code about 200 times. Or you could read on a bit, and learn about the magic of the **for loop**.

A for loop is not unlike the while loop that you learned about before (in the section with the unimaginative title 'While loops' in Chapter 4). In fact, you can write a while loop that does exactly the same as a for loop:

```
# for loop                      # while loop
for i in range(10):             i = 0
    print(i)                    while i < 10:
                                    print(i)
                                    i = i + 1
```

If you understand the for loop from this example, you really got that while loop down. If you are still a bit lost, don't worry. The while loop example is here to improve your understanding of both for and while loops. Now open an Interpreter and break down that for loop! Start with the range function:

```
print(range(10))
```

If you type that into an Interpreter (NOT in experiment.py; you will get back to that later!), the outcome should be a list with the numbers 0 to 9:

```
[0, 1, 2, 3, 4, 5, 6, 7, 8, 9]
```

Now type:

```
for i in range(10):
    print(i)
```

If you did this correctly, you should see the numbers 0 to 9, each printed on a new line. To better understand what the for loop is doing, type the following:

```
import time
for i in range(10):
     print(i)
     time.sleep(1)
```

The `sleep` function from the `time` module allows you to pause for a number of seconds (1, in this case). If all went well, you should have seen the numbers 1 to 9 get printed to the Interpreter, each separated by one second.

This is what a for loop does: *it takes one value at a time from a list/tuple/vector, and runs indented code with that value.* Often, the value is a number and is named `i` (short for **iterator**), but this does not have to be the case:

```
my_letters = ['k', 'i', 'e', 'k', 'e', 'b', 'o', 'e']
for letter in my_letters:
     print(letter)
     time.sleep(1)
```

An alternative way of running through a list, is by creating a range with all its index numbers. That is: from 0 (for the first value) to its length minus one (for the last value). Run this example to see for yourself:

```
my_letters = ['k', 'i', 'e', 'k', 'e', 'b', 'o', 'e']
for i in range(0, len(my_letters)):
     print(my_letters[i])
     time.sleep(1)
```

A for loop works its way through a list of values, and really doesn't care about what those values are. They could be numbers or strings (like in the examples above), but they can also be nested lists:

```
a = [ [1, 2, 3], ['a', 'b', 'c']]
for l in a:
     print(l)
     time.sleep(1)
```

You could even for-loop through a list of nested lists, and then for-loop through each nested list:

```
a = [ [1, 2, 3], ['a', 'b', 'c']]
for l in a:
     for thing in l:
          print(thing)
          time.sleep(1)
```

As you could see from the last example, the 'outer' for loop is run with its first value (the value of `a[0]`, which is list `[1, 2, 3]`). Then the 'inner' (the more indented) for loop is run with all values of a[0], thus printing 1, 2, and 3. After the inner for loop runs out of values, it's the outer for loop's turn again. This time, it gives variable l the value of a[1] (which is the list ['a', 'b', 'c']). Then the inner list gives the variable thing a new value on each iteration, starting with 'a', then 'b', and finally 'c'.

Perhaps a more structured way of moving through nested lists, is by using the range function to for-loop through all their index numbers:

```
a = [ [1, 2, 3], ['a', 'b', 'c']]
for i in range(len(a)):
     for j in range(len(a[i])):
          print(a[i][j])
          time.sleep(1)
```

This looks slightly more organised, and can be preferred in some situations. For example, when you want to use the values of the index numbers i and j for other purposes.

For loop through trials

Close the Interpreter and return to the experiment.py script from the 'A single trial' section. To illustrate the power of a for loop in experiment programming, add the following code to experiment.py. Place it before the first disp.fill(fixscr) line:

```
for cueside in ['left', 'right']:
```

To make this for loop work, you will have to indent all of the single-trial code. That is: all lines from disp.fill(fixscr) or intstim.draw() until timer.pause(FEEDBACKTIME) or wait(FEEDBACKTIME) must be indented by one indent. To remind you: one indent is one tab, two spaces, or four spaces – with a strong preference for four spaces!

After indenting your code, change the line disp.fill(cuescr['left']) (PyGaze) or the line cuestimp['left'].draw() (PsychoPy) to:

PyGaze code
```
     disp.fill(cuescr[cueside])
```

PsychoPy code
```
     cuestim[cueside].draw()
```

As you can see, you changed the **hard-coded** cue side 'left' to a reference to the cueside variable. cueside is defined by your for loop. It should refer to the value 'left' on the first iteration, and 'right' on the second.

If you run the current code, you should see one trial with a cue on the left, followed by a trial with a cue on the right. Please do check if that is the case with your script. If your code does something else, look back through the last chapters to make sure you copied everything correctly!

For loop through conditions

The term 'conditions' is used rather loosely in this chapter. Here, it means 'parameters that are variable in your experiment', referring to the location of cues and targets, as well as the type of target and the SOA.

Most experiments have a number of **unique trials**. These are all the possible combinations of the aforementioned variable parameters (cue location, target location, target letter, SOA). In the current example, there are two cue locations × two target locations × two target letters × two SOAs = 16 unique trials. Because this kind of Posner cueing task is supposed to have a 50 per cent validity, all unique trials should occur equally (thus making sure that there will be equal numbers of valid and invalid trials).

Each trial has more than one parameter. The most elegant solution, would be to store all of these in a single dict. See the example below (but *do not* copy it to your script):

```
trial = {'cueside':'left', 'tarside':'right', \
         'target':'E', 'soa':100}
```

Of course, you do not want only one **trial dict**. You want a dict for every single (unique) trial! You could collect all of these dicts in a list. This list could start out empty, and fill up when you loop through all variable parameters. That is: for each unique combination of parameters, you append a new trial dict to a list.

Add the following code to your experiment.py, directly after the line `fbscr[1].draw_text(text='Correct!', colour=(0,255,0), fontsize=24)` (PyGaze) or `fbstim[1] = TextStim(disp, text='Correct!', height=24, color=(-1, 1, -1))` (PsychoPy) line:

Same code for PyGaze and PsychoPy

```
# create an empty list to contain all unique trials
alltrials = []

# loop through all parameters
for cueside in CUELOCS:
    for tarside in TARLOCS:
        for soa in SOAS:
            for tar in TARGETS:

                # create a unique trial dict
                trial = {'cueside':cueside, \
                         'tarside':tarside, \
                         'target':tar, 'soa':soa}
                # add the trial dict to the
                # list
                alltrials.append(trial)
```

This code will create a list of all 16 unique trials. Before you can see them in action, you will need to make some further changes, though. Start with the line that reads `for cueside in ['left', 'right']:` and replace it with:

Same code for PyGaze and PsychoPy
```
tor trial in alltrials:
```

This for loop will run through the entire `alltrials` list. On every iteration of the loop, the variable `trial` will refer to the value of a new trial dict. This is great, because it means that you can use `trial['cueside']` to refer to the location of the cue, or `trial['soa']` to refer to the SOA. Of course, you will need to make some changes in your code to reference the trial dict.

Replace `disp.fill(cuescr[cueside])` (PyGaze) or `cuestim[cueside].draw()` with:

PyGaze code
```
    disp.fill(cuescr[trial['cueside']])
```

PsychoPy code
```
    cuestim[trial['cueside']].draw()
```

Replace `timer.pause(100 - CUETIME)` (PyGaze) or `wait(0.1 - CUETIME)` (PsychoPy) with:

PyGaze code
```
    timer.pause(trial['soa'] - CUETIME)
```

PsychoPy code
```
    wait(trial['soa'] - CUETIME)
```

Replace `disp.fill(tarscr['right']['E'])` (PyGaze) or `tarstim['right']['E'].draw()` (PsychoPy) with:

PyGaze code
```
    disp.fill(tarscr[trial['tarside']][trial['target']])
```

PsychoPy code
```
    tarstim[trial['tarside']][trial['target']].draw()
```

Finally, replace `if response == 'E':` with:

Same code for PyGaze and PsychoPy
```
    if response == trial['target']:
```

Now run experiment.py, and see whether your code works. If you did everything correctly, you should be running through 16 unique trials.

Logging values

Even though you just ran through 16 trials, no evidence of this remains. This is because all important variables were overwritten in each new trial. To store a few, you could use PyGaze's Logfile class. By creating a **Logfile** instance, you can open a new text file (with a .txt extension). You can write lists of values to this text file, which will appear as tab-separated values.

PsychoPy offers several options for logging data, most of which are very useful in a specific context. The general format, the `TrialHandler` class in PsychoPy's `data` module, requires you to store information on trials and responses in a dict. This is very similar to what you did in this experiment, and the TrialHandler offers good functionality for trial randomisation and logging data to different formats. Despite these benefits, you'll not be using it.

Instead of the high-level PsychoPy class, you will learn how to do basic writing to a text file. This is a hassle-free and straightforward way of logging data, and has a bonus advantage of being more generalisable. Being able to open, write, and close files by using code is a very good skill to have, which is why this book focuses on these basics rather than on the TrialHandler class.

If you do want to know more about the TrialHandler class, PsychoPy's documentation website is a good place to look: www.psychopy.org/api/data.html.

To use PyGaze's Logfile class, you must first import it. Add this line to the start of your experiment. For the logging you will implement in PsychoPy, you don't have to import anything.

PyGaze code
```
from pygaze.logfile import Logfile
```

After the `kb = Keyboard(keylist=None, timeout=None)` (PyGaze) line or the `disp = Window(size=DISPSIZE, units='pix', color=BGC, fullscr=True)` line (PsychoPy), add:

PyGaze code
```
# create a new log file
log = Logfile()
```

PsychoPy code
```
# open a new file instance
log = open(LOGFILE + '.tsv', 'w')
```

The LOGFILE constant in the PsychoPy code is something we will return to later (it isn't defined yet, but will be shortly). You add '.tsv' to the file name to give it a 'tab-separated values' extension, which your computer will recognise. The 'w' is for 'writing' (overwriting any existing data), and indicates the access mode of the open file. Other options include 'r' for 'reading' (to load existing data), and 'a' for 'appending' (to add new to existing data).

The `Logfile` and `file` classes have two methods of interest: `write` and `close`. The `close` method should always be called at the end of an experiment. (It's a bad coding habit to leave files open when you no longer need them, so close those bad boys.) Add the following directly before the `disp.close()` line at the bottom of your script:

Same code for PyGaze and PsychoPy
```
# close the log file
log.close()
```

The Logfile's `write` method requires you to pass a single list of all values that you want to write to the log file. It is useful to start with a **header**, which will appear on the first row of your log file. This will help you to recognise the values.

In the PsychoPy example, where you write the data file yourself, some additional trickery is required. Actually, it's not really trickery, it's just string management. You can only write a single string to the open file instance at a time, but your data will be stored in separate variables.

There is a quick, four-step solution to turn the contents of several variables into a single string. The first step is to collect all the data into a single list. This allows the second step to work: using Python's `map` function to turn every value in the list into a string. The `map` function allows you to apply a function of your choice on a large set of values at once. You can use the `str` function to turn values into strings. This is necessary, because of step 3: using the `join` method to merge all values in a list into a single string, separated by tabs ('\t'). Finally, a new line ('\n') needs to be added, to make sure that the next line you log will actually start on the next line in the log file. If you don't add a newline, all your data will end up in a single, really long line.

In sum, you take all relevant values, stick 'em in a list, convert them to strings, and then merge all individual values into a single string that ends with a newline.

Add the following directly after the `log = Logfile()` (PyGaze) or `log = open(LOGFILE + '.tsv', 'w')` (PsychoPy) line.

PyGaze code

```
# define a header
header = ['fixonset', 'cueonset', 'cueoffset', 'taronset', \
          'cueside', 'tarside', 'valid', 'soa', 'target', \
          'response', 'correct', 'RT']

# write the header to the log file
log.write(header)
```

PsychoPy code

```
# define a header
header = ['fixonset', 'cueonset', 'cueoffset', 'taronset', \
          'cueside', 'tarside', 'valid', 'soa', 'target', \
          'response', 'correct', 'RT']

# make all values in the header into strings
# (all values are strings already, but this is an example)
line = map(str, header)

# join all string values into one string, separated by tabs
# ('\t')
line = '\t'.join(line)

# add a newline ('\n') to the string
line += '\n'
```

```
# write the header to the log file
log.write(line)
```

Easy enough, right? The same principle applies when you want to log data. You generally do this at the end of a trial, or at least after a response has been given. In your case, you could do the logging directly after the feedback. This is a good place, because there you know about all trial parameters (cue location, validity, etc.) and about the response (accuracy time).

However, before you add data logging, it is important to add one additional thing to your script. Although the validity is a crucial aspect in a Posner cueing task, your script does not mention it once (for overly anal nerds: yes, it is mentioned in the header). It doesn't really matter to your computer, because it simply needs to know where to display the cue and where to display the target, but not whether those locations match. You care about whether both locations match, because then you know that the trial is valid. You need this in the analysis.

Of course, it would be easy enough to add checking the validity to an analysis script, or in an analysis with a spreadsheet editor or SPSS. However, it is even easier to add it to your experiment script. *Sometimes you create and log variables that are not useful in your experiment script, but only in the analysis.* Validity is one of those: you don't need it within the experiment, but it's great to have it logged for analysis-related purposes. After the RT = presstime - taronset line, add the following:

Same code for PyGaze and PsychoPy

```
     # check if the cue was valid
     if trial['cueside'] == trial['tarside']:
          validity = 1
     else:
          validity = 0
```

Now it's time to log! Directly after the timer.pause(FEEDBACKTIME) (PyGaze) or wait(FEEDBACKTIME) (PsychoPy) line, add the following:

Pygaze code

```
     # log all interesting values
     log.write([fixonset, cueonset, cueoffset, taronset, \
          trial['cueside'], trial['tarside'], validity, \
          trial['soa'], trial['target'], response,
          correct, RT])
```

PsychoPy code

```
     # collect all interesting values in a single list
     line = [fixonset, cueonset, cueoffset, taronset, \
          trial['cueside'], trial['tarside'], validity, \
          trial['soa'], trial['target'], response, \
          correct, RT]

     # turn all values into a string
```

```
⎵⎵⎵⎵    line = map(str, line)

⎵⎵⎵⎵    # merge all individual values into a single string,
⎵⎵⎵⎵    # separated by tabs
⎵⎵⎵⎵    line = '\t'.join(line)

⎵⎵⎵⎵    # add a newline ('\n') to the string
⎵⎵⎵⎵    line += '\n'

⎵⎵⎵⎵    # write the data string to the log file
⎵⎵⎵⎵    log.write(line)
```

If you run your script now, PyGaze would create a logfile called 'default.txt', because that is the default name. In PsychoPy, the program wouldn't even run at all, due to a reference to the undefined variable LOGFILE. You can change this by adding the following to your constants.py:

Same code for PyGaze and PsychoPy
```
LOGFILENAME = raw_input('Participant name: ')
LOGFILE = LOGFILENAME
```

The `raw_input` function will allow you to type into the terminal that you use to run the experiment.py script. You can type any text or number you like, but it is wise to *keep file names short and sweet, and free of weird interpunction* (underscores and dashes are fine, the rest is not).

That last line, `LOGFILE  =  LOGFILENAME`, is a bit weird. Why have both a LOGFILENAME and a LOGFILE variable? In PyGaze, they have different meanings. LOGFILENAME refers to just the name of the log file (e.g. 'subject-0'), whereas LOGFILE could contain a complete file path, e.g. 'C:\my_data\subject-0'. In addition, LOGFILENAME is used to name other log files too, for example when eye-tracking data is also collected.

Display timing

Run experiment.py again. You should *run through 16 unique trials*, and at the end a log file should be created. As usual, if this is not the case, retrace your steps and fix your code.

After running the experiment, open your log file in a spreadsheet editor (Open/Libre Office Calc, Microsoft Excel, etc.). Text files can have .txt, .csv, and .tsv extensions, and you might not be familiar with these. To open such files, simply start your spreadsheet editor, click on the 'File' option in the menu (at top of the window), and then select 'Open...'. In the menu that opens, make sure that the option 'All files (*.*)' is highlighted. Next, browse to the text file you would like to open, click on it, and then click on the 'Open' button.

Once you open the file, you are presented with a text import menu. The only thing you really need to worry about here, is that you *select only the Tab as the separator*.

It is possible that the file opens automatically and does not give you a menu, but instead shows all its contents in the first column. In that case, select the first column (click on the letter A), then select 'Data' from the menu. Under 'Data', there should be a 'Text to columns …' option. Click that, and follow the instructions as above.

Important note for people with non-English language settings: In some languages (such as French, Italian, German, and Dutch), mathematical symbols are different from English conventions. In English, decimal numbers are indicated with a full stop: 4.5. However, in some other notation systems, decimal numbers are indicated with a comma: 4,5. This particular symbol is called the **decimal separator**. Python abides by English conventions, so the decimal separator will be a full stop (or dot, or point, or period, or however you want to call it). *Make sure that your spreadsheet editor is using a full stop (".") as the decimal separator!*

Now that you have the data open, it's time to do some calculations. The first thing you want to check, is whether your display timing is accurate. Particularly important are the cue duration and the stimulus onset asynchrony (SOA).

To calculate the actual cue duration, *subtract the cueonset from the cueoffset*. If you did everything according to the example, the cueoffset should be in column C and the cueonset in column B. To calculate the difference, type in cell O2:

```
=C2-B2
```

If you copy this along the entire dataset (from O2 to O17), you are likely not seeing values around 50 milliseconds, but around 67. This may seem weird, but was entirely predictable.

The monitor is refreshed at a certain rate. On most computers, this is around 60 Hertz. This means that the monitor is fully updated 60 times in every second. That leaves 16.67 milliseconds per monitor refresh. The monitor starts refreshing in the top-left corner, and updates every pixel from left-to-right, from top-to-bottom. This process ends 16.67 ms after it started, in the bottom-right corner of the monitor. And then starts again from the top left.

In PsychoPy and in PyGaze (if you use the PsychoPy display type, and often if you use PyGame too, but not always), sending a new Display or Window to the monitor is halted until the monitor refresh starts in the top-left corner. Halting further processing until a new refresh cycle starts, is called a **blocking flip** or **vertical sync**. It is useful, because it makes sure that a full screen is always presented.

What you should be careful about, is allowing too little time for the Display to be updated. When you call `disp.show()` or `disp.flip()`, due to a variety of different reasons, there will be a little lag between the function being called and the monitor being updated.

Consider the following example: You call `disp.show()` and update the monitor at timepoint 0. You then wait precisely 50 ms (which is the duration of exactly three monitor-refresh cycles at 60 Hz), then fill the Display with a new Screen, and then call `disp.show()` again. Although you call `disp.show()` around timepoint 50, it is very likely that you just missed the 'refresh deadline'. Due to the blocking flip, the script will now wait until the next refresh cycle starts to update the monitor with the new Display. That means that your pause was 66.67 ms instead of 50.

The solution is actually really simple. *Do not wait precisely 50 ms if you want to display a Screen for exactly 50 ms. Instead, allow for a bit of wiggle-room.* Usually, 5 to 10 milliseconds should be enough.

You can test this in your own script. *Open constants.py, and take 7 ms off each time* (including the SOAs!). 50 becomes 43, 100 becomes 93, 900 becomes 893, 1500 becomes 1493, and so on.

After doing this, run your script again, and recalculate the cue duration and the SOAs in a spreadsheet editor. This should have solved your problem. If you do have SOAs that are about 16.67 (one refresh cycle) too long, try adjusting a line in experiment.py, `timer. pause(trial['soa'] - CUETIME)` (PyGaze) or `wait(trial['soa'] - CUETIME)` (PsychoPy), to:

PyGaze code
```
    timer.pause(trial['soa'] - CUETIME - 10)
```
PsychoPy code
```
    wait(trial['soa'] - CUETIME - 0.01)
```
That should solve your issues!

Small print

Even when you use PychoPy, you can sometimes get weird onset times. This could be due to a variety of reasons, including having multiple monitors attached to a single computer, not using a full-screen experiment, or having a thoroughly messed-up system.

The most important thing is to *always check your timing, before your timing wrecks you,* preferably using external instruments like photo-diodes or high-speed cameras to test your monitor's timing. It is highly recommended to check your experiment's timing after a pilot run, and not after testing a couple of participants. You don't want to lose actual data over programming mistakes or hardware issues!

Of course, not all experiments require millisecond-accurate display precision. If you present a questionnaire or a reinforcement learning task, an extra refresh cycle here or there should usually not make a difference. Keep in mind what the point of your experiment is, and look out for potential ways in which timing errors could affect your work.

Randomisation

At this point, you probably ran through your experiment quite a few times. You might have noticed that the trials are presented in the same, predictable order. This is a by-product of the neat and organised way in which you produced a list of unique trials.

Make one last change to constants.py. Add the following:

Same code for PyGaze and PsychoPy
```
TRIALREPEATS = 20
```

This will be the amount of times each unique trial is repeated. Some quick arithmetic shows that there will be 16 unique trials × 20 repeats = 320 trials in total. That leaves you with 180 trials per SOA, and 180 trials per validity condition. That is 90 valid trials at each SOA, and 90 invalid.

To make the randomisation happen, you will need the `random` module. This is a native part of Python, and it contains the `shuffle` function. This function can randomise the order of a list. Make sure to import the module at the beginning of experiment.py:

Same code for PyGaze and PsychoPy

```
import random
```

Now scroll down in experiment.py, and change the `alltrials.append(trial)` line to the following (the indentation is because it is embedded in four for loops!):

Same code for PyGaze and PsychoPy

```
                    alltrials.extend( TRIALREPEATS \
                    * [trial] )
```

Instead of adding a single trial to your list of all trials, it will add 20 (or whatever value TRIALREPEATS is). The only thing left to do, is to shuffle all trials. Do this by adding the following lines directly after the preceding addition. Note that there should not be any indentation, as the following lines should not be part of the for loops that create your unique trials.

Same code for PyGaze and PsychoPy

```
# randomise the order of all trials
random.shuffle(alltrials)
```

This will randomise the order of your alltrials list. Do not make the mistake of typing `alltrials = random.shuffle(alltrials)`. The `shuffle` function works 'in place': it simply adjusts the list that you passed, without returning anything.

Now you can run your experiment again, and enjoy all 320 trials of it. Have fun!

MAKE SOME NOISE

In this section, you will learn how to make a musical instrument out of a joystick. You can also use the keyboard, if you don't have a joystick. Although this might seem like a weak excuse to make some noise, it will actually be a very good programming exercise. If you manage to annoy the people around you with obnoxious noise, that's just a bonus.

Turning your joystick or keyboard into a musical instrument won't require you to be a modern-day MacGyver. Instead, you can write a script that responds to a button press by making a sound. That's not to say this is easy: writing a script that responds to events requires some abstract thinking.

Before you start with the fun stuff, create a new folder. Within that folder, create a new Python script and name it 'constants.py'. Open it in an editor, to define some defaults:

```
# set the display type to 'pygame'
DISPTYPE = 'pygame'
# make sure that the DISPSIZE matches your monitor
# resolution!
DISPSIZE = (1920, 1080)
```

Do you have a joystick?

Of course, not everyone will have a joystick lying around. Some people might even wonder about what a joystick is.

The term 'joystick' in a strict sense applies to devices that have a pivoting stick that allows users to, for example, fly an aeroplane. In a broader sense, the term 'joysticks' often applies to any gaming controller. In this section, the term 'joystick' will refer to this broader class of input devices. Joysticks are not only useful for playing computer games, but can also be used in psychological research.

A lot of joysticks have two **control sticks** (mini-joysticks) that each cover two **axes** (movement directions), a couple of **buttons**, and a **hat**. That's not a fancy top hat, a baseball cap, or something that was knitted by your grandmother. For joysticks, a hat is a special button that you can push in four directions. If you ever owned a GameBoy, you might recall the four-point button that controlled your movement. That button was a 'hat'.

Some joysticks will also carry '**balls**'. The concept behind these is very similar to that of an old computer mouse: you can roll a ball, and the joystick will convert the roll into a movement in a two-dimensional plane.

Another cool thing about joysticks, is that some offer a '**rumble**' feature. It allows programmers to make the controller vibrate to give vibrotactile feedback. You can find this feature in games, for example if you ram a car or shoot a gun, but you can also use it to give feedback to participants in your psychological experiment.

In this section, the focus is on the joystick's buttons. If you don't have a joystick, you can substitute the buttons with the number keys.

Using a joystick

Programming for a joystick is easier than you might think, and it is very similar to using the mouse or a keyboard through PyGaze or PsychoPy. There are a few libraries that offer excellent functionality for joysticks, including PyGame, PyGaze, and PsychoPy. In this chapter, PyGaze is used for no particular reason at all. It's a nice library, and it offers everything you need for this project to work.

You can import the Joystick class from PyGaze's `joystick` module:

```
from pygaze.joystick import Joystick
```

You could then initialise a Joystick object, for example called `js`:

```
js = Joystick()
```

PyGaze will automatically detect and engage the first joystick attached to your computer. Obviously, this only works if one is actually plugged in. After initialising the joystick, you can poll the buttons with a single function:

```
js.get_joybuttons()
```

This works in the same way as the Keyboard class `get_key` method. You can specify a list of allowed buttons, and a response timeout in milliseconds:

```
button, presstime = js.get_joybuttons(joybuttonlist \
     =[0,4,6], timeout=3000)
```

The `get_joybuttons` method will return which button was pressed, and at what time it was pushed. In the above example, `button` is an integer that indicates what button was pressed, or None when no button was pressed. `presstime` will be a float with a timestamp that is relative to when PyGaze was imported.

If you have a joystick at your disposal, now would be the time to start coding. In the same folder as the constants.py you created a bit earlier, create a new Python script. You could call it 'noisemaker_joystick.py'. Start by importing the Joystick and the Sound classes:

```
from pygaze.joystick import Joystick
from pygaze.sound import Sound
from pygaze.display import Display
```

Now you want to initialise a Joystick instance to be able to use it as an input device. You should also initialise a Display. This isn't strictly necessary, but is for the sake of consistency with the keyboard implementation (which does require a Display to be active).

```
# initialise a Display instance
disp = Display()

# create a Joystick instance
# ('dev' is short for 'device')
dev = Joystick()
```

The next step is to create a function that checks if any buttons were pressed. The function's input should be the device that you want it to use, which is the joystick. The function's output should be the number of the button that was pressed (or None when no button was pressed). You might wonder why you would want to create a custom function for this, while the Joystick class `get_joybutton` does almost exactly the same thing. There is no programming-related reason to do it, but it's a good practice exercise!

As you might remember from the 'Functions' section in Chapter 2, a function definition always starts with `def`, followed by the function's name, then the inputs between round brackets, and it ends with a colon. Like so:

```
# definition of a function to get user input
def get_input(device):
```

The code that makes up the function should be indented, preferably by four spaces per line. It should check whether a button is pressed, but with a low timeout:

```
    # wait for a button press for about 10 ms
    button, presstime = device.get_joybutton(timeout=10)
```

The result should be returned as an output:

```
    # return the button number (or None)
    return button
```

That's it for now. Skip over the next section on using a keyboard, and continue with the section on 'Playing sounds on button presses'.

Using a keyboard

If you don't have a joystick at hand, you can use your keyboard instead. You've used PyGaze's Keyboard class before, but let's start with a reminder.

You can import the `Keyboard` class from PyGaze's `keyboard` module:

```
from pygaze.keyboard import Keyboard
```

To initialise an instance of the class, you can use the following:

```
kb = Keyboard()
```

As with the Joystick class, you can specify a default key list and timeout. You can use the `range` function to generate a list of the numbers between 0 and 10, which are the names for the number keys. Because the Keyboard class requires a list of strings to be passed as key names, you should convert the generated numbers to strings. You might remember the `map` function, which can apply a function of your choice to an entire list at once. You might also remember the `str` function, which can convert numeric values into strings. Combined, you could do the following:

```
numbers = range(0, 10)
stringnumbers = map(str, numbers)
kb = Keyboard(keylist=stringnumbers)
```

This would produce a Keyboard instance that only allows you to press the number keys. Remember: these are not the number pad keys, but the numbers above the letter keys.

Let's start programming to implement the above example. In the same folder as the constants.py script that you created a bit earlier, create a new Python script. You can name it 'noisemaker_keyboard.py'. First, import the Keyboard and Sound classes:

```
from pygaze.keyboard import Keyboard
from pygaze.sound import Sound
```

You should also import the Display class, because the Keyboard only works if there is an active Display (this is not true for the Joystick and Sound classes, by the way).

```
from pygaze.display import Display
```

Time to initialise a Display and a Keyboard instance. Remember, the Keyboard instance should only respond to number keys!

```
# initialise a Display instance
# (required for the Keyboard to work)
disp = Display()

# create a range of numbers
numbers = range(0,10)

# turn the numbers from integer values into strings
numbers = map(str, numbers)

# create a Keyboard instance
dev = Keyboard(keylist=numbers)
```

The next step is to create a function that checks if any keys were pressed. The function's input should be the device that you want it to use, which is the keyboard. The function's output should be the number of the key that was pressed (or None when no key was pressed). You might wonder why you would want to create a custom function for this, while the Keyboard class's get_key does almost exactly the same thing. There is no programming-related reason to do it, but it's a good practice exercise!

As you might remember from the 'Functions' section in Chapter 2, a function definition always starts with def, followed by the function's name, then the inputs between round brackets, and it ends with a colon. Like so:

```
# definition of a function to get user input
def get_input(device):
```

The code that makes up the function should be indented, preferably by four spaces per line. It should check whether a button is pressed, but with a low timeout:

```
    # wait for a button press for about 10 ms
    key, presstime = device.get_key(timeout=10)
```

The result will be a key name, or None. A key name will be a string, and it will be one of the number keys. In this function, you want the output to be an integer value. So

TABLE 5.2   Notes and frequencies

Keynote	Frequency (Hz)
A4	440
B4	494
C5	523
D5	587
E5	659
F5	698
G5	784
A5	880
B5	988

you should convert the key name (a string) into a number. You can do this by using the `int` function, which turns numeric values into integer numbers. Unfortunately, the `int` function will produce an error when you ask it to convert a None, because a None is not a numeric value. This means you should check whether the value of the key variable is not None, before converting it to an integer:

```
    # check if a key was pressed
    # (this results in a value that is not None)
    if key != None:
        # convert the key name (a string) into an
        # integer
        key = int(key)
    # return the key name (or None)
    return key
```

This lays the ground work for the next bit: making noises when keys are pressed!

Playing sounds on button presses

Sounds from actual instruments are composed of a keynote and several harmonics that are based on the keynote. The relative contributions of the keynote and each harmonic determine the sound's *timbre* (also referred to as tone colour). This book is a bit of a philistine, and shall proceed to completely ignore the concept of timbre. Instead, this book will use pure tones. These are sounds with only a keynote, and no harmonics.

As you know, sounds are the vibrations of air (or a different medium). Sounds can be characterised by their frequency: the amount of vibrations that occur per second. The frequencies of a few musical notes are listed in Table 5.2. (Note for overly anal nerds: Yes, these are rounded off to the nearest integer.) You can use them to create Sound instances that can play a certain keynote.

Let's start with a single note: A4, or 440 Hertz. You can specify this frequency by using the Sound class's `freq` keyword argument. A pure tone is a sine wave, so you should use a sinusoid oscillator when creating the Sound instance (specified by the `osc` keyword argument). You can use the `length` keyword argument to specify the sound's duration in milliseconds. In addition, you can use the `attack` and `decay` keywords to specify the fade-in and fade-out times in milliseconds. An attack of 10 milliseconds means that the sound will take 10 milliseconds to reach its peak volume, and a decay of 10 milliseconds means that the sound will take 10 milliseconds to go from peak volume down to no volume.

As an example, think of a Sound with a length of 100 milliseconds, an attack of 10 milliseconds, and a decay of 10 milliseconds. The sound will take 10 milliseconds to build up to full volume, then play at full volume for 80 milliseconds, and will then reduce to no volume during 10 milliseconds.

Now initialise a Sound instance in your script to create A4 notes with a duration of 250 milliseconds:

```
a4 = Sound(osc='sine', freq=440, length=250, \
      attack=10, decay=10)
```

The following step is to monitor whether button presses occur, and then play the sound whenever they do. A while loop is perfect for this! As you might remember, a while loop can run indefinitely. You can make it stop by flipping its associated Boolean variable from True to False. You could use the following while loop in your script:

```
# run a while loop until
stop = False
while not stop:
```

Within the loop, you should check whether a button is pressed. Then you should decide whether to play a sound or not, depending on whether a button was pressed or not. You can do this by using the `get_input` function you defined earlier:

```
    # check if a button was pressed
    number = get_input(dev)
    # if a button was pressed, number will not be None
    if number != None:
        # if a button was pressed, play the sound
        a4.play()
```

This loop could go on forever, because you never specified when it should stop! To mend this, you could make the loop stop if a button was pressed. Each joystick will have a button that's labelled 0 (which button this is, depends on your joystick), so that would be the ideal button to use for stopping the loop.

```
    # check if a button was pressed
    number = get_input(dev)

    # if a button was pressed, number will not be None
```

```
        if number != None:

                # check if number is 0
                if number == 0:

                        # make the while loop stop if number is 0
                        stop = True

                    # if the number is not 0, play the sound
                    else:
                            a4.play()
```

That should do it! Your while loop will keep looping through the code that is indented. This code will first check if a button is pressed by using the `get_input` function. It will set the `number` variable to None if no key was pressed, or to the number of the button that was pressed. The first if statement will check if the `number` variable is not None. If it is None, the code will simply move to the next loop of the while loop. If `number` is not None, the next if statement will check if the `number` was 0. If it was, then the `stop` variable is set to True, which will make the while loop stop at the start of its next iteration. If number was not 0, the sound will be played.

There is one final thing to do before you try to run this code. It is crucial that you close the Display, otherwise it might stay on when your script stops running:

```
# close the Display
disp.close()
```

Now run the script, and punch the buttons to make some noise! (Press the button that's numbered 0 to stop.)

Unexpected instrument

The script you created in the previous chapter might have bored you quite quickly, because it can only produce a single note. To make it a bit more exciting, you can change the script to make it play a different note for every button.

To do this, you should first create a whole bunch of different Sounds. The quickest way to do this, is by creating a set of all the sound frequencies that you want to use. You can define these in a dict, where you can use the button numbers as the dict's keys. Replace the lines where you defined the `a4` variable in the previous chapter, by the following:

```
# create a dict with the frequency for each button
freqs = {1:440, 2:494, 3:523, 4:587, 5:659, \
     6:698, 7:784, 8:880, 9:988}
```

Now that you specified all the frequencies, it's time to create a Sound instance for each frequency. To do this, you could use a for loop to loop through the `freqs` dict's keys. You can use the dict's `keys` method to generate a list of all key names. The best way of storing the Sound instances is in a dict with the same keys as the `freqs` dict. Add the following code to your script, directly after the lines where you define the `freqs` variable:

```
# create an empty dict for the sounds
sounds = {}
# loop through the keys of the freqs dict
for button in freqs.keys():
    # create a new Sound instance with the right
    # frequency
    sounds[button] = Sound(osc='sine', freq=freqs[button],\
        length=250, attack=10, decay=10)
```

Now only one thing needs to be changed to make your script work. The current script still references the a4 variable, even though you've replaced that by the sounds variable. To fix this, replace the a4.play() line by the following:

```
            sounds[number].play()
```

This uses the pressed button's number to pick the right Sound from the sounds dict, and plays it. Run your script to test it out!

6

ANALYSING BEHAVIOURAL DATA

Now that you have a nice dataset, it's time to learn how to analyse it. Almost all analyses go through the same steps: importing data, storing it in a more usable format, data processing (calculating means, standard deviations, maybe fitting some models), statistics, and making pretty graphs.

In this chapter, you will start by analysing the **behavioural data** from your own experiment. In the next chapter, you will turn to **trace analyses**. The example will be pupil data, but the principles are applicable to any kind of continuous data (EEG, grip force, movement velocity, etc.).

Analysis plan

You can get a dataset by running your own Posner cueing task, or by downloading the example data file from the companion website: www.routledge.com/cw/dalmaijer. Your focus should be on the difference between the valid (cue and target on the same location) and the invalid condition (cue and target on different locations). You have two variables of interest: reaction time and accuracy.

Before starting on the code, think about the analysis process for a bit. You will need to extract your data from the text file. This data can be read line-by-line, and the result of that is that it will be organised per trial. That is, with a single value for each variable (trial 1 validity, trial 1 reaction time, etc.). That's not ideal. To calculate means it would be easier to have the data organised per variable, with a single value for each trial (for example, trial 1 reaction time, trial 2 reaction time, etc.). So you need to convert the data so that it is organised per variable, ideally with a single vector per variable (for example: all reaction times in one long list).

Once you have a single vector for each variable, you can start selecting trials. You have a variable for the validity of each trial, which you can use to select all valid trials. You also have a variable for accuracy, so you can use that to select all correct trials (researchers generally do not use incorrect trials when calculating mean reaction times).

After selecting the correct trials, you can calculate descriptive statistics: mean, standard deviation, and standard error of the mean. You could also opt for calculating a median instead of a mean (more on that later).

Once you have calculated the means (for reaction times and accuracy) per condition (valid and invalid), you can average these over the entire sample (= your group of participants). In addition, you could do statistical tests to see whether there is a difference between the conditions.

After calculating the group mean and standard error of the mean, you can use these values to draw a nice graph. Additionally, you can add the results of your statistics to show whether there is a significant difference.

Extracting data

It's good to separate your analysis completely from your experiment, in terms of organisation. So start by creating a new folder, and a new script that you could name **analysis.py**. In your new folder, create a folder called **data**, and copy your data file to the new data folder.

Now open analysis.py in an editor, and write the following:

```
import os
import numpy
from matplotlib import pyplot
from scipy.stats import ttest_rel
```

By now, you should already be familiar with NumPy, and you have even seen Matplotlib on several occasions (if you have read the 'Make some noise' sections). You can use NumPy to read and process the data, Matplotlib to make pretty plots, and `ttest_rel` from SciPy's `stats` module to do a related-samples t-test.

The other module, `os`, is useful to do stuff that relates to the **o**perating **s**ystem. This includes folder and file management, which is very useful when you're dealing with data files. Let's start by making your script recognise the current folder:

```
# get the path to the current folder
DIR = os.path.dirname(os.path.abspath(__file__))
```

That looks confusing, so let's break it down. `__file__` is a special variable. You don't have to create it, Python does that for you. It contains a **path** to the Python script file. This could be, for example, 'C:\example\analysis.py'. The inner (and thus the first!) function you use on `__file__` is abspath, which transforms the path into an absolute path. You do this, because paths can be defined in two ways: relative and absolute. A relative path would be 'the folder that contains the folder that this script is in' ('.\.\this_script.py'), whereas absolute is 'C:\top_level\second_level\this_script.py'. `__file__` usually refers to an absolute path, but in some cases it does not. Because you need the absolute path, you use abspath to convert a relative path to an absolute path. Just to be sure.

The second function is `dirname`. This takes the path to a file, and strips the file's name out of it. What you are left with, is the path to the folder that contains the script file. If the file path was 'C:\example\analysis.py', `dirname` will turn that into 'C:\example'.

Why do you do this? Well, you need the path to the data folder! You can construct this by combining the name to the script's folder and 'data':

```
DATADIR = os.path.join(DIR, 'data')
```

The `join` function takes all individual strings that you pass, and turns them into a path that makes sense to your operating system. If your directory was 'C:\example', the above line will turn that into 'C:\example\data'.

To construct the name of your data file, you can use the same function:

```
# construct the name of your data file
datafile = os.path.join(DATADIR, 'example.txt')
```

Change 'example.txt' to the name of your own data file (you placed it in the data folder earlier). Now that you have the path to your data file, you can finally load its contents:

```
# load the raw contents of the data file
raw = numpy.loadtxt(datafile, dtype=str, unpack=True)
```

The `loadtxt` function takes the contents of a file (one big string), and **parses** this. Parsing means to analyse a string, and to recognise relevant information. `loadtxt` needs the name of the file that you want to read, for obvious reasons. The first keyword argument you pass is `dtype`, which specifies the data type. You set it to `str` (for 'string'), because some of the data in your file is formatted as a string (the header, for example). This means that all numbers in your data file will also be loaded as strings, but you can fix this later on.

The second keyword you passed is `unpack`, which tells loadtxt to **transpose** the data in your file. Basically, this means that your data is rotated counter-clockwise by 90 degrees. The result is that your data's columns become rows, and rows become columns. This means that your data is no longer ordered per trial (as in the data file's lines), but per variable. So all reaction times are in one vector, and all accuracies in another, and so on.

Run the script within your Editor, to an interpreter. In Spyder, open a new interpreter: click 'Consoles' in the menu, then click 'Open a new Python console'. Now click 'Run' in the menu, then 'Configure...'. Then select 'Execute in current Python or IPython interpreter', and click on the 'Run' button. In IDLE, select 'Run' in the menu, then 'Run Module'.

Now, in the interpreter (=console), type `raw` and press Enter. You should see a NumPy array. Now type `raw[0]` and press Enter. This should print a NumPy array (the first within the variable raw) that contains the string 'fixonset', and then a whole bunch of numbers. These are the timestamps of the onset of the fixation Screen in each trial. Finally, type `raw[11]` and press Enter. This prints a single NumPy array with the string 'RT' and the reaction times for all trials.

The current format is a bit unwieldy: a single NumPy array that contains twelve other NumPy arrays (one for each variable you logged in the experiment). The most annoying thing is that the name of each variable is still in each NumPy array.

So let's think of a better format: how about a dict, with an informative key for every variable that you logged? Something like:

```
data = {'fixonset':array(['5485', '9575', ..., \
        '1188518', '1191807'],
...
'RT':array(['690', '748', ..., '689', '689']}
```

That would make sense, right? You could simply type data['RT'] to get all reaction times. The first step is to create an empty dict:

```
# create new empty dict
data = {}
```

Now, you could manually convert the NumPy array raw into the dict data. That would take you quite a few lines, and a lot of copy-pasting code. Alternatively, you could loop through all NumPy arrays within raw by using a for loop:

```
# loop through all vectors in raw
for i in range(len(raw)):
```

On each iteration of this for loop, i will be the index number of a NumPy array within raw. The first value of every NumPy array in raw is the name of a variable, so raw[i][0] will be a different name in each iteration. Include print(raw[i][0]) to see for yourself:

```
# loop through all vectors in raw

for i in range(len(raw)):
    print(raw[i][0])
```

You could use raw[i][0] as keys in your data dict. The rest of each array in raw contains the data. In code, raw[i][1:] means 'all values in raw[i] from the second index until the end'. To create your data dict, use the following for loop:

```
for i in range(len(raw)):

    # the first index of each array is the variable name
    varname = raw[i][0]
    # the rest of the array is the data
    values = raw[i][1:]

    # create a new entry in the data dict
    # and make it hold the values
    data[varname] = values
```

Run the script in your editor, using a console. Then, in the console, type data and press Enter. You should see a massive amount of numbers. This means that you probably did it right! In the console, type data['RT'] and press Enter. You should see a NumPy array with all reaction times. However, all of them are still string values. If you want to do calculations with them, you will have to convert them to numbers.

Besides the NumPy arrays with numbers-as-strings, there are also arrays with meaningful string data (the location of the cue, for example). Those should not be converted to floats. In fact, trying to do so will result in an error. The easiest solution is to loop through all arrays, and simply try to convert their values into numbers. If you can, that's great. If you can't, then don't convert them.

To try something, and to do something else if it fails, you can use Python's **try-except** statements. These can be used to try one thing, and do a different thing when the thing you tried first caused an **Exception** (= an error). You could implement this in your for loop.

```
for i in range(len(raw)):

    # the first index of each array is the variable name
    varname = raw[i][0]

    # try to convert the values to numbers
    try:
        values = raw[i][1:].astype(float)

    # if conversion to numbers fails, do not convert
    except:
        values = raw[i][1:]

    # create a new entry in the data dict
    # and make it hold the values
    data[varname] = values
```

NumPy arrays have an `astype` method that can change the data type of all the values in the array. If you have an array of numbers that are formatted like strings, you can convert them to floating point numbers by using `astype(float)`. However, using the same on an array of strings (that are not numbers) will raise an Exception.

In the above code, you first try to convert all values in an array to floats. This will raise an Exception if there are non-numerical strings in the array. In that case, the code under the try statement fails, and the code under the except statement is run instead.

If you copy the for loop into analysis.py (instead of the for loop on the in the previous example!) and run the script, you should be able to type `data['RT']` in the console. Unlike before, it should now contain numerical values rather than strings. Score!

Selecting data

Now that you have all your data in a manageable format, it's time to start splitting it up according to your conditions. You have two important conditions: the SOA, which was either 100 ms or 900 ms; and the validity, which was either 1 (valid) or 0 (invalid).

You would like to be able to select four groups: 100 ms, valid; 100 ms, invalid; 900 ms, valid; and 900 ms, invalid. As you can see, these depend on two different variables: `data['soa']` can be either 100 or 900, and `data['valid']` either 1 or 0.

To make a selection based on the content of a variable, you can use the operators that you learned about in the 'Booleans' section in Chapter 2. To select all valid trials, you can use the following:

```
valid = data['valid'] == 1
```

This will create a variable `valid`, which will be a **Boolean vector**. That's a fancy term for a list of True and False values. Here, you compare the vector `data['valid']` with the integer 1. The result will be a Boolean vector with the same length as `data['valid']`. It will be True at every index number of `data['valid']` that is equal to 1, and False where `data['valid']` is not 1. For example, if `data['valid']` was [1, 0, 1, 0], the Boolean vector created above would be [True, False, True, False].

You can use Boolean vectors to select values from NumPy arrays:

```
data['RT'][valid]
```

This will select only the values in a vector for which the corresponding value (at the same index number) in the Boolean vector is True. In this case, that means you select only the reaction times from valid trials. For example, if `valid` was [True, False, True, False], and `data['RT']` was [512, 535, 505, 570], then `data['RT'][valid]` would be [512, 505].

Now make some Boolean vectors for your data by adding the following code to your analysis.py script:

```
# make Boolean vectors for valid and invalid trials
sel = {}
sel['valid'] = data['valid'] == 1
sel['invalid'] = data['valid'] == 0

# make Boolean vectors for 100 and 900 ms SOAs
sel[100] = data['soa'] == 100
sel[900] = data['soa'] == 900
```

After running analysis.py again, you can calculate the average accuracy (proportion of correct responses) of each condition! In the interpreter, type:

```
numpy.mean(data['correct'][sel['valid']])
numpy.mean(data['correct'][sel['invalid']])
```

Those are the means of all valid and all invalid trials. You can also combine multiple Boolean vectors, for example to select only the valid trials with a 100 ms SOA:

```
numpy.mean(data['correct'][sel[100] & sel['valid']])
numpy.mean(data['correct'][sel[100] & sel['invalid']])
```

In the next section, you will find out how to calculate means, medians, standard deviations, and standard errors.

Averaging data

In the previous section, you made Boolean vectors that could select four groups: 100 ms, valid; 100 ms, invalid; 900 ms, valid; and 900 ms, invalid. For each of these groups, you could calculate the basic descriptives: mean, standard deviation, and standard error of the mean (pedantic remark: that last one isn't actually a descriptive statistic, as it tells you something about the sampling process, and not just about the distribution of your data).

Unfortunately, using these measures is only appropriate when you are dealing with normally distributed data. And you might not be.

The accuracy per trial has two potential values: 1 (correct) and 0 (incorrect). This type of data is referred to as dichotomous or binary. You can calculate a mean of all of these ones and zeros, and that will give you the **proportion of correct responses**. However, it would not be appropriate to calculate a standard deviation or the standard error of the mean in the ways that you are used to. There are correct ways of calculating confidence intervals (see: http://en.wikipedia.org/wiki/Binomial_proportion_confidence_interval), but let's ignore those for now. The solution here is to simply not calculate the standard deviation or error for each individual participant's error rate (you will be able to do so for the whole group later on).

Reaction times are a different story, and the correct way of analysing them can be debated. The reason for this is that reaction times are not normally distributed. This makes sense: a reaction time cannot be lower than 0, but it can always be longer (to infinity, and perhaps beyond?). In most datasets, the distribution of reaction times has a positive skew (a longer tail on the right).

Why does this matter? Well, if you calculate a mean, you assume that the distribution is not skewed. So when you calculate a mean of a skewed distribution, it might not correctly represent the centre of that distribution. Rather, the mean will be pulled towards the tail.

One alternative option is to calculate a **median**. This is the value that is in the centre when you make an ordered list of all the reaction times, and can be a better reflection of the centre of a skewed distribution.

A more fancy alternative is to fit an ExGaussian distribution to your reaction time data. This is a combination of a normal distribution and an exponential decay function, so it matches the typical profile of a distribution of reaction times. The ExGaussian provides you with a centre parameter (equivalent to the mean), and a deviation parameter (equivalent to the standard deviation). The downside of using an ExGaussion fit is that you need a lot of data for a good parameter estimation.

For simplicity's sake, here you can calculate a median and use the regular way of calculating the standard deviation and the standard error. In fact, you should find that these will do a very good job of describing the example datasets. That's because the examples were completely fabricated by sampling random numbers from a normal distribution. Note that this was done only for teaching purposes! Fabricating data for other purposes is bad, m'kay?

Let's return to the actual programming. You stuck all your Boolean vectors in a single dict, so you can loop through them a bit easier. You can do this by creating two for loops: one to go through the SOA conditions, and one nested loop to go through the validity conditions:

```
# loop through all SOAs
for soa in [100, 900]:
     # loop through all validities
     for val in ['valid', 'invalid']:
```

Within these for loops, you can calculate all the descriptives you need:

```
          # calculate statistics
          rt_m = numpy.median(data['RT'][sel[soa] & \
               sel[val]])
          rt_sd = numpy.std(data['RT'][sel[soa] & \
               sel[val]])
          rt_sem = rt_sd / numpy.sqrt(len(data['RT'] \
               [sel[soa] & sel[val]]))
          acc_m = numpy.mean(data['correct'][sel[soa] & \
               sel[val]])

          # report statistics
          print('condition %d ms SOA, %s:' % (soa, val))
          print('median RT=%.2f, SD=%.2f, SEM=%.2f' % \
               (rt_m, rt_sd, rt_sem))
          print('proportion correct=%.2f\n' % (acc_m))
```

Calculating medians, standard deviations (SD), and means is easy: a single NumPy function can take care of it. The standard error of the mean (SEM) is a bit more unclear, perhaps. The standard error of the mean can be calculated by dividing the standard deviation by the square root of the number of observations (trials, in this case). You can count the number of samples by using the len function, which gives you the number of values in a NumPy array. The square root can be calculated with NumPy's sqrt function.

As it is now, you simply print the results to an interpreter. That is useful for you, because you can read them there, but it is less useful to your computer. Because you keep overwriting the same variable names, the results of your calculations do not persist. That's annoying, because you will need them later on (for plotting, for example).

A nice solution is to store the descriptives that you calculated in a dictionary. Add the following code *before* the first for loop:

```
# create an empty dict to hold descriptives
descr = {}
```

This creates an empty dictionary. It makes sense to order the data per SOA, and then per validity (because we are primarily interested in the difference between the valid and invalid conditions within each SOA condition). This means that the descr dict should have two keys, each with two new dicts: 100 and 900. The easier way to achieve this, is by adding the following directly after the for soa in [100, 900]: line:

```
     # create a new empty dict within the descr dict
     descr[soa] = {}
```

Now within the second for loop, after `for val in ['valid', 'invalid']:`, add code to add yet another dict to `descr` (this time with keys for each validity condition):

```
        # nest another empty dict within descr
        descr[soa][val] = {}
```

Finally, after calculating the values, you can now store them. After line `acc_m  = numpy.mean(data['correct'][sel[soa] & sel[val]]:`, add:

```
        # store the calculated values in descr
        descr[soa][val]['rt_m'] = rt_m
        descr[soa][val]['rt_sd'] = rt_sd
        descr[soa][val]['rt_sem'] = rt_sem
        descr[soa][val]['acc_m'] = acc_m
```

Run your current script within an Editor. In the Interpreter you can now type, for example, `descr[100]['valid']` (and Enter) to get all measures for the 100 ms SOA and valid condition.

Nesting dicts in dicts within dicts might not always be the best option for a flexible data analysis. Other ways include storing data in a multi-dimensional NumPy array, with a dimension for each factor (SOA and validity). You will get to know this method in section 'Combining datasets', where you can run through data from multiple participants.

Plotting data

Now that you have calculated the mean and standard error of the mean for a single participant, you can plot them. Matplotlib's `pyplot` library provides a whole range of functions to create high-quality graphs. The amount of customisation options might be a little overwhelming at first, but you will get used to it.

The recipe for a graph is quite straightforward: you start with creating a new (empty) figure, then you draw the means and standard errors for each condition, and you end by adding axis labels and a legend.

Let's start with creating a new figure. Matplotlib has a very useful function to create figures with one or more subplots in them. You can create one subplot for the 100 ms SOA, and one for 900 ms. You can add the following lines to analysis.py. Make sure to add them at the very end, and without indentation!

```
# create a new figure with two subplots
fig, (ax100, ax900) = pyplot.subplots(nrows=1, ncols=2, \
    sharey=True, figsize=(19.2, 10.8), dpi=100.0)
```

The subplots function creates a single **figure**, with multiple **axes**. In Matplotlib, a figure is the background that contains a single or multiple subplots. Each subplots is called an **axis**. The axes can be used to plot data.

When you call the subplots function, you can pass a number of keywords. Two of the keywords determine the amount of axes (subplots): `nrows` is the number of horizontal rows of plots, and `ncols` is the number of vertical columns of plots. You ask for one row and two columns, which results in two plots next to one another. Further keywords are concerned with the lay-out. `sharey` and `sharex` are Booleans that indicate whether all subplots should have the same *y*- and *x*-axis. `figsize` determines the size of the figure (the background containing all subplots) in inches, while `dpi` determines the amount of dots (pixels) per inch. A figure of 19.2 inches wide and 10.8 inches high, with a DPI of 100 results in a figure of 19.2 ★ 100 = 1920 pixels wide and 10.8 ★ 100 = 1080 pixels high.

You can create a bar plot. Before you start, it is important that you know how wide your bars are going to be, and how much distance you want between them. Matplotlib considers the x-axis in a bar plot to be no different from the x-axis in a scatter plot, which means that you can define the start and width of each bar in numbers. For example, your bars could be 0.4 wide, and the distance between them could be 0.1 (these values correspond to the values on the x-axis in your plot).

```
# define the bar plot parameters
width = 0.4
intdist = 0.1
```

While drawing bars, you will need to update the starting position of the next bar. For example, if your draw the first at 0.1, you will want to draw the second on 0.6. That is the position of the first bar, plus its width, plus the distance between bars.

```
# define the starting position (left edge) of the first bar
barpos = 0.1
```

The final thing to decide, is which colour you want to use for which condition. You can store these in a dict. Matplotlib recognises all sorts of colour formats: built-in colour abbreviations (e.g. 'b' for blue, or 'g' for green), RGB guns with values between 0 and 1 (e.g. (1,0,0) for red), html colour names (e.g. 'red', 'burlywood', or 'charteuse'), and hex values (e.g. '#ff69b4' for hot pink). See http://matplotlib.org/api/colors_api.html for more info.

```
# define the bar colours
cols = {'valid':'#4e9a06', 'invalid':'#ce5c00'}
```

Time to plot your results. Create a new for loop, to go through the validity conditions:

```
for val in ['valid', 'invalid']:
```

Within the for loop, draw a bar by using the `bar` method of axis. This requires the starting point of the bar, its height, and its width. The width and position were already determined. The height is determined by the data (that's the median reaction time here). You can also pass a value to create error bars by using the `yerr` keyword. Usually, you want this to be the standard error. Finally, you can also define a label, which can be any string. Labels appear in the legend.

```
    # draw the 100 ms SOA median reaction time
    ax100.bar(barpos, descr[100][val]['rt_m'], \
        width=width, yerr=descr[100][val]['rt_sem'], \
        color=cols[val], ecolor='black', label=val)
```

You should also do this for the 900 ms SOA:

```
    # draw the 900 ms SOA median reaction time
    ax900.bar(barpos, descr[900][val]['rt_m'], \
        width=width, yerr=descr[900][val]['rt_sem'], \
        color=cols[val], ecolor='black', label=val)
```

After drawing the bars, you should update the position of the next bars. If you neglect this, all bars will be drawn on top of each other!

```
    # update the bar position
    barpos += width + intdist
```

After drawing the data within a for loop, you should make the plots more clear. Start by adding a y-axis label (only for the first subplot, because both plots have the same y-axis). Add the following line, but without indentation!

```
# add y-axis label to the left plot
ax100.set_ylabel('Median reaction time (ms)')
```

You can add a legend simply by calling each axis's `legend` method. This adds a legend to the figure, listing only the data that you explicitly labelled. You can choose the position yourself, or have it automatically set to the best position. The position label is a combination of 'upper', 'center', or 'lower' to indicate the vertical position; and 'left', 'center' or 'right' for the horizontal position. It can also be 'best' to auto-select the best-fitting location (Matlplotlib will try to avoid drawing the legend on top of anything else).

```
# add a legend to the right axis
ax900.legend(loc='upper right')
```

Because you added a legend, the x-axis becomes unnecessary (they both reflect the validity). You can hide it by using the following code:

```
# hide x-axes
ax100.get_xaxis().set_visible(False)
ax900.get_xaxis().set_visible(False)
```

In addition, you can add a title to each individual plot, to clarify which SOA they represent:

```
# give the plots a title
ax100.set_title('100 ms SOA')
ax900.set_title('900 ms SOA')
```

Finally, you can set the scale in which you want to show the graph. You could set the x-axis to run from 0 to the next bar position (leaving equal space left and right). The y-axis could run from 100 to 1000, which is the range that reaction times are normally in.

```
# set x-axis limits
ax100.set_xlim([0, barpos])
ax900.set_xlim([0, barpos])
```

```
# set y-axis limits
ax100.set_ylim([100, 1000])
ax900.set_ylim([100, 1000])
```

Now the only thing left to do, is to save your figure. You can do this by calling the figure's `savefig` method. This will create an image in the same folder as the script:

```
# save the figure
fig.savefig('reaction_times.png')
```

Cool. Cool, cool, cool. Run the current analysis.py, and enjoy the plot. If you run into errors, track back and check where you made a mistake.

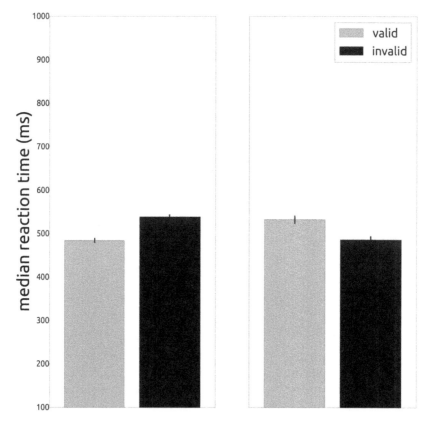

FIGURE 6.1 This is what a bar plot of the reaction times for the valid (light) and invalid (dark) conditions looks like. The left panel is with an SOA of 100 milliseconds, and the right panel for an SOA of 900 milliseconds

Combining datasets

Now that you have the code to read, process, and plot an individual participant's data, you can start thinking about doing the same for a group of participants. You can download an example dataset of ten participants from the companion website: www.routledge.com/cw/dalmaijer. In essence, you could simply take your current code to analyse one participant's data, and put it in a for loop to analyse multiple participants in a row.

With a for loop, you can run through all participants. For each participant, you calculate the values you need: median reaction time and accuracy for each condition. You should store these values in a variable, so that you can use them to calculate group statistics later on.

While going through all participants, you will be creating a bar graph for each. At the end, you will also create a graph for the group. This quickly amounts to a lot of figures, which makes it worthwhile to neatly store them in a separate folder to prevent cluttering. Let's start by creating a new folder, using code.

Open analysis.py (you created it in the previous chapters). Add the following code directly after the `DATADIR = os.path.join(DIR, 'data')` line:

```
# construct a path to the output directory
OUTDIR = os.path.join(DIR, 'output')
```

This will construct the path to your output directory, for example 'C:\example\output'. This folder will not exist the first time you run your script, so you will need to make it. You can do this by using the `os` module's `mkdir` function. However, if you think ahead a bit, you will realise that the output directory will exist after you ran the script once. Calling `mkdir` to create a folder that already exists will result in an error. Therefore, you should include a line to check whether the output directory does not exist *yet*. You can use the `os` module's `isdir` function for that:

```
# check if the output folder does not exist
if not os.path.isdir(OUTDIR):
     # only create an output directory if it doesn't
     # exist yet
     os.mkdir(OUTDIR)
```

Because you will be creating a lot of plots for individual participants, it is a good idea to separate those from the group average plots. You could create a new folder for all individual participants' output:

```
# construct a path to the individual output directory
IOUTDIR = os.path.join(OUTDIR, 'individual')

# check if the individual output folder exists
if not os.path.isdir(IOUTDIR):
     # create an individual output directory
     os.mkdir(IOUTDIR)
```

Now that you took care of the folder infrastructure, let's get on with the actual analysis. First, you need to create a single variable that can hold data for all ten participants. For each participant, there will be two conditions, each with two levels: SOA with 100 ms and 900 ms, and validity with valid and invalid. For each of these conditions, and for each of the participants, you will have two values: the median reaction time and the proportion of correct responses.

You could stick all of those values in dicts (one for each participant), nested in other dicts (one for each SOA condition), nested in some more dicts (one for each validity condition), nested in even more dicts (one for RT and one for accuracy). But that seems like quite a complicated mess, and it will not be optimal for further calculations due to a lack of flexibility.

Instead, you would rather have all data in vectors, where you can indicate what values to incorporate in a calculation. For example, sometimes you might want to access all participants' median reaction times only in the valid condition, but of both SOA conditions. Or you might want to have a look at the reaction times of only the first five participants.

To make this possible, you could create two empty multi-dimensional NumPy arrays. This sounds complicated, but it comes down to the following: for each condition, you need a dimension in your NumPy array. And one additional one for the participant numbers.

For a single subject, you can visualise this as a two-dimensional 'sheet' of four values:

	Valid	*Invalid*
100 ms SOA	500	560
900 ms SOA	550	500

You can imagine the collection of participants' data as a stack of sheets, each containing similar numbers to the example above. In this stack, the first dimension is the validity, the second is the SOA, and the third is the participant number. The first two dimensions will have a depth of two (100 ms and 900 ms, or valid and invalid), whereas the third dimension will have a depth of ten (10 participants).

In Python, you can create such a stack by creating a multi-dimensional NumPy array. Initially, this will be full of zeros, but you will fill it up with data as you run through all participants. Create two such arrays, one for reaction times and one for accuracy:

```
# define the number of participants
N = 10

# create an empty multi-dimensional array to store data
all_rt = numpy.zeros((2, 2, N))
all_acc = numpy.zeros((2, 2, N))
```

Add the above code directly after the `os.mkdir(IOUTDIR)` line. NumPy's `zeros` function can be used to create multi-dimensional arrays filled with zeros.

Now that you have variables to store data in, it's time to loop through all participants. Directly after the above code, add a new for loop:

```
# loop through all participant numbers
for pnr in range(0, N):
```

`range(0, N)` will create a list of all numbers from 0 to 9. These are all participant numbers, so the for loop will run through all of them, using `pnr` as the variable that points to the participant number.

The next step is very important. To make the for loop work, *increase the indentation of all code below the for loop by one indent* (one tab or four spaces, depending on your preference). In Spyder, select the block of code and press the Tab key; or in IDLE, select the block of code and press the Ctrl and] keys at the same time.

If you did everything correctly, *all analysis code from reading a data file until saving a bar graph is now indented.* This means the for loop will run through all of it. That's great, because you want it to read, process, and plot the data of every participant in a row. There are a few more adjustments to make in the current code, though.

The first is in constructing the data file's name. The current line is:

```
    datafile = os.path.join(DATADIR, 'example.txt')
```

But it should refer to the current participant number. Therefore, change it to this:

```
    datafile = os.path.join(DATADIR, 'pp%d.txt' % (pnr))
```

You should recognise the notation `'pp%d.txt'`, which is a string with a wildcard for a decimal number. The wildcard is replaced by `pnr`, which is the participant number in each iteration of the for loop. Thus, using this notation will make sure that you read a new data file on each iteration of the for loop.

Another change you should make, is in the line that saves the figure. It currently is:

```
    fig.savefig('reaction_times.png')
```

If you leave it like this, you will simply overwrite the same figure on each iteration of the for loop. Instead, you should incorporate the participant number in the file name. In addition, you could save the individual graph in the folder for individual graphs (IOUTDIR). Change the above line to the following lines:

```
    savefilename = os.path.join(IOUTDIR, \
        'reaction_times_%d.png' % (pnr))
    fig.savefig(savefilename)
    pyplot.close(fig)
```

That last line, `pyplot.close(fig)`, ensures that the plotting library (Matplotlib) closes the figure. This is necessary, because open plots take up space in your computer's temporary memory. If you leave too many figures open, Matplotlib will run out of available memory, and your script will crash.

There is one more addition required to the current code. You need to store the median reaction time and accuracy for each participant in the multi-dimensional NumPy arrays you created before. Directly after the above code (to save and close the figure), add the following:

```
    # store all median reaction times
    all_rt[0, 0, pnr] = descr[100]['valid']['rt_m']
    all_rt[1, 0, pnr] = descr[100]['invalid']['rt_m']
    all_rt[0, 1, pnr] = descr[900]['valid']['rt_m']
    all_rt[1, 1, pnr] = descr[900]['invalid']['rt_m']

    # store all proportion corrects
    all_acc[0, 0, pnr] = descr[100]['valid']['acc_m']
    all_acc[1, 0, pnr] = descr[100]['invalid']['acc_m']
    all_acc[0, 1, pnr] = descr[900]['valid']['acc_m']
    all_acc[1, 1, pnr] = descr[900]['invalid']['acc_m']
```

To see how the multi-dimensional NumPy arrays help you, you can run the current script in an Editor (to the current Interpreter/console). After running, in the Interpreter type `descr[100]['valid']['rt_m']; descr[100]['invalid']['rt_m']` and hit Enter. This prints out the median reaction times for the last participant, for the 100 ms SOA, and the valid and invalid conditions. Now type `all_rt[:,0,9]`. Translated to English, this means "from the `all_rt` variable, take all values in the first dimension (the colon, :, means 'all'), and the first (index 0) position in the second dimension, and on the tenth (index 9) position in the third dimension". The first dimension indicated the validity (0=valid, 1=invalid). The second indicated the SOA (0=100 ms, 1=900 ms), and the third indicated the participant number. Thus `all_rt[0,0,9]` contains the same values as `descr[100]['valid']['rt_m']`.

Because of the flexible nature in which you can access values in NumPy arrays, they are ideal to calculate averages. To average all reaction times in the 100 ms SOA and valid cue condition, simply type the following in the Interpreter:

```
numpy.mean(all_rt[0,0,:])
```

You could also calculate the average reaction time in both the valid and invalid conditions, in the 100 ms SOA condition:

```
numpy.mean(all_rt[:,0,:])
```

Or in the 900 ms condition:

```
numpy.mean(all_rt[:,1,:])
```

Or the same of only the first five participants:

```
numpy.mean(all_rt[:,1,0:5])
```

You can also calculate the means of both the valid 100 ms and the valid 900 ms conditions at the same time, by using the mean function's `axis` keyword. Do so by specifying the number of the axis you want to calculate the averages of. That's the second (with index number 1) in the following selection:

```
numpy.mean(all_rt[0, :, :], axis=1)
```

Now that you played around with the data for a bit, it's time to return to your analysis.py script. You could calculate four means and four standard errors of the mean, and you could visualise these in a clear way. One way of visualising the means, is to plot two lines: one for the valid condition, and one for the invalid. Each line will have two points: one at 100 ms, and one at 900 ms. In this way, the interaction effect (on reaction time and accuracy) between SOA and validity will be represented the clearest. If you do not quite follow, the graph you produce in the end will hopefully clear things up.

All the way at the end of analysis.py, *without indentation*, include the following code:

```
# create a new figure with a two subplots
fig, (rt_ax, acc_ax) = pyplot.subplots(nrows=2, \
      sharex=True, figsize=(19.2, 10.8), dpi=100.0)
```

One of the subplots will present the reaction times, and the other will present the accuracy. These plots will have a few things in common: the x-axis and the colouring. The x-axis will represent the SOA, so there will be two values: 100 ms and 900 ms. You can choose the colours for valid and invalid yourself, by replacing the hex values (e.g. '#4e9a06' for green) in the code below:

```
# the x-axis will be the SOAs
x = [100, 900]
# the colours the valid and invalid conditions
cols = {'valid':'#4e9a06', 'invalid':'#ce5c00'}
```

Now it's time to plot the actual values as lines. There are two plots: one for reaction times and one for accuracy. Each will show two lines: one for valid and one for invalid. Each line will be drawn between two values: one for 100 ms and one for 900 ms. These will be calculated by NumPy's mean function, using the axis keyword (as before). You also need the standard error of the mean to create error bars. (Because this is a sample standard error, you use the square root of the number of participants minus one.) Add the following code:

```
# the y-axes will be the valid and invalid means
rt_valid = numpy.mean(all_rt[0, :, :], axis=1)
rt_invalid = numpy.mean(all_rt[1, :, :], axis=1)

# calculate the SEM (=SD/sqrt(N-1))
rt_valid_sem = numpy.std(all_rt[0,:,:], axis=1) \
      / numpy.sqrt(N - 1)
rt_invalid_sem = numpy.std(all_rt[1,:,:], axis=1) \
      / numpy.sqrt(N - 1)
```

You can plot a line with error bars by using each axis' errorbar method. This requires a few arguments, of which the most important are the *x* values and the *y* values (to indicate where to draw a line, and where the error bars should be). In addition, the errorbar method requires the values that indicate the size of the error bars (yerr), the colour of the line (`color`), and the colour of the error bars (`ecolor`). Of course, you can also provide a label to indicate what the line describes:

```
# plot the means for valid and invalid as lines,
# including error bars for the standard error of the mean
rt_ax.errorbar(x, rt_valid, yerr=rt_valid_sem, \
     color=cols['valid'], ecolor='black', label='valid')
rt_ax.errorbar(x, rt_invalid, yerr=rt_invalid_sem, \
     color=cols['invalid'], ecolor='black', \
     label='invalid')
```

Finally, you need to clarify the plot: add a label to the y axis, and put in a legend:

```
# add y-axis label
rt_ax.set_ylabel('reaction time (ms)')
# add legend
rt_ax.legend(loc='upper right')
```

After averaging and plotting the reaction times, you can do the same for the accuracy. First, calculate means and standard errors of the means:

```
# calculate the accuracy means
acc_valid = numpy.mean(all_acc[0, :, :], axis=1)
acc_invalid = numpy.mean(all_acc[1, :, :], axis=1)

# calculate the SEM (=SD/sqrt(N-1))
acc_valid_sem = numpy.std(all_acc[0,:,:], axis=1) \
     / numpy.sqrt(N - 1)
acc_invalid_sem = numpy.std(all_acc[1,:,:], axis=1) \
     / numpy.sqrt(N - 1)
```

Then plot lines with error bars:

```
# plot the means for valid and invalid as lines,
# including error bars for the standard error of the mean
acc_ax.errorbar(x, acc_valid, yerr=acc_valid_sem, \
     color=cols['valid'], ecolor='black', label='valid')
acc_ax.errorbar(x, acc_invalid, yerr=acc_invalid_sem, \
     color=cols['invalid'], ecolor='black', \
     label='invalid')
```

And add labels to both axes:

```
# add axis labels
acc_ax.set_xlabel('stimulus onset asynchrony (ms)')
acc_ax.set_ylabel('proportion correct')
```

Finally, set the limits of the x-axis. You want the axis to include both 100 and 900 ms, so a lower limit of 0 and an upper limit of 1000 seem appropriate. The x-axes of both subplots are coupled, so you only have to change one to change both:

```
# set x limits
acc_ax.set_xlim([0, 1000])
```

Now add the code to save the figure:

```
# save the figure as a PNG image
savefilename = os.path.join(OUTDIR, 'averages.png')
fig.savefig(savefilename)
```

Now run the script, and BOOM! You created ten individual bar plots, and a line plot for the group averages.

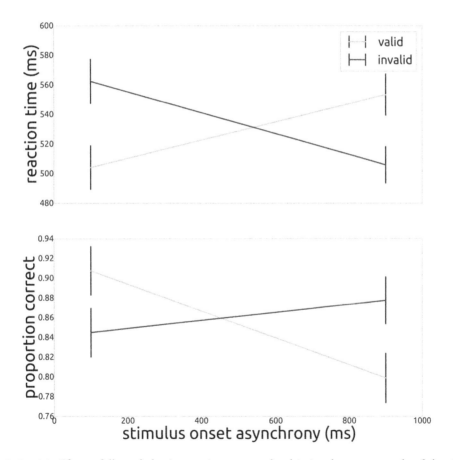

FIGURE 6.2 If you followed the instructions correctly, this is what your graph of the data should look like

One thing to note for the future: because it is easier, you calculated the between-participants standard error of the mean. However, the comparisons you will make in the next section will test within-participant differences between the conditions. Therefore, computing and plotting the within-participants standard error of the mean would have been more appropriate.

Statistical testing

The comparisons you would like to make are within each SOA, between the valid and the invalid condition.

Officially, with a design like this, you should do a repeated-measures analysis of variance (ANOVA) with SOA and validity as factors (each with two levels). This test could demonstrate a significant main effect of validity and/or of SOA, and it could show a significant interaction effect between the two. If you find such a significant effect, you could also compare individual *cells* (pairs of groups you can make from the factors and levels). For example, you could test whether there was a significant difference in reaction times between the valid and invalid conditions within the 100 millisecond SOA condition. Importantly, if the repeated-measures ANOVA did not show any significant effects, it might be inappropriate to do such follow-up tests (provided you don't have a good reason to do so, for example a very strong hypothesis).

Also, before even doing the repeated-measures ANOVA, you should check whether all of its underlying assumptions are met. For example, the variances in all cells should be equal, and you should test for this using Mauchly's test of sphericity.

(Please note that some stats nerds might propose a different analysis, such as a linear mixed effects model, or something else entirely. When in doubt, consult Google. When still in doubt after Google, consult a statistician.)

For now, you can be a rebel and completely ignore the rules. Instead, you could do two related-samples t-tests. One to test if the reaction times to valid cues and invalid cues are different in the 100 ms SOA condition, and another to test if reaction times to valid and invalid cues are different in the 900 ms SOA condition.

You should not take this as advice to not do appropriate statistics! The reason for not doing a more appropriate test, is that this book is not on statistics. You're reading this to be able to get started with Python programming, not to get acquainted with the ins and outs of within-participant statistical testing.

If you learned about statistics before, you might be able to implement the tests of your choice. If you forgot and need to refresh your memory, Wikipedia has pretty decent articles on most statistical tests, including all the formulae you need.

Now back to what you were doing: related-samples t-tests in Python. Open the analysis.py script from the previous sections. To perform a related-samples t-test, you can use the `ttest_rel` function from SciPy's `stats` module. This function requires two arguments: one NumPy arrays of data in one condition, and another NumPy array of data from the other condition. This could be, for example, the reaction times from the valid condition, and the reaction times from the invalid condition.

`ttest_rel` will calculate and return a t-statistic and a p-value. For those not in the know: the t-statistic indicates how far apart two distributions are, and the p-value indicates how likely it is to find a more extreme t-statistic than you did (assuming there is no difference between the distributions).

In your case, one array will contain valid reaction times and the other will be of invalid reaction times, split out according to SOA. Add the following lines to the end of analysis.py:

```
# perform two related-samples t-test
t100, p100 = ttest_rel(all_rt[0,0,:], all_rt[1,0,:])
t900, p900 = ttest_rel(all_rt[0,1,:], all_rt[1,1,:])
```

In addition, add code to report the values:

```
print('\nstats report:')
print('SOA 100ms, valid vs invalid: t=%.2f, p=%.3f' % \
    (t100, p100))
print('SOA 900ms, valid vs invalid: t=%.2f, p=%.3f' % \
    (t900, p900))
```

Of course, you can do the same for the accuracy:

```
t100, p100 = ttest_rel(all_acc[0,0,:], all_acc[1,0,:])
t900, p900 = ttest_rel(all_acc[0,1,:], all_acc[1,1,:])
print('SOA 100ms, valid vs invalid: t=%.2f, p=%.3f' % \
    (t100, p100))
print('SOA 900ms, valid vs invalid: t=%.2f, p=%.3f' % \
    (t900, p900))
```

If this was real, you would have demonstrated the facilitatory effects of exogenous attention: lower reaction times and higher accuracy after a valid cue that was presented 100 milliseconds prior to a target. However, if the stimulus-onset asynchrony was 900 milliseconds, the results would be opposite: longer reaction times and lower accuracy. This is inhibition of return. (Please remember that this data was completely fabricated for educational purposes; don't expect such strong effects in actual experiments!)

7

ANALYSING TRACES

Now that you know how to analyse reaction time and accuracy data, it's time to move on to something a bit more complicated: trace analysis. A trace can be any type of data that you collect continuously: pupil size, EEG, fMRI, force output, movement velocity, and so on. It doesn't really matter where the trace comes from, the basic steps of the analysis are always the same: you collect the traces for individual trials, average them per condition, and then test where the traces are different between conditions.

Introduction

Pupil size

In this section, you will use an example dataset of pupillometry measurements. You can download it from the companion website www.routledge.com/cw/dalmaijer. Put this file in a new empty folder.

The data was collected in a very straightforward experimental design: participants looked at a computer monitor that had a grey fixation dot. Every few seconds the display changed from black to white, or vice versa.

The effect of lighting on pupil size is rather strong: The pupil contracts when the eyes are exposed to bright light, and it dilates when there is little light. The pupil is a bit slow to respond, though. Usually, a change in pupil size becomes apparent after about half a second (or a little under).

The data in the example file was collected with an EyeLink 1000 (SR Research Ltd). This is an eye tracker: a fancy camera that can recognise and follow eyes, and can measure the diameter (and surface area) of pupils. The EyeLink 1000 operates at 1000 Hz, which means that it provides one snapshot of the pupil diameter every millisecond.

PyGaze Analyser

To read the EyeLink's data file, you can use PyGaze Analyser. You can download the package from www.routledge.com/cw/dalmaijer. After downloading the zipped archive, unzip it and copy the folder called 'pygazeanalyser' to your new analysis folder (where the example data file is).

PyGaze Analyser is currently a relatively simple library that can extract data from EyeLink, EyeTribe, and SensoMotoric Instruments (SMI) files. In addition, it provides functions for high-level plotting of gaze fixation data, which can produce fancy pictures. You will encounter these in a later section.

Read eye-tracker data

You currently have two things in your new analysis folder: the example data file (`ED_pupil.asc`), and the pygazeanalyser folder. Now add another file: an empty Python script that you could name analysis.py. Open analysis.py in a script Editor. Start by importing the relevant libraries and functions:

```
import numpy
from matplotlib import pyplot
from scipy.stats import ttest_rel
from pygazeanalyser.edfreader import read_edf
```

You should recognise the first three from Chapter 6. The fourth one is new, and it is specifically designed to read data from EyeLink files. These files have a **.edf** extension, which is why the function is called `read_edf`. The data file you have has a **.asc** extension. This is a converted EDF file; it contains the same data, but in a more readable format.

Data files from eye trackers (and most other traces) consist of at least two types of data. The first type is **samples**. In this case, that is data on the gaze location and the pupil diameter. Each of these samples comes with a timestamp. The second type of data are **events**. These are strings of information that appear between the samples. Usually, they indicate that something happened in the experiment. They provide anchors within the data file. Without these, you would not have known at what point in the experiment the samples were collected.

In the current data file, there are four events of interest. The first indicates the start of a trial: `PUPIL_TRIALSTART, colour='black'`. It can also end with `'white'`. The colour indicates the colour of the monitor during that trial. The second kind of event was logged about 200 milliseconds before the monitor changed colour: `baseline_start`. The third event was `pupdata_start`. It was logged when the monitor changed colour. Finally, the event `pupdata_stop` was logged 2.5 seconds after the monitor changed colour.

The `read_edf` function takes at least two arguments: the name of (or path to) the data file, and the event that indicated a trial start. This does not need to be a full event. In your case, you can pass `PUPIL_TRIALSTART` and neglect the second bit (that indicated the colour and was not the same for every trial). You can also pass the event that indicated the end of a trial. If you do not provide this, read_edf will continue reading until it encounters the next trial start. By not passing the ending event, you risk reading irrelevant data. Add the following code to your analysis.py:

```
# read data file
data = read_edf('ED_pupil.asc', 'PUPIL_TRIALSTART', \
     stop='pupdata_stop')
```

This reads the file, and stores its contents in a new variable (data). This variable is quite large and quite complex, so an explanation is in order. data is a list that contains values of single trials (one trial per index). In this case there were 50 trials, so len(data)==50. You can refer to a single trial by using data[n], where n is the trial number.

Each single trial is represented by a dict. These dicts always have the same six keys. The first are 'trackertime' and 'time'. Both of these are NumPy arrays that contain the timestamps of all data samples. The timestamps in 'trackertime' are in the time that the eye tracker reported. The timestamps in 'time' start at 0 in every trial.

The next three keys are 'x', 'y', and 'size'. These are all NumPy arrays. 'x' contains samples of the horizontal gaze position, and 'y' of the vertical gaze position (that is: at which pixel on the monitor a participant was looking). 'size' contains samples of the pupil size. These can represent either the pupil surface area, or the pupil diameter (which depends on the EyeLink's settings during testing). Pupil size was measured in arbitrary units, which are relative to the specific setup and participant. Note that these units do not quite mean anything in the real world, and that you can't compare them between participants.

Finally, there is the 'events' key. In eye movement recordings, events can specify eye movements (fixations, saccades, and blinks; these will be explained in the 'Eye tracking – the basics' section in Chapter 8), or messages that are logged in the data file. The 'events' key refers to another dict, which contains the following keys: 'Sfix' (indicates fixation start), 'Efix' (indicates fixation end), 'Sblk' (indicates the start of a blink), 'Eblk' (indicates the end of a blink), 'Ssac' (indicates the start of a saccade), and 'Esac' (indicates the end of a saccade). All these events are lists that contain a timestamp, and data that is specific to the event (saccade starting and ending location, and duration, for example). The last key in the 'events' dict is the 'msg' key. This contains a list of logged messages and their timestamps.

Let's look at the 'msg' key a bit closer. Run the current analysis.py (with only the imports and the read_edf call) in an Editor, with the output to an Interpreter. Now type the following into the Interpeter:

```
print(data[0]['events']['msg'])
```

If you did everything correctly, you should see the following:

```
[[476461, 'PUPIL_TRIALSTART, colour=black\n'], \
     [476461, 'baseline_start\n'], [476661, \
     'pupdata_start\n']]
```

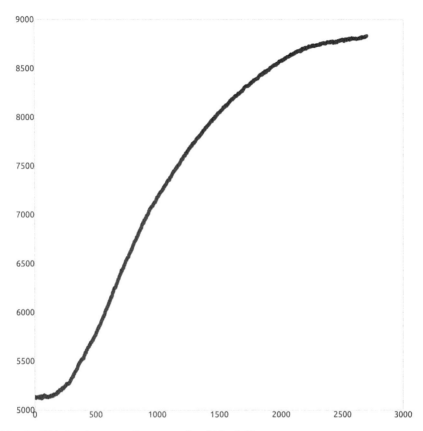

FIGURE 7.1   This is what your first trace should look like

As you can see, this is a list of all logged events. Each event is a list itself, containing a timestamp (in trackertime!) and the actual message.

Plot your first trace

Now that you know the format of your data, it's time to plot your first trace! Type the following into the interpreter:

```
pyplot.plot(data[0]['size'], 'o')
pyplot.show()
```

This plots the pupil size in the first trial, and marks every sample with a circle marker ('o'). In the graph, you see *a lot* of samples (2701, to be precise). They show an increase in pupil size, which is what you expected based on the previous section (where you saw that the first trial was of a black screen).

You can check what happened in the trial, by typing the following into the Interpreter:

```
data[0]['events']['msg'][0]
```

This shows the logged event that signals the trial start and the screen colour ('black'). The other two events in this trial signal the start of the baseline period (during which the monitor was still white), and the exact time at which the monitor changed colour. You can see them by typing the following into the Interpreter:

```
data[0]['events']['msg'][1]
data[0]['events']['msg'][2]
```

You can also save their timestamps, by typing the following into the Interpreter:

```
t1, msg = data[0]['events']['msg'][1]
t2, msg = data[0]['events']['msg'][2]
```

The variables t1 and t2 each contain timestamps in tracker-time. So now you know when events happened, but you don't know what pupil size samples correspond with those timestamps yet. For that, you need to know how to index the data[0]['size'] vector. To find out which samples you need, you can use data[0]['trackertime'] to check at which index numbers your timestamps occur. These index numbers can then be used to select samples from data[0]['size']. With NumPy's where function, you can find the index numbers for which a certain logical statement is True. Type this into the Interpreter:

```
numpy.where(data[0]['trackertime'] == t1)
```

The output format is a bit weird: it's a tuple that contains a NumPy array that in turn contains all index values for which data[0]['trackertime']==t1. To store this value, use the following in the Interpreter:

```
t1i = numpy.where(data[0]['trackertime'] == t1)[0]
t2i = numpy.where(data[0]['trackertime'] == t2)[0]
```

The variables t1i and t2i now refer to the index number of sample arrays ('time', 'trackertime', 'x', 'y', and 'size') that correspond to t1 (baseline start) and t2 (monitor change). You can use these indices to select the baseline, and the pupil response to a monitor change. Type the following in the Interpreter:

```
baseline = data[0]['size'][t1i:t2i]
trace = data[0]['size'][t2i:]
```

It was mentioned before that the pupil size is in arbitrary units. This is of little use, because you don't know what they mean. In theory, you could recalculate the arbitrary units to millimetres, but only if you can compare your data with data that was recorded from an artificial pupil in the same setup. This works, because you know the exact size of the artificial pupil in millimetres, and you know its size in arbitrary units (if you use the same setup to measure it).

However, you don't have to use an artificial eye. Pupil size is known to fluctuate over time. In fact, it decreases quite dramatically during the course of most (boring) experiments. Therefore, researchers often calculate the proportional change in pupil size. This is the

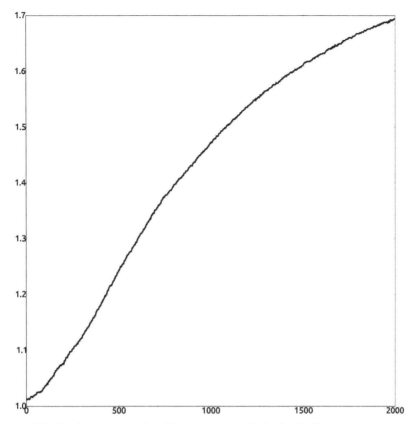

FIGURE 7.2   This is what a proportional increase in pupil size looks like

pupil size divided by the average (or median) pupil size during a baseline period. It reflects the relative increase or decrease in pupil size. You can calculate this by typing the following line in the Interpreter, and hitting Enter.

```
prop_trace = trace / numpy.median(baseline)
```

Now plot this trace by typing the following lines into the Interpreter. The '-' in the first line indicates that the data should be drawn as a line.

```
pyplot.plot(prop_trace, '-')
pyplot.show()
```

Averaging traces

The next step is to loop through all traces, and collect all pupil responses to changes in monitor luminance. These changes would be light-to-dark in black screen trials, and dark-to-light in white screen trials. Open your analysis.py from the previous chapter in an Editor. Add the following lines:

```
# create a new dict to contain traces
traces = {'black':[], 'white':[]}
```

This creates a new dict with two keys. Each key contains an empty list. You can use a for loop to run through all trials. For each trial, you could calculate the proportional pupil change, and add it to the appropriate list. Start with the for loop that goes through all trials:

```
# loop through all trials
n_trials = len(data)
for i in range(n_trials):
```

For each trial, start by checking the first event. From this event, you can determine the trial type: if 'black' was in the event's message, the trial was a light-to-dark monitor change. If 'white' was in the event's message, the trial was a dark-to-light change.

```
    # check the trial type
    t0, msg = data[i]['events']['msg'][0]
    if 'black' in msg:
        trialtype = 'black'
    elif 'white' in msg:
        trialtype = 'white'
```

Now, as you did in the previous section, you need to check the times of the baseline start, and the actual monitor change. You also need the index numbers that correspond to those timestamps (this is the same as in the 'Plot your first trace' section).

```
    # get the timestamps of baseline and monitor change
    t1, msg = data[i]['events']['msg'][1]
    t2, msg = data[i]['events']['msg'][2]
    # turn the timestamps into index numbers
    t1i = numpy.where(data[i]['trackertime'] == t1)[0]
    t2i = numpy.where(data[i]['trackertime'] == t2)[0]
```

The next step, as in the previous section, is to separate out the baseline and the rest of the pupil trace. There is one little extra, though: you should cut the trace a bit short. Every pupil size trace will contain around 2500 samples (that is excluding the baseline). Due to sampling insecurity, sometimes there will be a bit more, and sometimes a bit less. Later on, when you get to averaging traces, it will be important that all traces have the same length.

In order to make sure this is the case, you can cut the length of each trace down to 2000. This corresponds with two seconds, and that is more than enough time to see the pupillary light reflex. Add the following code to your analysis.py:

```
    # get the baseline trace
    baseline = data[i]['size'][t1i:t2i]
    # get the pupil change trace (2000 samples)
    trace = data[i]['size'][t2i:t2i+2000]
```

The baseline is from `t1i` to `t2i`, which is the same as before. The actual trace starts at `t2i`, just as before but this time, however, it ends at `t2i+2000`. This is exactly 2000 samples after it begins, to ensure that all traces will be of that same length.

Now that you have the baseline and the actual trace, divide the trace by the median of the baseline. This will result in a trace that reflects the proportional change in pupil size.

```
    # divide the pupil trace by the baseline median
    trace = trace / numpy.median(baseline)
```

The only thing that's left to do in the for loop, is to add the trace for this trial to the appropriate list:

```
    # add the trace to the list for this trial type
    traces[trialtype].append(trace)
```

When the for loop is completed, you are left with two lists that contain all trials for trials with black-to-white and white-to-black monitor changes. Because NumPy arrays are easier to work with, it would be good to convert these lists to NumPy arrays. You can do this with NumPy's array function. Add the following code at the end of analysis.py, *without any indentation:*

```
# convert lists to NumPy arrays
traces['black'] = numpy.array(traces['black'])
traces['white'] = numpy.array(traces['white'])
```

There are a few cool things you can do now to turn the lists of traces into arrays. The first is to calculate the average trace. For this, it is important to understand the way in which your traces are stored. They are in a multi-dimensional NumPy array, with the first axis being all trial numbers and the second being all sample numbers. To calculate the average trace, you should average over all trials, but not over all timepoints. That is: you have to average each trials' timepoint 1, and each trials' timepoint 2, all the way to each trials' timepoint 2000. The array that contains all 2000 of these averages is the **average trace**.

Using NumPy, you don't have to calculate 2000 averages individually. Instead, you can simply use the `mean` function's `axis` keyword to indicate that you want to calculate the averages of all points in the first dimension of your trace array. Example:

```
numpy.mean(traces['black'], axis=0)
```

This produces an average trace just like the one discussed above. The trace has 2000 values, each of which is an average of all samples at an index. For example, the value at index 5 (that's the sixth value!) is the average of all black trials' sixth samples. This average trace characterises the average pupillary light response to a light-to-dark transition of the computer monitor.

You can use NumPy's `std` function in the same way:

```
numpy.std(traces['black'], axis=0)
```

Instead of the average, this gives you the standard deviation of all traces. If you divide this trace by the square root of the number of trials, you end up with the standard error of the mean for each timepoint. This tells you roughly how reliable your estimate of the average is across time. This should be relatively constant, so seeing large deviations at some points might require a closer look at your data!

The len function can tell you how many trials there are in each array. As mentioned before: by dividing the standard deviation by the square root of the number of trials, you can calculate the standard error of the mean. Add the following code to your analysis.py, to calculate the average traces of both the black and white condition, and their standard errors. As usual, you can store these in a dict for easy access:

```
# create an empty dict to contain mean and SEM
avgs = {'black':{}, 'white':{}}

# loop through both conditions
for con in ['black', 'white']:

    # calculate the number of trials in this condition
    n_trials = len(traces[con])

    # calculate the average trace in this condition
    avgs[con]['M'] = numpy.mean(traces[con], axis=0)

    # calculate the standard deviation in this condition
    sd = numpy.std(traces[con], axis=0)

    # calculate the standard error in this condition
    avgs[con]['SEM'] = sd / numpy.sqrt(n_trials)
```

As with the mean and std functions, you can also use the axis keyword in the ttest_rel function to perform multiple tests at once. Use this to check at which time points the pupil's response to a light-to-dark change is significantly different from the pupil's response to a dark-to-light change:

```
# do a t-test on every timepoint
t, p = ttest_rel(traces['black'], traces['white'], axis=0)
```

Because you just did 2000 t-tests, you cannot simply use a p-value significance cutoff (alpha) of 0.05. The idea behind an alpha of 0.05, is that you accept that five per cent of the time your conclusion will be wrong. With 2000 tests, each with an alpha of five per cent, you would expect at least 100 significant differences to occur purely by chance.

Instead, you could use a Bonferroni correction. This requires you to divide alpha by the number of tests you performed, so that the overall chance of an accidental error is still only five per cent.

```
# Bonferroni-corrected alpha
alpha = 0.05 / len(t)
```

You consider differences to be significant only when their t-test's p-value is below the new alpha level. That is, where p is less than alpha, the 'black' and 'white' traces are actually different from each other.

The next step is to create a pretty plot. First, define the colour of each condition, and create a new figure with a single axis (that's what a subplot is called in Matplotlib):

```
# define the plotting colours
cols = {'black':'#204a87', 'white':'#c4a000'}

# create a new figure with a single axis
fig, ax = pyplot.subplots(figsize=(19.2,10.8), dpi=100.0)
```

Next, loop through the conditions with a for loop:

```
# loop through the conditions
for con in ['black', 'white']:
```

For each condition, plot the average trace. You can also plot a shaded area, by using the axis' fill_between method. This method requires you to put in x values (the numbers 0 to 1999 in this case: the elapsed time since a monitor change in milliseconds), as well as two y values. The first array of *y* values will be the mean trace plus the standard error of the mean trace. The second will be the mean trace minus the standard error of the mean trace. By specifying the alpha keyword, you can set the transparency: a value of 1 means completely opaque, whereas a value of 0 means invisible. (Note that this alpha is completely different from the significance threshold discussed earlier!) Add the following code in the for loop:

```
    # create x-values
    x = range(len(avgs[con]['M']))
    # plot the mean trace
    ax.plot(x, avgs[con]['M'], '-', color=cols[con], \
        label=con)
    # plot the standard error of the mean shading
    y1 = avgs[con]['M'] + avgs[con]['SEM']
    y2 = avgs[con]['M'] - avgs[con]['SEM']
    ax.fill_between(x, y1, y2, color=cols[con], \
        alpha=0.3)
```

The last thing to plot, is a shaded area that indicates where the two traces differ significantly from each other. You can do this using the same fill_between method that you used to indicate the standard error of the mean. The function has a where keyword that will make sure the shading is only drawn at locations where a conditional statement is True. For example, when p < 0.05.

To do this, you need to know the limits of your *y*-axis. Let's set those at 0 and 2 (the proportional change in pupil size will likely be between those numbers). You can use these to create the top and bottom y traces. The bottom trace will simply be an array of all zeros. The top trace will be an array of all 2s.

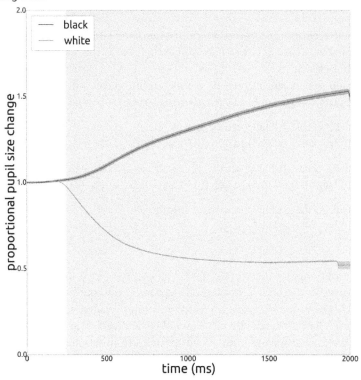

FIGURE 7.3 This is what the average traces should look like. The dark line indicates the average pupillary response to a light-dark luminance transition, and the light line indicates the average pupillary response to a dark-to-light luminance transition. Shading around the lines indicates the standard error of the mean, and the grey shading indicates where the lines differ significantly from each other (point-wise related-samples t tests, Bonferroni corrected)

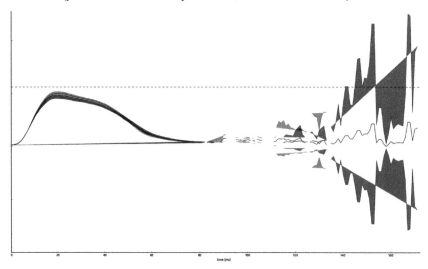

FIGURE 7.4 This is what happens when something goes wrong when you're trying to plot a trace. Or when a participant's eye explodes during testing. Either way: Oops!

```
# create y arrays
y1 = numpy.zeros(len(x))
y2 = numpy.ones(len(x)) * 2

# shade significant difference between traces
ax.fill_between(x, y1, y2, where=p<alpha, \
        color='#babdb6', alpha=0.2)
```

Now finish the plot by setting the labels and limits of the axes, and by adding a legend:

```
# set axes limits
ax.set_xlim([0, 2000])
ax.set_ylim([0, 2])
# set axis labels
ax.set_xlabel('time (ms)')
ax.set_ylabel('proportional pupil size change')

# add legend
ax.legend(loc='upper left')
```

And finally save the figure:

```
fig.savefig('pupil_traces.png')
```

8

EYE TRACKING

Eye tracking is a popular technique in experimental psychology and cognitive neuroscience. It is applied to humans, other primates, and even to some non-primate animals. (That's no joke; see for example a study in rats by Wallace et al., 2013 – the videos in the supplementary materials are amazing!) Eye tracking usually involves pointing a camera at someone's face, and using it to estimate where they are looking.

Eye tracking offers a lot of things to measure: where people look (fixations), how people move their eyes (saccadic trajectories), how quickly they do it (saccadic response time and velocity), and how big their pupils are (pupillometry). These metrics can give us insight into many things, including what people attend to, how motivated they are, and how attentive they are during tasks. Some eye-movement characteristics are affected in unique ways by a variety of diseases and disorders, and can provide early diagnostic information or deeper insight into patients' conditions. My personal take on this, is the following half-witty variation of an age-old cliché:

Not the eyes, but eye movements are the window to the soul.

Eye movements are not only of interest in science and medicine, but also in usability testing and marketing. Usability experts like to record the eye movements of people while they are using websites and graphical user interfaces. The eye-movement patterns can tell experts how intuitive an interface is. Marketing professionals employ the same methods, but are primarily interested in whether people see their advertisements, products, and brand names.

Another application of eye tracking is in software engineering. Eye movement characteristics are relatively unique, and can be combined to form a 'finger print' that is specific to a user. Techniques have been developed to recognise people by their eye movements, and some experts think this technology can replace passwords in the future. In addition, eye movements can be used to navigate a computer's operating system, which can be a tool to assist the disabled or to play video games. Eye tracking is also a promising new addition to virtual reality headsets, as it allows for more realistic rendering of a virtual environment.

Introduction

The basics

When you look at an image, you will show (mostly) three types of eye movements: fixations, saccades, and blinks. **Blinks** happen when you close your eyelids and see nothing. **Saccades** occur when you quickly move your eyes. When you do, your vision is largely suppressed (if it wasn't, you would see a blur during saccades). **Fixations** are the times when your eyes stay relatively still, and you can actually see what you are looking at.

Because most of your conscious vision happens during fixations, a lot of research focuses on them. Most researchers assume that when you look at something, that something is also what you attend to. This means that mapping where you are (or have been) looking at, can provide crucial information about what draws your attention.

The most simple experiment you could do, is to show participants an image, and simultaneously record their gazing behaviour. Afterwards, you can map where participants had been looking, and that will hopefully tell you what parts of the image were interesting to a human observer.

To record participants' gaze behaviour, you need an eye tracker. This is nothing more than a camera with a filter, some infrared lights, and software that can quick image processing through algorithmic magic. The concept is simple: the infrared lights illuminate your face, while the camera makes a snapshot of your eyes. Image processing software then tries to find your pupil and the reflection of the infrared light on your cornea (the front part of your eye). When you look around, the corneal reflection is relatively constant, but the pupil moves with your gaze. Using the difference between the pupil and the corneal reflection, and settings derived from a calibration, an algorithm can convert the location of your pupil within your eye to your point-of-regard on the computer monitor. In other words: the eye tracker manages to estimate where you are looking.

Creating an eye-tracking experiment

In this section, you are going to script a simple eye-tracking experiment like the one described before. It will show images for a couple of seconds, and it will record eye movements while the images are being shown. The idea is to get you acquainted with the basics of recording and analysing fixation behaviour. The library of choice in this section is PyGaze, because it has a native and very usable class that deals with eye trackers. In other libraries, even PsychoPy, collecting eye-movement data is more of a hassle. PyGaze supports a wide variety of systems, including most devices from EyeLink (SR Research), the EyeTribe, SensoMotoric Instruments (SMI), and Tobii.

FIGURE 8.1 This is one of the example images. It's a picture I took during a holiday on Texel, one of the islands north of the Netherlands. Where do you expect most fixations to occur?

Materials

To see this kind of eye tracking in practice, you need two things: an eye tracker, and some images. Example images can be downloaded from the companion website: www.routledge.com/cw/dalmaijer but you are also welcome to use your own holiday snaps. An eye tracker might be harder to come by, but don't worry if you don't have one: PyGaze offers a dummy mode that allows you to use the mouse cursor to simulate eye movements.

A data file will be produced through your experiment, but an example is also available if you don't have an eye tracker. The example data and analysis software can be downloaded from the companion website www.routledge.com/cw/dalmaijer. More on that later.

constants.py

The first step of any experiment, is to create a file that contains the settings of your experiment. Create a new folder, and create a new Python script in it. Name the script 'constants.py', and add the following code:

```
# The DISPTYPE can be either 'pygame' or 'psychopy'
DISPTYPE = 'pygame'

# The DISPSIZE should match your monitor's resolution!
DISPSIZE = (1024, 768)
```

Now on to a new constant: TRACKERTYPE, which establishes the type of eye tracker that you will be using. This can be a specific brand of supported eye trackers, or one of two dummy substitutes. At the time of writing, PyGaze supports SR Research's EyeLink systems ('eyelink'), the EyeTribe tracker ('eyetribe'), SensoMotoric Instruments' systems ('smi'), and Tobii's systems ('tobii'). There is also a dummy mode that allows you to simulate eye movements with the mouse ('dummy'), and there is a really simple dummy mode ('dumbdummy') that provides bogus values. In this example, the TRACKERTYPE will be set to 'eyelink'. Please change this to whatever type of tracker you actually wish to use.

```
# Set the TRACKERTYPE to the brand you use
TRACKERTYPE = 'eyelink'
```

Another new constant is DUMMYMODE. This is a Boolean that allows you to easily test your scripts without an eye tracker having to be attached. Setting DUMMYMODE to True does the same thing as setting TRACKERTYPE to 'dummy'.

```
# DUMMYMODE should be True if no tracker is attached
DUMMYMODE = False
```

Back to stuff you know. Let's set the default foreground and background colour for the experiment. White on black should be fine:

```
# Foreground colour set to white
FGC = (255, 255, 255)
```

```
# Background colour set to black
BGC = (0, 0, 0)
```

You should also think about timing. In the experiment you are about to create, there will be a presentation of a fixation mark, followed by the presentation of an image. Two seconds of fixation followed by ten seconds of gazing seem appropriate:

```
# Fixation mark time (milliseconds)
FIXTIME = 2000
```

```
# Image time (milliseconds)
IMGTIME = 10000
```

Finally, let's turn to the images. Download them from the companion website www. routledge.com/cw/dalmaijer (if you hadn't already), or use your own. Wherever you got them from, make sure to copy them to a folder named 'images'. This folder should be located within the same folder as where your 'constants.py' is. Make sure you get the folder locations right, because this is crucial!

The following bits are going to be a bit of file and folder management, not unlike the things you've seen before. To do this, you will need the os module. So start by importing it:

```
import os
```

Let's get the path to the folder that contains your scripts. You can do this by getting the absolute path (by using the abspath function) to the current script (this is stored in the __file__ variable). You can get the folder's name with the dirname function (folders are also called directories):

```
# Get the path to the current folder
```

```
DIR = os.path.dirname(os.path.abspath(__file__))
```

Now let's construct the name of the image folder. You can create it by combining the current folder's path (associated with the DIR variable) and the string 'images'. You can do this using the join function, which automatically uses the correct directory separator (this is a backward slash in Windows, but can differ between operating systems):

```
# Get the path to the image folder
IMGDIR = os.path.join(DIR, 'images')
```

The last thing you should do, is get a list of the file names of your images. You don't have to construct this list yourself. Instead, you can use the listdir function to get a list of all files in a directory:

```
# Get a list of all image names
IMGNAMES = os.listdir(IMGDIR)
```

Note that this function creates a list of *all* files, including files that are not images. Make sure that there are *only* actual image files in your 'images' folder to prevent any unwelcome crashes! (These could occur if you try to present a non-image file.)

As a final trick, you can sort the image names to be sorted in alphabetical order by using the list's sort method:

```
# Sort IMGNAMES in alphabetical order
IMGNAMES.sort()
```

Screens

Time to start coding the experiment. You will need the Display class to interact with the monitor, the Screen class to create stimuli, the Keyboard class to monitor key presses, the EyeTracker class to interact with the eye tracker, and the libtime module to tell the time. You will also need the os module to deal with the image files, and some of the constants you defined. In the same folder as your constants.py script, create a new Python script and name it 'experiment.py'. Start by importing the classes you need:

```
import os
from constants import *
from pygaze.display import Display
from pygaze.screen import Screen
from pygaze.keyboard import Keyboard
from pygaze.eyetracker import EyeTracker
import pygaze.libtime as timer
```

Now, to get things started, you can initialise a Display and a Keyboard instance:

```
# Initialise a Display to interact with the monitor
disp = Display()

# Initialise a Keyboard to collect key presses
```

```
kb = Keyboard(keylist=None, timeout=None)
```

In the experiment, you only need a few different Screens: one with task instructions, one with a central fixation mark, and one to draw the images on.

Let's start with the instructions:

```
# Create a Screen for the image task instructions
inscr = Screen()
inscr.draw_text(text='Please look at the images. \
     \n\n(Press any key to begin)', fontsize=24)
```

Next is the fixation Screen. You can show this between the images, to allow people some rest. It also standardises the starting fixation position. People will always start with a central gaze when the images are preceded with a central fixation mark.

```
# Create a Screen with a central fixation cross
fixscr = Screen()
fixscr.draw_fixation(fixtype='cross', diameter=8)
```

The last Screen is the one you can use to draw images on. Earlier, you learned that drawing during timing-critical phases of the experiment is a bad idea. One solution is to draw all possible Screens before the experiment begins. Another option is to draw the Screens in the trial that you need them in. In this case, you could draw the image on a Screen at the start of each trial. Timing isn't critical there yet, as participants will still be looking at the fixation mark (a few milliseconds more or less of that aren't going to have an impact on their behaviour).

For now, simply create an empty Screen. You can draw the images later:

```
# Create a Screen to draw images on later
imgscr = Screen()
```

The eyetracker class

PyGaze offers a unified class to communicate with eye trackers of different brands, all with the same functions. This is useful, as it means you don't have to reprogram your experiments every time you want to use a different eye tracker.

The name of this class is, rather unimaginatively, the `EyeTracker` class. It's part of the equally unoriginally named `eyetracker` module. The class offers a relatively simple way to communicate with an eye tracker. It allows you to start recording and pause recording, and it can send messages to the log file (e.g. to signal the onset of events).

In addition, the EyeTracker class allows you to access samples while its recording. This means that you can know where a participant is looking (with the `sample` method), or how big their pupils are (with the `pupil_size` method). There are also methods to wait for the starts and ends of saccades, fixations, and blinks. For example the `wait_for_fixation_start` will wait for a fixation to start, and return the starting time and position. These methods allow you to make your experiments contingent on your participants' eye movements.

Finally, the EyeTracker class offers methods that allow you to calibrate the eye tracker, and to check whether a calibration is still accurate. An eye tracker's estimate of where someone looks, is based on parameters that differ between people, and between experimental setups. Therefore, devices need to be calibrated to each individual participant. To start a calibration routine, you need only call an EyeTracker instance's `calibrate` method.

Throughout the experiment, you can check whether a calibration is still accurate by using the `drift_correct` method. This offers one keyword argument, `pos`, which determines the position of a fixation target. The `drift_correct` method will show a fixation target, wait for a participant to look at it (indicated by the participant pressing the Space bar), and will then check whether the tracker's gaze position estimate is near the fixation target. If it is within a certain range, then the tracker's calibration is still fine.

Calibrations can suffer from drift over time, which can cause them to become inaccurate. Therefore, it is important to check whether a calibration is still accurate every so often. How often is subject to personal preference, participant compliance, and the quality of your setup. When accuracy is of utmost importance, you could call `drift_correct` every trial. You could also call it every 20 or so trials, when you are more confident in your setup.

Initialising a new EyeTracker instance, requires you to pass the active Display as an argument. This is because the EyeTracker needs to know where it can display its calibration routine. Add the following to your experiment.py script:

```
# Initialise a new EyeTracker
tracker = EyeTracker(disp)

# Calibrate the eye tracker
tracker.calibrate()
```

This will initialise a connection with your eye tracker, and then calibrate it at the start of your experiment.

After the calibration, you could show the instructions to your experiment. You could also do this before you calibrate the system. This depends on your personal preference, and maybe on how much faith you have in your participant's memory.

```
# Feed the instructions to the Display
disp.fill(inscr)

# Show the instructions
disp.show()

# Wait until the participant presses any key
# (Allowing them to read the instructions at their own
# pace)
kb.get_key()
```

Single trial

A single trial in this experiment should show a fixation, followed by an image, and it should record eye movements throughout. Before showing the image, you need to make sure that the eye tracker is recording data. You also need to signal (in the data file) when the image was visible, and which image it was (this helps you to make sense of the data afterwards). Speaking of the data file: this is automatically created by the EyeTracker instance. You don't have to do anything, other than occasionally logging messages (if you need them), and closing the file in the end (this is done when you close the connection to the tracker).

Before you can show the image, you need to load it from its file and draw it on a Screen. As an example, just take the first image from the IMGNAMES (that's the list of all images you created earlier). You can load and draw it using the imgscr instance's draw_ image method. This requires the full path to an image, which you can construct using the os.path module's join method:

```
# Choose the first image for now
imgname = IMGNAMES[0]

# Construct the path to the image
imgpath = os.path.join(IMGDIR, imgname)

# Draw the image on imgscr
# (clear imgscr first, to be sure it's clean)
imgscr.clear()
imgscr.draw_image(imgpath)
```

That's it for the preparation. Now let's get this trial on the road! Start by asking the tracker to start recording gaze data:

```
# Start recording gaze data
tracker.start_recording()
```

If you're using an EyeLink, you can use the EyeTracker class's status_msg method to display the name of this trial's image on the EyeLink computer. This is a different computer from the one that is presenting the experiment, and it allows a researcher to monitor a participant's eye movements in real time. In the bottom right, it also displays a 'status message', which can be set by the experiment script:

```
# Display a status message on the EyeLink computer
# (EyeLink only; doesn't do anything for other brands)
tracker.status_msg('Trial with %s image' % (imgname))
```

Next, log a message to the tracker to indicate that the trial has started:

```
# Log trial start
tracker.log('TRIALSTART')
```

Now, time to actually start presenting something. The fixation screen should be shown first. It's important to log the onset of each new Screen to the log file, so you can make sense of your gaze data afterwards. If you don't log anything, all you have at the end of the experiment is a large heap of data, with no clues about what was on the screen when that data was collected!

```
# Feed the fixation Screen to the Display
disp.fill(fixscr)

# Update the monitor to show the fixation mark
disp.show()

# Log the fixation onset to the gaze data file
tracker.log('fixation_onset')

# Wait for the right duration
timer.pause(FIXTIME)
```

The exact same principle applies to the image Screen:

```
# Feed the image Screen to the Display
disp.fill(imgscr)

# Update the monitor to show the image
disp.show()

# Log the image onset to the gaze data file
# Include the image name in the message!
tracker.log('image_onset, imgname=%s' % (imgname))

# Wait for the right duration
timer.pause(IMGTIME)
```

After showing the image, you should clear the display. You can do this by calling its fill method to fill the Display with the current background colour. Then call its show method to update the monitor, and make sure to record the image's offset in the log file:

```
# Clear the Display
disp.fill()

# Update the monitor to show a blank screen
disp.show()

# Log the image offset
tracker.log('image_offset')
```

That's the end of the trial. You can pause the recording of gaze data by calling the tracker instance's stop_recording method.

```
# Log the end of the trial
tracker.log('TRIALEND')

# Pause recording
tracker.stop_recording()
```

At the end of your experiment script, you might want to notify the participant that they are finished. You can recycle the instructions Screen for this:

```
# Clear the instructions Screen
inscr.clear()

# Write a new message
inscr.draw_text(text='All done!', fontsize=24)

# Feed the new message to the Display
disp.fill(inscr)

# Show the message
disp.show()

# Wait until the participant presses any key
# (Allowing them to read at their own pace)
kb.get_key()
```

After the message, make sure to close the connection to the eye tracker by calling the EyeTracker instance's `close` method:

```
# Close the connection to the eye tracker
# (This will also close the log file!)
tracker.close()
```

The final thing to do is to close the Display:

```
# Close the Display
disp.close()
```

If you want to, you can run the current script to show a single image, and record your own gaze data. In the next section, you can learn how to modify the current script to show all your images in one long slide show.

Whole experiment

Essentially, you want your experiment to run through all images in your 'images' folder (`IMGDIR`). You have a list that contains all their names, `IMGNAMES`, and you have a script to do eye tracking on a single image. All you need to do now, is run through the list of images, and make your code run with each image.

You might recall the 'For loop' section in Chapter 5, where you used a for loop to cycle through a list of trials. In the current experiment, you can use the same approach. The first thing to do, is to replace the following part of your script:

```
# Choose the first image for now
imgname = IMGNAMES[0]
```

This only selects the first image, but you want it to run through all images in a for loop. Replace the above two lines by the following:

```
# Loop through all image names
for imgname in IMGNAMES:
```

As you might remember, indentation is really important when using for loops. Every line of code that needs to be run within the loop, needs to be indented by one unit of indentation more than the for loop. You might also remember that the preferred unit of indentation is four spaces.

In your script, *increase the indentation of every line from*

⎵⎵⎵⎵ ```imgpath = os.path.join(IMGDIR, imgname)```

to (and including!)

⎵⎵⎵⎵ ```tracker.stop_recording()```

The lines from `inscr.clear()` should not be indented, nor should any line be before the for loop.

With this relatively minor change, you've made your experiment work with all your images. Note that the experiment takes about twelve seconds per image, so make sure that you don't include too many of them. Or do include your entire vacation album, if you have an afternoon to waste.

Processing gaze data

In this section, you can learn how to visualise fixation data. If you had an eye tracker at your disposal, you can make your own data from the experiment in the previous section. If you didn't have an eye tracker, you can download a sample dataset from the companion website www.routledge.com/cw/dalmaijer.

As in the Chapter 7 'Analysing traces', you can use the PyGaze Analyser library to extract data from a data file. In that chapter, we focused on pupil size, and used logged events to separate out the data from several conditions. In this chapter, you will learn about a different type of logged events: **fixations**.

Fixations occur when people hold their eyes relatively stable. Most conscious vision happens during fixations, and a lot of animals (including humans) tend to fixate their gaze on whatever has their interest.

In this example, a participant was allowed to look at several images. The participant's fixations can inform you about what parts of each image piqued their interest. Because this is highly exploratory research, you won't have to go into statistics here. Instead, your task is to visualise the participant's gaze behaviour in several ways. (Do note that this is not a general advice. Always ask for the statistics behind visualisations!)

Gaze data visualisations provide qualitative rather than quanitative evidence, and should not be interpreted with too much confidence. However, visualisations are rather useful to guide further quantitative research, and they are very popular in marketing and usability research. Therefore, it's good to learn how to create them!

In this section, you can do two things: either use your own data and images from the previous section (where you created an eye-tracking experiment), or download the example data and images from the companion website.

In addition, it is important that you are using the correct constants.py script. In constants.py, the file names for your images were defined and ordered. In the analysis, the images and their order need to be the same as in the experiment, otherwise you could end up plotting data on the wrong image!

In sum, if you would like to use your own data, then use the 'images' folder and constants.py from the previous section ('Creating an eye-tracking experiment'). If you prefer to use the example data from the companion website, then make sure you also download the 'images' folder from the companion website. If you are using the example data, you should also create a 'constants.py' script with the following code:'

If you are using the example data file, make sure to download the example images for this section from the companion website www.routledge.com/cw/dalmaijer. Place these images in a folder called 'images'. In addition, create a new Python script, and name it constants.py. Add the following code:

```python
import os

# The DISPTYPE can be either 'pygame' or 'psychopy'
DISPTYPE = 'pygame'

# The DISPSIZE should match your monitor's resolution!
DISPSIZE = (1024, 768)

# Set the TRACKERTYPE to the brand you use
TRACKERTYPE = 'eyelink'

# DUMMYMODE should be True if no tracker is attached
DUMMYMODE = False

# Foreground colour set to white
FGC = (255, 255, 255)

# Background colour set to black
BGC = (0, 0, 0)

# Fixation mark time (milliseconds)
FIXTIME = 2000

# Image time (milliseconds)
IMGTIME = 10000

# Get the path to the current folder
DIR = os.path.dirname(os.path.abspath(__file__))

# Get the path to the image folder
IMGDIR = os.path.join(DIR, 'images')

# Get a list of all image names
```

```
IMGNAMES = os.listdir(IMGDIR)

# Sort IMGNAMES in alphabetical order
IMGNAMES.sort()
```

If you are using the example data, create a new folder, and copy in the following things: the data file (downloaded from the companion website), the images folder (downloaded and unzipped archive from the companion website), and the constants.py you just created.

Extracting gaze data

Gaze data files are enormous, usually with anything between 60 to 1000 samples for every second of data collection. Making sense of these files by manually processing them, is a complete nightmare. Never do it! Instead, use programming libraries to do the work for you.

One of the libraries you could use, is PyGaze Analyser. This is a relatively simple library that can read data from several types of eye trackers. Supported are SR Research's EyeLink files (EDF converted to ASCII using SR's own edf2asc software), EyeTribe tracker files (as produced by PyTribe or PyGaze), and SensoMotoric Systems' files (IDF converted to TSV using SMI's own conversion software). You can download PyGaze Analyser from the companion website www.routledge.com/cw/dalmaijer.

After downloading pygazeanalyser.zip, extract its contents, and copy it to the same folder as where constants.py is saved. This is crucial!

If you haven't done this yet, now would also be the time to download the example data file. Make sure that you copy it to the same folder as where constants.py is located.

The next step is to start programming. In the same folder as where constants.py is located, open a new script. You can name it 'analysis.py'.

The contents of your folder should now be:

- images (folder that contains all images used in the experiment)
- pygazeanalyser (folder that contains PyGaze Analyser)
- default.asc (gaze data file)
- constants.py (script with all constants)
- experiment.py (only if you did previous section)
- analysis.py (empty for now)

Open analysis.py in an Editor, and start by importing the relevant libraries. You will need the `os` module to handle files and folders. You will also need to import the constants. From PyGaze Analyser, you will need the `gazeplotter` module, and the correct reader. In this example, the `read_edf` function from the `edfreader` module will be used, which is for EyeLink files. If you have an EyeTribe file, you will instead need the `read_eyetribe` function from the `eyetribereader` module. If you have an SMI file, you need the `read_idf` function from the `idfreader` module. Finally, whatever you used, you also need the `close` function from Matplotlib's `pyplot` module.

```
import os
from constants import *
from pygazeanalyser.edfreader import read_edf
from pygazeanalyser import gazeplotter
from matplotlib.pyplot import close
```

Your script will create and save quite a lot of data visualisations, which will be stored in separate image files. It's a good idea to stick all of them in a separate folder to keep things organised. You could name that folder 'output', and construct the path using the DIR constant and the `os.path` module's `join` function:

```
# Construct the name of the output directory
OUTPUTDIR = os.path.join(DIR, 'output')
```

You don't have to go through the effort of manually creating a new folder. Instead, you can create a new one using the `mkdir` function from the `os` module.

One downside of using `mkdir`, is that it causes an error if you try to make a new folder when that folder already exists. To prevent any kind of accidents, it's good practice to find out whether the folder you were about to make already exists. You can do this with the `os.path` module's `isdir` function. Use the following code in your script to combine these functions:

```
# Check if the output directory exists yet
if not os.path.isdir(OUTPUTDIR):
    # If the output directory does not exist yet, make it
    os.mkdir(OUTPUTDIR)
```

If the output folder already exists, `os.path.isdir` will return True. The if statement used here will only run if False is returned, though, due to the use of `not`. Thus, if no output directory exists, `mkdir` will create one.

Time to actually read the data. You can do this using the `read_edf`, `read_eyetribe`, or `read_idf` function, depending on what data file you have. They all return the same data structure, so if you need, you can simply substitute for `read_edf` in the following example:

```
# Read the data
data = read_edf('default.asc', 'image_onset', \
    stop='image_offset')
```

The `read_edf` function requires two input arguments: the name of the data file, and a string that indicates what event signalled the start of a trial. This does not have to be the actual start of a trial; it can also be the start of the period within a trial that you want to extract. In addition, you can also pass the keyword argument `stop`. This allows you to specify the string that indicates what event signalled the end of a trial.

In your data file (which is named default if you didn't specify a file name) the event that indicates the onset of an image is 'image_onset'. There was more to that string (it also included the presented image's name), but you don't have to specify a full event string for `read_edf` to work. Finally, the event that signalled the image's offset was 'image_offset'.

The `read_edf` function returned a variable that you named data. This variable is a list of all trials that were extracted from the data file. Each trial is represented by a dict. Within each trial dict, there are six different keys: 'x' and 'y' for the horizontal and vertical gaze position, 'size' for the pupil size, 'trackertime' and 'time' for the absolute and relative time, and 'events' for all detected and logged events.

With the exception of 'events', all keys point to NumPy arrays that contain data samples. How to process these is the topic of Chapter 7 'Analysing traces'. The 'events' key points to another dict, which has seven keys. These keys are 'Sfix' and 'Efix' for fixation starts and ends, 'Ssac' and 'Esac' for saccade starts and ends, 'Sblk' and 'Eblk' for blink starts and ends, and 'msg' for logged messages.

Each of the 'events' keys points to a list. Each of these lists contains even more lists! What those lists contain, depends on which event you look at. For example, the 'msg' key points to a list that contains lists for every event that was logged. Each individual event list consists of a timestamp, and of the actual message. One individual list within the 'msg' list could look like this example: [399495, 'image_onset\n'].

Of importance here, is the 'Efix' key. This points to a list of lists, where each individual list represents a fixation end. Each fixation end is a list that contains the start time, the end time, the duration, the ending x position, and the ending y position of a fixation. One such an individual list could look like this: [399928, 400063, 136, 327.5, 371.1].

The quickest way to get a feeling for what is in the data, is by running your current script within a code editor's console (for example within Spyder). After loading the data by running your script, you can print several event lists. For example, you could print all messages from the first trial (at index 0):

```
print(data[0]['events']['msg'])
```

You could also print all fixation end events from the second trial (at index 1):

```
print(data[1]['events']['Efix'])
```

For now, you don't have to become familiar with the 'events' lists too intimately. Instead, you can rely on several visualisation functions to do the work for you. More about that in the next chapter!

Analysing gaze data

Before running through all trials, you need to know how many there are. To check how many trials there are in the data variable, you can use the `len` function:

```
# Get the amount of trials in this dataset
ntrials = len(data)
```

Now you can use a for loop to run through all of the trials:

```
# Loop through all trials
for trialnr in range(ntrials):
```

Note that all code following the for loop will be indented! (preferably by 4 spaces.)

The first thing you need, is the name of the image that was presented in a trial. In the experiment, you simply ran through the list of images you produced in the constants. You sorted this list in alphabetical order, which means that the list's order will be the same in the experiment and in the analysis. You can use this to your advantage, by simply using the trial number to index the list of image names:

```
    # Get the image name
    imgname = IMGNAMES[trialnr]
```

You also need the path to the image file, because some of the plotting functions can use the actual image in their visualisations. You can construct the path to each image file by using the IMGDIR constant and the image's name:

```
    # Get the path to the image
    imgpath = os.path.join(IMGDIR, imgname)
```

Now for the actual data: you need the fixations. As mentioned before, these are stored in the 'events' dict of each trial, specifically as a list that is associated with the 'Efix' key. You can access it like you would any other dict:

```
    # Get the fixations in this trial
    fixations = data[trialnr]['events']['Efix']
```

Remember, in the experiment you used a central fixation mark before each image was presented. This means that the initial fixation on each image will be in the centre, precisely where the fixation mark was. Because of this, the first fixation does not reflect a participant's response to the image, and you should get rid of it. You can remove it by popping it out of the fixations list. To do so, use the list's pop method to remove the fixation at index 0:

FIGURE 8.2 These are the raw samples (grey dots) superimposed on the image they were collected with

```
     # Delete the first fixation
     fixations.pop(0)
```

In addition to the fixations, you can also get the x and y coordinates of each sample. These are associated with the 'x' and 'y' keys of each trial's dict. Accessing them is really easy:

```
     # Get the raw x and y gaze coordinates
     x = data[trialnr]['x']
     y = data[trialnr]['y']
```

Analysing fixations

It's time to finally plot something! Let's start by plotting all the collected (raw) samples on the presented image. Having a look at your raw data is always a good idea. It should provide you with a rough idea of your data quality, especially about how much drift there was. In the example figure, you can already somewhat see fixations and saccades (and blinks, if the samples suddenly jump to the bottom of the image).

If you want to save the image, you need to create a path to the intended save file's location first. To do so, you can construct a new name for the raw data plot, for example by using the stimulus image's name:

```
     savename = 'raw_%s' % imgname
```

Then you need to combine the raw data plot's name with the output directory:

```
     savepath = os.path.join(OUTPUTDIR, savename)
```

Finally, you can call the draw_raw function from the gazeplotter module. This function requires three arguments: the x coordinates of your raw samples (from your x

FIGURE 8.3 These are the fixations (white dots) superimposed on the image they were collected with

variable), the y coordinates of your raw samples (from your y variable), and the size of the original display (from your `DISPSIZE` constant).

In addition, you can specify two keyword arguments. The first is `imagefile`, which allows you to specify the image on which your raw samples were collected. This image will be the background on which the raw samples are plotted. If you don't specify an image, a black background will be used instead. The second keyword argument is `savefilename`, which allows you to indicate where you want to save the produced plot. If you don't specify a name (or None), no plot will be saved.

To create a plot of your raw samples, and save it in the output directory, use the following code:

```
     fig = gazeplotter.draw_raw(x, y, DISPSIZE, \
          imagefile=imgpath, savefilename=savepath)
```

The `draw_raw` (and all other plotting functions in this chapter) returns a Matplotlib Figure instance. You can use it to further manipulate your plot, and you can close it by using the `close` function from Matplotlib's `pyplot` module:

```
     close(fig)
```

Regularly closing your figures is good practice. Keeping too many open will flood Matplotlib's memory, which will cause it to crash!

Now, let's move on to something more fancy: time to plot the fixations on an image! Fixations can be representing as (transparent) dots on the original image. You can create such a plot with the gazeplotter module's `draw_fixations` function. It requires two arguments: the fixations (a list of 'Efix' events), and the display size.

You can also specify some keyword arguments. These include the `imagefile` and `savefilename`, which work in the same way as they did with the `draw_raw` function.

FIGURE 8.4 This is a heatmap of the fixations superimposed on the image they were collected with

In addition, you can use the `durationsize` keyword to specify a Boolean. If set to True, dots will be sized according to how long a fixation was: the longer a fixation, the larger a dot will be. If `durationsize` is set to False, all dots will have the same size. A similar keyword argument is `durationcolour`, which also requires a Boolean. If you set it to True, longer fixations will have a 'hotter' colour. If `durationcolour` is set to False, all dots will be green. For an example, see Figure 8.3.

For this plot, you should also create a name and a path for the intended save file. After doing it, you can create the plot by using the `draw_fixations` function. As before, close the Figure after creating and saving it:

```
     # Plot the fixations
     savename = 'fixations_%s' % imgname
     savepath = os.path.join(OUTPUTDIR, savename)
     fig = gazeplotter.draw_fixations(fixations, DISPSIZE, \
          durationsize=True, durationcolour=False, \
          imagefile=imgpath, savefilename=savepath)
     close(fig)
```

The final plot is the most fancy one: a heatmap. This visualisation is rather popular in eye-tracking research, primarily because it looks really pretty. The idea is that you represent areas where fixations were denser with hotter colours. You can also weigh in the duration of fixations, to make long fixations count more than short fixations. The result is a visualisation that can instantly tell you where fixations occurred most (see Figure 8.4).

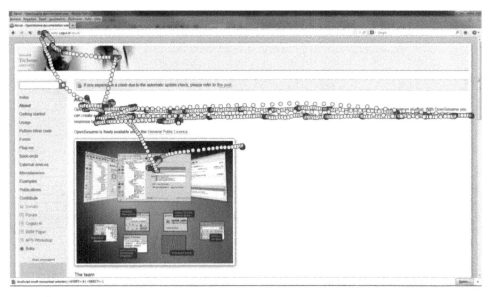

FIGURE 8.5 Raw gaze samples (grey dots) on a screenshot of a documentation website. You can see that the participant followed the text with their eyes. Note how the overlap is not one-to-one, especially in the central-right part of the image. This indicates some drift occurred, reducing the quality of the data. This is very common

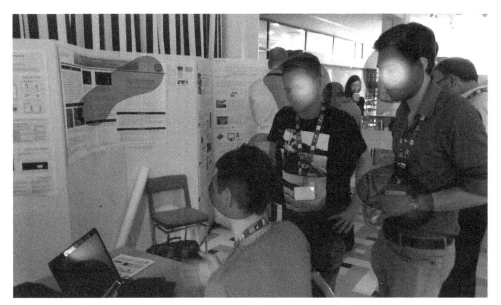

FIGURE 8.6 Heatmap on a picture of a scientific conference. This picture was taken at the European Conference on Eye Movements in 2013, where a bunch of nerds was discussing some software. Curiously, the fixations concentrated mostly on the man on the right, and not on the super-handsome guy in the centre

FIGURE 8.7 Fixations (white dots) on picture of a building at night. Fixations are concentrated around the high-contrast areas in the picture

To draw a heatmap, you can use the `draw_heatmap` function from the `gazeplotter` module. It requires the same two arguments as the `draw_fixations` function: a list of 'Efix' events, and the display size.

The `draw_heatmap` function can take four keywords, of which two are the same as for the `draw_raw` and `draw_fixation` functions: `imagefile` to specify the original image, and `savefilename` to store the produced heatmap. Another keyword is `alpha`, which allows you to set the transparency of the heatmap that will be superimposed on the image. If set to 0, the heatmap will be fully transparent, and if set to 1, the heatmap will be completely opaque. The default value is 0.5. The final keyword is `durationweight`, which requires a Boolean. If you set it to True, the duration of fixations will be weighted into the heatmap construction, with longer fixations being assigned more weight. If set to False, all fixations will be treated as equally important. The default value is True.

To draw and save a heatmap, and to close it afterwards, use the following code:

```
# Plot a heatmap
savename = 'heatmap_%s' % imgname
savepath = os.path.join(OUTPUTDIR, savename)
fig = gazeplotter.draw_heatmap(fixations, DISPSIZE, \
        imagefile=imgpath, savefilename=savepath)
close(fig)
```

And with that, your script should be finished. Run it to loop through all trials, creating three data visualisations per trial. When the script finishes, you can admire all of these plots in the output folder.

The example images include a screenshot of a documentation website. The text on that webpage was clearly being scanned by the participant. You can see this in the raw data plot and in the fixation plot, where fixations land on consecutive parts of the text. Interestingly, people rarely fixate all words in a sentence, and instead skip common words that they can read from the corner of their eye.

There were quite a few pictures with faces in the examples. The fixation plots and heatmaps for these tell a clear story: our participant liked to look at faces. This is a common pattern, and you can see it in most humans who are allowed to look at a picture freely. The affinity for faces is not set in stone, though. If you ask a participant to look for your keys in a picture, it's likely they will pay a lot less attention to the faces in it.

The final example highlighted here, is of a building at night. It is the Van Unnik building, on Utrecht University's campus. Most of it was decommissioned in 2014, but it was my place of work at the time this picture was taken. The top-right window used to be my office.

What's interesting about the visualisation, is that the fixations are concentrated on the lighter parts of the image. This reflects a very common tendency in human gazing behaviour: differences in contrast are very potent in grasping our attention. In this image, the lights in the offices, in the university logo, and on the street contrast with the generally dark background. Our eyes are drawn to these parts. Don't go away thinking that our eyes are like moths, though! If the contrast was inverted, participants would have been looking at the dark parts against a generally light background.

One final thing to note here, is that it is somewhat unusual to create heatmaps from a single participant's viewing data. It was great for teaching purposes, but normally one would collect fixations from a larger group of participants. When testing participants, it's always *the more, the merrier*. Unless you're testing overly anal nerds, of course.

9

GETTING HELP

After working your way through this book, you should be able to do quite a bit of research with Python. However, there will inevitably be moments where you get stuck on something. This is when you turn to the internet!

Stack Overflow

Stack Overflow is a programming forum. It is populated by an interesting mix of complete beginners who will ask basic questions, highly qualified and experienced nerds who can fix any bug, and every kind of programmer in between. If you have a question, chances are that you will find someone else has already asked it, and that another someone has already provided an answer. You can find this wondrous website at www.stackoverflow.com.

Documentation websites

Every Python package that was used in this book provides at least some documentation on their website. You can find out more about PyGaze on www.pygaze.org, more on PsychoPy can be found on www.psychopy.org/api/api.html, and more on PyGame can be found on www.pygame.org/docs. NumPy and Matplotlib are both part of the SciPy project, and documentation can be found through the project's website: www.scipy.org.

PyGaze forum

If you have a query that is specific to PyGaze, you can always turn to the PyGaze forum. This is available via www.forum.cogsci.nl, and is a platform where psychologists can help each other. In addition, the package's developers regularly check it, and provide help wherever they can.

Contact the author

If you're absolutely stuck, and have exhausted all of the above resources, you can contact the author of this book. Note that public resources are a preferred way of communicating your questions and issues. Using a public forum is beneficial to you, because help is quicker via forums than directly from the author (the author and other people are active on the forum, whereas only the author responds to his own email). More importantly, the answer to your question might help other people, if they run into the same issue.

To email the author, fill out the contact form here: www.pygaze.org/contact.

APPENDIX: CODE LISTING

Make some noise (1)

```
import numpy
from matplotlib import pyplot

noise = numpy.random.rand(500, 500, 3)
pyplot.imshow(noise)

pyplot.show()
```

Chapter 3: Display

Pygaze

constants.py

```
# Display settings (type and resolution).
DISPTYPE = 'pygame'
DISPSIZE = (1920, 1080)

# Default foreground and background colour.
FGC = (0, 0, 0)
BGC = (128, 128, 128)
```

experiment.py

```
from pygaze.display import Display
import pygaze.libtime as timer

# Initialise a new Display instance.
```

```
disp = Display()

# Update the display (this makes the grey background visible).
disp.show()

# Pause for two seconds.
timer.pause(2000)

# Close the Display again.
disp.close()
```

Pyschopy

constants.py

```
# Window resolution.
DISPSIZE = (1920, 1080)

# Default foreground and background colour.
FGC = (0, 0, 0)
BGC = (128, 128, 128)
```

experiment.py

```
from constants import DISPSIZE
from psychopy.visual import Window
from psychopy.core import wait

# Initialise a new Window instance.
disp = Window(size=DISPSIZE, units='pix', fullscr=True)

# Wait for two seconds.
wait(2)

# Close the Display again.
disp.close()
```

Chapter 3: Screen

Pygaze

constants.py

```
# Display settings (type and resolution).
DISPTYPE = 'pygame'
DISPSIZE = (1920, 1080)

# Default foreground and background colour.
FGC = (0, 0, 0)
BGC = (128, 128, 128)
```

experiment.py

```
from pygaze.display import Display
from pygaze.screen import Screen
import pygaze.libtime as timer

# Initialise a new Display instance.
disp = Display()

# Create a new Screen instance.
fixscreen = Screen()
# Draw a fixation dot on the new Screen.
fixscreen.draw_fixation(fixtype='dot')

# Create another Screen instance.
imgscreen = Screen()
# Draw an image on this screen.
imgscreen.draw_image('example.png')

# Fill the Display with the fixation screen.
disp.fill(fixscreen)
# Show the Display on the computer monitor.
disp.show()
# Pause for one seconds.
timer.pause(1000)

# Fill the display with the image screen.
disp.fill(imgscreen)
# Show the Display on the computer monitor.
disp.show()
# Pause for two seconds.
timer.pause(2000)

# Close the Display again.
disp.close()
```

PyschoPy

constants.py

```
# Window resolution.
DISPSIZE = (1920, 1080)

# Default foreground and background colour.
FGC = (-1, -1, -1)
BGC = (0, 0, 0)
```

experiment.py

```
from constants import DISPSIZE, FGC
from psychopy.visual import Window, Circle, ImageStim
```

```
from psychopy.core import wait

# Initialise a new Window instance.
disp = Window(size=DISPSIZE, units='pix', fullscr=True)

# Create a new circle stimulus.
# (This will serve as a fixation dot.)
fixmark = Circle(disp, radius=6, edges=64, \
     lineColor=FGC, fillColor=FGC)

# Create a new image stimulus
img = ImageStim(disp, image='example.png')

# Draw the circle stimulus.
fixmark.draw()
# Update the computer monitor.
disp.flip()
# Wait for one second.
wait(1)

# Draw the image.
img.draw()
# Update the computer monitor.
disp.flip()
# Wait for two seconds.
wait(2)

# Close the Display again.
disp.close()
```

Chapter 3: Grating

Pygaze

constants.py

```
# Set the Display size (this should match the resolution).
DISPSIZE = (1920, 1080)
# Set the Display type.
DISPTYPE = 'psychopy'
```

experiment.py

```
import pygaze
from pygaze.display import Display
from pygaze.screen import Screen
import pygaze.libtime as timer
import numpy
from psychopy.visual import GratingStim

# Create a new Display instance.
disp = Display()
```

```
# Create a new grating stimulus, using PsychoPy.
gabor = GratingStim(pygaze.expdisplay, tex='sin', mask='gauss', \
     sf=0.05, size=200)
# Create a new Screen instance.
gaborscreen = Screen()
# Add the GratingStim to the Screen's stimulus list.
gaborscreen.screen.append(gabor)

# Create some noise using NumPy.
noise = (numpy.random.rand(64, 64) * 2) - 1
# Create a new grating stimulus, using PsychoPy and the noise created
     before.
noisepatch = GratingStim(pygaze.expdisplay, tex=noise, mask='gauss', \
     size=200)
# Create a new Screen instance.
noisescreen = Screen()
# Add the GratingStim to the Screen's stimulus list.
noisescreen.screen.append(noisepatch)

# Fill the Display with the Gabor screen.
disp.fill(gaborscreen)
# Show the Display on the computer monitor.
disp.show()
# Wait for one second.
timer.pause(1000)

# Fill the Display with the noise screen.
disp.fill(noisescreen)
# Show the Display on the computer monitor.
disp.show()
# Wait for two seconds.
timer.pause(2000)

disp.close()
```

PsychoPy

constants.py

```
# Set the Window size (this should match the resolution)
DISPSIZE = (1920, 1080)
```

experiment.py

```
from constants import DISPSIZE
import numpy
from psychopy.visual import Window, GratingStim
from psychopy.core import wait

# Create a new Window instance.
disp = Window(size=DISPSIZE, units='pix', fullscr=True)
```

```
# Create a new grating stimulus.
gabor = GratingStim(disp, tex='sin', mask='gauss', sf=0.05, size=200)

# Create some noise using NumPy.
noise = (numpy.random.rand(64, 64) * 2) - 1
# Create a new grating stimulus, using the noise created before.
noisepatch = GratingStim(disp, tex=noise, mask='gauss', size=200)

# Draw the grating stimulus.
gabor.draw()
# Show the window on the computer monitor.
disp.flip()
# Wait for one second.
wait(1)

# Draw the noise stimulus.
noisepatch.draw()
# Show the window on the computer monitor.
disp.flip()
# Wait for two seconds.
wait(2)

disp.close()
```

Chapter 4: Keyboard

Pygaze

constants.py

```
# display resolution (should match monitor settings!)
DISPSIZE = (1920, 1080)
# display type (either 'pygame' or 'psychopy')
DISPTYPE = 'psychopy'
# foreground and background
FGC = (0, 0, 0)
BGC = (128, 128, 128)
```

experiment.py

```
import random
from constants import *
from pygaze.display import Display
from pygaze.screen import Screen
from pygaze.keyboard import Keyboard
from pygaze.sound import Sound

# create a new Display instance (to interact with the monitor)
disp = Display()
# create a new Screen (to use as a canvas to draw on)
scr = Screen()
```

```
# Create two Sounds, one for nice and one for stern feedback
sine = Sound(osc='sine', freq=4000, length=500)
noise = Sound(osc='whitenoise', length=500)

# a list of vowels
vowels = ['a', 'e', 'i', 'o', 'u', 'y']

# create a new Keyboard instance, to monitor key presses
kb = Keyboard(keylist=vowels, timeout=None)

# randomly choose one vowel
letter = random.choice(vowels)

# draw the vowel on a Screen
scr.draw_text(text=letter, fontsize=128)

# fill the Display with a Screen and update the monitor
disp.fill(scr)
disp.show()

# wait for a response
key, presstime = kb.get_key()

# check if the pressed key matches the displayed letter
if key == letter:
      correct = 1
else:
      correct = 0

# on a correct response...
if correct:
      # ...provide nice feedback
      feedback = 'Well done!'
      # (0,255,0) is green
      fbcolour = (0, 255, 0)
# on an incorrect response...
else:
      # ...provide nasty feedback
      feedback = 'You suck!'
      # (0,255,0) is red
      fbcolour = (255, 0, 0)

# construct an informative string by using variables
extrafb = 'The vowel was %s, and you typed %s.' \
      % (letter, key)

# first clear the Screen of its current content
scr.clear()
# then draw the feedback text
scr.draw_text(text=feedback, colour=fbcolour, fontsize=24)
# determine the position of the extra feedback
# (at half the screen width, and 60% of the screen height)
```

```
extrafbpos = (int(DISPSIZE[0]*0.5), int(DISPSIZE[1]*0.6))
# draw the extra feedback
scr.draw_text(text=extrafb, pos=extrafbpos, fontsize=24)


# show the Screen with feedback
disp.fill(scr)
disp.show()


# on a correct response...
if correct:
ⵧⵧⵧⵧ # ...play the sine Sound
ⵧⵧⵧⵧ sine.play()
# on an incorrect response...
else:
ⵧⵧⵧⵧ # ...play the harsh Sound
ⵧⵧⵧⵧ noise.play()


# wait for any keypress
kb.get_key(keylist=None, timeout=None)


# close the Display
disp.close()
```

Psychopy

constants.py

```
# display resolution (should match monitor settings!)
DISPSIZE = (1920, 1080)
# foreground and background
FGC = (-1, -1, -1)
BGC = (1, 1, 1)
```

experiment.py

```
import random
from constants import *
from psychopy.visual import Window, TextStim
from psychopy.event import waitKeys
from psychopy.sound import Sound

# create a new Display instance (to interact with the monitor)
disp = Window(size=DISPSIZE, units='pix', fullscr=True)

# create two Sounds: one for nice and one for stern feedback
high = Sound(value=4000, secs=0.5)
low = Sound(value=400, secs=0.5)

# a list of vowels
vowels = ['a', 'e', 'i', 'o', 'u', 'y']
```

```
# randomly choose one vowel
letter = random.choice(vowels)

# create a TextStim for the vowel
vowelstim = TextStim(disp, text=letter, height=128)

# draw the text stimulus
vowelstim.draw()
# update the monitor
disp.flip()

# wait for a response
resplist = waitKeys(maxWait=float('inf'), keyList=vowels, \
     timeStamped=True)
# select the first response from the list
key, presstime = resplist[0]

# check if the pressed key matches the displayed letter
if key == letter:
     correct = 1
else:
     correct = 0

# on a correct response...
if correct:
     # ...provide nice feedback
     feedback = 'Well done!'
     # (-1, 1, -1) is green
     fbcolour = (-1, 1, -1)
# on an incorrect response...
else:
     # ...provide nasty feedback
     feedback = 'You suck!'
     # (1, -1, -1) is red
     fbcolour = (1, -1, -1)

# construct an informative string by using variables
extrafb = 'The vowel was %s, and you typed %s.' \
     % (letter, key)

# create a stimulus for the feedback text
fbstim = TextStim(disp, text=feedback, color=fbcolour, \
     height=24)

# determine the position of the extra feedback
# (at half the screen width, and 60% of the screen height)
extrafbpos = (0, int(DISPSIZE[1]*-0.1))
# create a stimulus for the extra feedback
extrafbstim = TextStim(disp, text=extrafb, pos=extrafbpos, \
     height=24)

# show the feedback
```

```
fbstim.draw()
extrafbstim.draw()
disp.flip()

# on a correct response...
if correct:
      # ...play the high sine Sound
      high.play()
# on an incorrect response...
else:
      # ...play the low sine Sound
      low.play()

# wait for any keypress
waitKeys(maxWait=float('inf'), keyList=None)

# close the Display
disp.close()
```

Chapter 4: While loop

Pygaze

constants.py

```
# the display size should match the monitor's resolution
DISPSIZE = (1920, 1080)
# the display type can be 'pygame' or 'psychopy'
DISPTYPE = 'pygame'
# the foreground and background colour are (red, green, blue)
# the values are 0 (no colour) to 255 (full colour)
FGC = (255, 255, 255)
BGC = (0, 0, 0)
```

experiment.py

```
from constants import DISPSIZE
from pygaze.display import Display
from pygaze.screen import Screen
from pygaze.keyboard import Keyboard

# create a Display to show things on the monitor
disp = Display()

# create a Screen for drawing operations
scr = Screen()

# create a Keyboard to collect keypresses
kb = Keyboard(keylist=None, timeout=None)

# define a super-important question
question = 'What do you think of this question?'
```

```
# define the question's position
qpos = (int(DISPSIZE[0]*0.5), int(DISPSIZE[1]*0.2))
# draw it on the Screen
scr.draw_text(text=question, pos=qpos, fontsize=24)

# fill the Display with the Screen
disp.fill(scr)
# present the current Display
disp.show()

# start with an empty response string
response = ''
# start undone
done = False

# loop until done == False
while not done:

     # check for keypresses
     key, presstime = kb.get_key()

     # check if the length of the key's name equals 1
     if len(key) == 1:
          # add the key to the response
          response += key
     # check if the key is the Space bar
     elif key == 'space':
          # add a space to the response
          response += ' '
     # check if the key's name was 'backspace' and
     # check if the response has at least 1 character
     elif key == 'backspace' and len(response) > 0:
          # remove the last character of the response
          response = response[0:-1]
     # if the key was none of the above, check if it
     # was the Enter key
     if key == 'return':
          # set done to True
          done = True

     # clear the current content of scr
     scr.clear()
     # redraw the question
     scr.draw_text(text=question, pos=qpos, fontsize=24)
     # draw the current response on a Screen
     scr.draw_text(text=response, fontsize=24)
     # fill the Display with the response Screen
     disp.fill(scr)
     # show the Display on the monitor
     disp.show()

# close the Display
disp.close()
```

Psychopy

constants.py

```python
# the display size should match the monitor's resolution
DISPSIZE = (1920, 1080)
# the foreground and background colour are (red, green, blue)
# the values are -1 (no colour) to 1 (full colour)
FGC = (1, 1, 1)
BGC = (-1, -1, -1)
```

experiment.py

```python
from constants import DISPSIZE
from psychopy.visual import Window, TextStim
from psychopy.event import waitKeys

# create a Window to show things on the monitor
disp = Window(size=DISPSIZE, units='pix', fullscr=True)

# define a super-important question
question = 'What do you think of this question?'

# define the question's position
qpos = (0, int(DISPSIZE[1]*0.2))
# create a new text stimulus
qstim = TextStim(disp, text=question, pos=qpos, height=24)
# draw the question
qstim.draw()
# create an additional text stimulus for the response
# (this will be updated later)
respstim = TextStim(disp, text='', height=24)

# start with an empty response string
response = ''
# start undone
done = False

# loop until done == False
while not done:

    # check for keypresses
    resplist = waitKeys(maxWait=float('inf'), keyList=None, \
        timeStamped=True)
    # use only the first in the returned list of keypresses
    key, presstime = resplist[0]

    # check if the length of the key's name equals 1
    if len(key) == 1:
        # add the key to the response
        response += key
    # check if the key is the Space bar
```

```
    elif key == 'space':
        # add a space to the response
        response += ' '
    # check if the key's name was 'backspace' and
    # check if the response has at least 1 character
    elif key == 'backspace' and len(response) > 0:
        # remove the last character of the response
        response = response[0:-1]
    # if the key was none of the above, check if it
    # was the Enter key
    if key == 'return':
        # set done to True
        done = True

    # update the response stimulus
    respstim.setText(response)

    # re-draw the question stimulus
    qstim.draw()
    # draw the response stimulus
    respstim.draw()
    # update the monitor
    disp.flip()

# close the Display
disp.close()
```

Make some noise (2)

```
import wave
import numpy
import pygame

# maximal sound amplitude and sampling rate
MAXAMP = 16383
SAMPLERATE = 48000

# mono
NCHANNELS = 1

# sound length (seconds) and frequency (Herz)
SOUNDLEN = 3.0
SOUNDFREQ = 1000

# calculate the total amount of cycles
ncycles = SOUNDLEN * SOUNDFREQ

# calculate the total amount of samples
nsamples = SOUNDLEN * SAMPLERATE
# calculate the number of samples per cycle
spc = nsamples / ncycles
```

```python
# the stepsize is the distance between samples within a cycle
# (divide the range by the amount of samples per cycle)
stepsize = (2*numpy.pi) / spc
# create a range of numbers between 0 and 2*pi
x = numpy.arange(0, 2*numpy.pi, stepsize)
# make a sine wave out of the range
sine = numpy.sin(x)

# increase the sine wave's amplitude
sine = sine * MAXAMP

# repeat the sine wave!
allsines = numpy.tile(sine, int(ncycles))

# initialise the mixer module
# (it requires the sampling rate and the number of channels)
pygame.mixer.init(frequency=SAMPLERATE, channels=NCHANNELS)

# now create a sound out of the allsines vector
tone = pygame.mixer.Sound(allsines.astype('int16'))

# play the sinusoid sound
tone.play()

# create a series of random numbers
noise = numpy.random.rand(SOUNDLEN * SAMPLERATE)

# correct the value range (-1 to 1)
noise = (noise * 2) - 1

# increase the noise's amplitude
noise = noise * MAXAMP

# turn the noise vector into a sound
whitenoise = pygame.mixer.Sound(noise.astype('int16'))

# play the noise sound
whitenoise.play()

# open new wave file objects
tonefile = wave.open('pure_tone.wav', 'w')
noisefile = wave.open('noise.wav', 'w')

# set parameters for the pure tone
tonefile.setframerate(SAMPLERATE)
tonefile.setnchannels(NCHANNELS)
tonefile.setsampwidth(2)

# set the same parameters for the noise
noisefile.setframerate(SAMPLERATE)
noisefile.setnchannels(NCHANNELS)
noisefile.setsampwidth(2)
```

```
# get buffers
tonebuffer = tone.get_buffer()
noisebuffer = whitenoise.get_buffer()
# write raw buffer to the wave file
tonefile.writeframesraw(tonebuffer.raw)
noisefile.writeframesraw(noisebuffer.raw)

# neatly close the wave file objects
tonefile.close()
noisefile.close()
```

Chapter 5: Posner experiment

Pygaze

constants.py

```
# the Display size should match the monitor resolution
DISPSIZE = (1920, 1080)
# the Display type should be set to 'psychopy' for this one
DISPTYPE = 'psychopy'
# foreground and background
FGC = (0, 0, 0)
BGC = (128,128,128)

# potential cue locations
CUELOCS = ['right', 'left']
# potential target locations
TARLOCS = ['right', 'left']
# potential SOAs
SOAS = [93, 893]
# potential targets
TARGETS = ['E', 'F']

# fixation time at the start of a trial
FIXTIME = 1493
# duration of the cue Screen
CUETIME = 43
# duration of the feedback Screen
FEEDBACKTIME = 993

# ask for the log file's name
LOGFILENAME = raw_input('Participant name: ')
LOGFILE = LOGFILENAME

# number of times to repeat all unique trials
TRIALREPEATS = 20
```

experiment.py

```
import random
from constants import *
```

```python
from pygaze.display import Display
from pygaze.screen import Screen
from pygaze.keyboard import Keyboard
from pygaze.logfile import Logfile
import pygaze.libtime as timer

# create a Display to deal with the monitor
disp = Display()
# create a Keyboard to collect responses
kb = Keyboard(keylist=None, timeout=None)

# create a new log file
log = Logfile()
# define a header
header = ['fixonset', 'cueonset', 'cueoffset', 'taronset', \
    'cueside', 'tarside', 'valid', 'soa', 'target', \
    'response', 'correct', 'RT']
# write the header to the log file
log.write(header)

# define the instructions
instructions = 'Welcome!\n\nIn this experiment, Es and Fs \
will appear on either side of the screen. If you see \
an E, press the E key. If you see an F, press F. \
\n\nPlease try to be as fast and as accurate as \
possible.\n\nGood luck!'
# create a new Screen
instscr = Screen()
# draw the instructions on the Screen
instscr.draw_text(text=instructions, fontsize=24)

# create a new Screen
fixscr = Screen()
# draw a fixation cross in the centre
fixscr.draw_fixation(fixtype='cross', diameter=12)

# define the boxes' width and height (same number: they're square!)
BOXSIZE = 200
# define the boxes' centre coordinates
BOXCORS = {}
BOXCORS['left'] = (int(DISPSIZE[0]*0.25 - BOXSIZE*0.5), \
    int(DISPSIZE[1]*0.5 - BOXSIZE*0.5))
BOXCORS['right'] = (int(DISPSIZE[0]*0.75 - BOXSIZE*0.5), \
    int(DISPSIZE[1]*0.5 - BOXSIZE*0.5))

# draw the left box
fixscr.draw_rect(x=BOXCORS['left'][0], y=BOXCORS['left'][1], \
    w=BOXSIZE, h=BOXSIZE, pw=3, fill=False)
# draw the right box
fixscr.draw_rect(x=BOXCORS['right'][0], y=BOXCORS['right'][1], \
    w=BOXSIZE, h=BOXSIZE, pw=3, fill=False)
```

```
# create a dict with two new Screens for the cues
cuescr = {}
cuescr['left'] = Screen()
cuescr['right'] = Screen()
# copy the fixation Screen to both cue Screens
cuescr['left'].copy(fixscr)
cuescr['right'].copy(fixscr)
# draw the cue boxes with thicker penwidths
cuescr['left'].draw_rect(x=BOXCORS['left'][0], y=BOXCORS['left'][1], \
     w=BOXSIZE, h=BOXSIZE, pw=8, fill=False)
cuescr['right'].draw_rect(x=BOXCORS['right'][0], y=BOXCORS['right'][1], \
     w=BOXSIZE, h=BOXSIZE, pw=8, fill=False)

# create a dict to contain further dicts to contain target Screens
tarscr = {}
tarscr['left'] = {}
tarscr['left']['E'] = Screen()
tarscr['left']['F'] = Screen()
tarscr['right'] = {}
tarscr['right']['E'] = Screen()
tarscr['right']['F'] = Screen()
# copy the fixation Screen to each target Screen
tarscr['left']['E'].copy(fixscr)
tarscr['left']['F'].copy(fixscr)
tarscr['right']['E'].copy(fixscr)
tarscr['right']['F'].copy(fixscr)
# calculate the target positions
tarpos = {}
tarpos['left'] = (BOXCORS['left'][0] + BOXSIZE/2, \
     BOXCORS['left'][1] + BOXSIZE/2)
tarpos['right'] = (BOXCORS['right'][0] + BOXSIZE/2, \
     BOXCORS['right'][1] + BOXSIZE/2)
# draw all possible targets on the target Screens
tarscr['left']['E'].draw_text(text='E', pos=tarpos['left'], fontsize=48)
tarscr['left']['F'].draw_text(text='F', pos=tarpos['left'], fontsize=48)
tarscr['right']['E'].draw_text(text='E', pos=tarpos['right'],
fontsize=48)
tarscr['right']['F'].draw_text(text='F', pos=tarpos['right'],
fontsize=48)

# create two new feedback Screens in a dict
fbscr = {}
# draw the incorrect feedback (evil red letters!)
fbscr[0] = Screen()
fbscr[0].draw_text(text='Incorrect!', colour=(255,0,0), fontsize=24)
# draw the correct feedback (nice and green)
fbscr[1] = Screen()
fbscr[1].draw_text(text='Correct!', colour=(0,255,0), fontsize=24)

# create an empty list to contain all unique trials
alltrials = []
# loop through all parameters
```

```
for cueside in CUELOCS:
     for tarside in TARLOCS:
          for soa in SOAS:
               for tar in TARGETS:
                    # create a unique trial dict
                    trial = {'cueside':cueside, 'tarside':tarside,\
                         'target':tar, 'soa':soa}
                    # add the trial dict to the list
                    alltrials.extend( TRIALREPEATS * [trial] )
# randomise the order of all trials
random.shuffle(alltrials)

# present the instructions
disp.fill(instscr)
disp.show()
# wait for any old keypress
kb.get_key(keylist=None, timeout=None)

# loop through all trials
for trial in alltrials:

     # show the fixation Screen
     disp.fill(fixscr)
     fixonset = disp.show()
     # wait for a bit
     timer.pause(FIXTIME)

     # show a cue Screen
     disp.fill(cuescr[trial['cueside']])
     cueonset = disp.show()
     # wait for a little bit
     timer.pause(CUETIME)

     # show the fixation Screen again
     disp.fill(fixscr)
     cueoffset = disp.show()
     # wait for the SOA minus the cue duration
     timer.pause(trial['soa'] - CUETIME - 10)

     # show a target Screen
     disp.fill(tarscr[trial['tarside']][trial['target']])
     taronset = disp.show()

     # wait for a response
     response, presstime = kb.get_key(keylist=['e', 'f'], timeout=None)
     # turn the lowercase response into uppercase
     response = response.upper()

     # check if the response was correct
     if response == trial['target']:
          correct = 1
     else:
```

```
          correct = 0

     # calculate the reaction time
     RT = presstime - taronset

     # check if the cue was valid
     if trial['cueside'] == trial['tarside']:
          validity = 1
     else:
          validity = 0

     # show the appropriate feedback Screen
     disp.fill(fbscr[correct])
     disp.show()
     # wait for a bit to allow the participant to see the feedback
     timer.pause(FEEDBACKTIME)

     # log all interesting values
     log.write([fixonset, cueonset, cueoffset, taronset, \
          trial['cueside'], trial['tarside'], validity, trial['soa'], \
          trial['target'], response, correct, RT])

# close the log file
log.close()

# shut down the experiment
disp.close()
```

Psychopy

constants.py

```
# the Display size should match the monitor resolution
DISPSIZE = (1920, 1080)
# foreground and background
FGC = (-1, -1, -1)
BGC = (0, 0, 0)

# potential cue locations
CUELOCS = ['right', 'left']
# potential target locations
TARLOCS = ['right', 'left']
# potential SOAs
SOAS = [0.093, 0.893]
# potential targets
TARGETS = ['E', 'F']

# fixation time at the start of a trial
FIXTIME = 1.493
# duration of the cue Screen
CUETIME = 0.043
```

```
# duration of the feedback Screen
FEEDBACKTIME = 0.993

# ask for the log file's name
LOGFILENAME = raw_input('Participant name: ')
LOGFILE = LOGFILENAME

# number of times to repeat all unique trials
TRIALREPEATS = 20
```

experiment.py

```
import random
from constants import *
from psychopy.visual import Window, TextStim, Circle, Rect
from psychopy.event import waitKeys
from psychopy.core import wait

# create a Window to deal with the monitor
disp = Window(size=DISPSIZE, units='pix', \
     color=BGC, fullscr=True)

# open a new file instance
log = open(LOGFILE + '.tsv', 'w')
# define a header
header = ['fixonset', 'cueonset', 'cueoffset', 'taronset', \
     'cueside', 'tarside', 'valid', 'soa', 'target', \
     'response', 'correct', 'RT']
# make all values in the header into strings
# (all values are strings already, but this is an example)
line = map(str, header)
# join all string values into one string, separated by tabs ('\t')
line = '\t'.join(line)
# add a newline ('\n') to the string
line += '\n'
# write the header to the log file
log.write(line)

# define the instructions
instructions = 'Welcome!\n\nIn this experiment, Es and Fs \
will appear on either side of the screen. If you see \
an E, press the E key. If you see an F, press F. \
\n\nPlease try to be as fast and as accurate as \
possible.\n\nGood luck!'
# create a new text stimulus
inststim = TextStim(disp, text=instructions, color=FGC, height=24)

# create a Circle stimulus for fixation purposes
fixstim = Circle(disp, radius=6, edges=32, \
     lineColor=FGC, fillColor=FGC)

# define the boxes' width and height (same number: they're square!)
```

```
BOXSIZE = 200
# define the boxes' centre coordinates
BOXCORS = {}
BOXCORS['left'] = (int(DISPSIZE[0]*-0.25), 0)
BOXCORS['right'] = (int(DISPSIZE[0]*0.25), 0)

# create the left box
lboxstim = Rect(disp, pos=BOXCORS['left'], \
     width=BOXSIZE, height=BOXSIZE, lineColor=FGC, lineWidth=3)
# create the right box
rboxstim = Rect(disp, pos=BOXCORS['right'], \
     width=BOXSIZE, height=BOXSIZE, lineColor=FGC, lineWidth=3)

# create an empty dict to hold both cue stimuli
cuestim = {}
# create the left box
cuestim['left'] = Rect(disp, pos=BOXCORS['left'], \
     width=BOXSIZE, height=BOXSIZE, lineColor=FGC, lineWidth=8)
# create the right box
cuestim['right'] = Rect(disp, pos=BOXCORS['right'], \
     width=BOXSIZE, height=BOXSIZE, lineColor=FGC, lineWidth=8)

# create a dict to contain further dicts to contain target stimuli
tarstim = {}
tarstim['left'] = {}
tarstim['right'] = {}
# draw all possible target stimuli
tarstim['left']['E'] = TextStim(disp, text='E', pos=BOXCORS['left'],
     height=48, color=FGC)
tarstim['left']['F'] = TextStim(disp, text='F', pos=BOXCORS['left'],
     height=48, color=FGC)
tarstim['right']['E'] = TextStim(disp, text='E', pos=BOXCORS['right'],
     height=48, color=FGC)
tarstim['right']['F'] = TextStim(disp, text='F', pos=BOXCORS['right'],
     height=48, color=FGC)

# create a dict to hold two feedback stimuli
fbstim = {}
# draw the incorrect feedback (evil red letters!)
fbstim[0] = TextStim(disp, text='Incorrect!', height=24, \
     color=(1, -1, -1))
# draw the correct feedback (nice and green)
fbstim[1] = TextStim(disp, text='Correct!', height=24, \
     color=(-1, 1, -1))

# create an empty list to contain all unique trials
alltrials = []
# loop through all parameters
for cueside in CUELOCS:
     for tarside in TARLOCS:
          for soa in SOAS:
               for tar in TARGETS:
```

```
                             # create a unique trial dict
                             trial = {'cueside':cueside, 'tarside':tarside,\
                                'target':tar, 'soa':soa}
                             # add the trial dict to the list
                             alltrials.extend( TRIALREPEATS * [trial] )
# randomise the order of all trials
random.shuffle(alltrials)

# present the instructions
inststim.draw()
disp.flip()
# wait for any old keypress
waitKeys(maxWait=float('inf'), keyList=None, timeStamped=True)

# loop through all trials
for trial in alltrials:

     # draw the fixation mark, and the left and right boxes
     fixstim.draw()
     lboxstim.draw()
     rboxstim.draw()
     # update the monitor
     fixonset = disp.flip()
     # wait for a bit
     wait(FIXTIME)

     # draw the fixation mark, and the left and right boxes
     fixstim.draw()
     lboxstim.draw()
     rboxstim.draw()
     # draw a cue
     cuestim[trial['cueside']].draw()
     # update the monitor
     cueonset = disp.flip()
     # wait for a little bit
     wait(CUETIME)

     # draw the fixation mark, and the left and right boxes
     fixstim.draw()
     lboxstim.draw()
     rboxstim.draw()
     # update the monitor
     cueoffset = disp.flip()
     # wait for the SOA minus the cue duration
     wait(trial['soa'] - CUETIME - 0.01)

     # draw the fixation mark, and the left and right boxes
     fixstim.draw()
     lboxstim.draw()
     rboxstim.draw()
     # draw a target stimulus
     tarstim[trial['tarside']][trial['target']].draw()
```

```python
        # update the monitor
        taronset = disp.flip()

        # wait for a response
        resplist = waitKeys(maxWait=float('inf'), keyList=['e','f'], \
            timeStamped=True)
        # select the first response from the response list
        response, presstime = resplist[0]
        # turn the lowercase response into uppercase
        response = response.upper()

        # check if the response was correct
        if response == trial['target']:
            correct = 1
        else:
            correct = 0

        # calculate the reaction time
        RT = presstime - taronset

        # check if the cue was valid
        if trial['cueside'] == trial['tarside']:
            validity = 1
        else:
            validity = 0

        # show the appropriate feedback stimulus
        fbstim[correct].draw()
        disp.flip()
        # wait for a bit to allow the participant to see the feedback
        wait(FEEDBACKTIME)

        # collect all interesting values in a single list
        line = [fixonset, cueonset, cueoffset, taronset, \
            trial['cueside'], trial['tarside'], validity, trial['soa'], \
            trial['target'], response, correct, RT]
        # turn all values into a string
        line = map(str, line)
        # merge all individual values into a single string, separated by
        #tabs
        line = '\t'.join(line)
        # add a newline ('\n') to the string
        line += '\n'
        # write the data string to the log file
        log.write(line)

# close the log file
log.close()

# shut down the experiment
disp.close()
```

Make some noise (3)

Pygaze

constants.py

```
# set the display type to 'pygame'
DISPTYPE = 'pygame'
# make sure that the DISPSIZE matches your monitor resolution!
DISPSIZE = (1920, 1080)
```

noisemaker_joystick.py

```
from pygaze.joystick import Joystick
from pygaze.sound import Sound
from pygaze.display import Display

# initialise a Display instance
disp = Display()

# create a Joystick instance
# ('dev' is short for 'device')
dev = Joystick()

# definition of a function to get user input
def get_input(device):

    # wait for a button press for about 10 ms
    button, presstime = device.get_joybutton(timeout=10)

    # return the button number (or None)
    return button

# create a dict with the frequency for each button
freqs = {1:440, 2:494, 3:523, 4:587, 5:659,
    6:698, 7:784, 8:880, 9:988}

# create an empty dict for the sounds
sounds = {}
# loop through the keys of the freqs dict
for button in freqs.keys():
    # create a new Sound instance with the right frequency
    sounds[button] = Sound(osc='sine', freq=freqs[button], \
        length=250, attack=10, decay=10)

# run a while loop until
stop = False
while not stop:

    # check if a button was pressed
    number = get_input(dev)
```

```
        # if a button was pressed, number will not be None
        if number != None:
            # check if number is 0
            if number == 0:
                # make the while loop stop if number is 0
                stop = True
            # if the number is not 0, play the sound
            else:
                sounds[number].play()

# close the Display
disp.close()
```

noisemaker_keyboard.py

```
from pygaze.keyboard import Keyboard
from pygaze.sound import Sound
from pygaze.display import Display

# initialise a Display instance
# (required for the Keyboard to work)
disp = Display()

# create a range of numbers
numbers = range(0,10)
# turn the numbers from integer values into strings
numbers = map(str, numbers)
# create a Keyboard instance
dev = Keyboard(keylist=numbers)

# definition of a function to get user input
def get_input(device):

    # wait for a button press for about 10 ms
    key, presstime = device.get_key(timeout=10)

    # check if a key was pressed
    # (this results in a value that is not None)
    if key != None:
        # convert the key name (a string) into an integer
        key = int(key)
    # return the key name (or None)
    return key

# create a dict with the frequency for each button
freqs = {1:440, 2:494, 3:523, 4:587, 5:659,
    6:698, 7:784, 8:880, 9:988}

# create an empty dict for the sounds
sounds = {}
# loop through the keys of the freqs dict
for button in freqs.keys():
```

```
     ⎵⎵⎵⎵ # create a new Sound instance with the right frequency
     ⎵⎵⎵⎵ sounds[button] = Sound(osc='sine', freq=freqs[button], \
     ⎵⎵⎵⎵ ⎵⎵⎵⎵ length=250, attack=10, decay=10)

# run a while loop until
stop = False
while not stop:

     ⎵⎵⎵⎵ # check if a button was pressed
     ⎵⎵⎵⎵ number = get_input(dev)
     ⎵⎵⎵⎵ # if a button was pressed, number will not be None
     ⎵⎵⎵⎵ if number != None:
     ⎵⎵⎵⎵ ⎵⎵⎵⎵ # check if number is 0
     ⎵⎵⎵⎵ ⎵⎵⎵⎵ if number == 0:
     ⎵⎵⎵⎵ ⎵⎵⎵⎵ ⎵⎵⎵⎵ # make the while loop stop if number is 0
     ⎵⎵⎵⎵ ⎵⎵⎵⎵ ⎵⎵⎵⎵ stop = True
     ⎵⎵⎵⎵ ⎵⎵⎵⎵ # if the number is not 0, play the sound
     ⎵⎵⎵⎵ ⎵⎵⎵⎵ else:
     ⎵⎵⎵⎵ ⎵⎵⎵⎵ ⎵⎵⎵⎵ sounds[number].play()

# close the Display
disp.close()
```

Chapter 6: Analysing behaviour

Pygaze

analysis.py

```
import os
import numpy
from matplotlib import pyplot
from scipy.stats import ttest_rel

# get the path to the current folder
DIR = os.path.dirname(os.path.abspath(__file__))
# construct the path to the data folder
DATADIR = os.path.join(DIR, 'data')

# construct a path to the output directory
OUTDIR = os.path.join(DIR, 'output')
# check if the output folder does not exist
if not os.path.isdir(OUTDIR):
     ⎵⎵⎵⎵ # only create an output directory if it doesn't exist yet
     ⎵⎵⎵⎵ os.mkdir(OUTDIR)

# construct a path to the individual output directory
IOUTDIR = os.path.join(OUTDIR, 'individual')
# check if the individual output folder exists
if not os.path.isdir(IOUTDIR):
```

```
      # create an individual output directory
      os.mkdir(IOUTDIR)

# define the number of participants
N = 10
# create an empty multi-dimensional array to store data
all_rt = numpy.zeros((2, 2, N))
all_acc = numpy.zeros((2, 2, N))

# loop through all participant numbers
for pnr in range(0, N):

      # construct the name of your data file
      datafile = os.path.join(DATADIR, 'pp%d.txt' % (pnr))

      # load the raw contents of the data file
      raw - numpy.loadtxt(datafile, dtype=str, unpack=True)

      # create new empty dict
      data = {}

      # loop through all vectors in raw
      for i in range(len(raw)):
            # the first index of each array is the variable name
            varname = raw[i][0]
            # try to convert the values to numbers
            try:
                  values = raw[i][1:].astype(float)
            # if conversion to numbers fails, do not convert
            except:
                  values = raw[i][1:]
            # create a new entry in the data dict
            # and make it hold the values
            data[varname] = values

      # make Boolean vectors for valid and invalid trials
      sel = {}
      sel['valid'] = data['valid'] == 1
      sel['invalid'] = data['valid'] == 0
      # make Boolean vectors for 100 and 900 ms SOAs
      sel[100] = data['soa'] == 100
      sel[900] = data['soa'] == 900

      # create an empty dict to hold descriptives
      descr = {}

      # loop through all SOAs
      for soa in [100, 900]:
            # create a new empty dict within the descr dict
            descr[soa] = {}
            # loop through all validities
            for val in ['valid', 'invalid']:
```

```
                            # nest another empty dict within descr
                            descr[soa][val] = {}
                            # calculate statistics
                            rt_m = numpy.median(data['RT'][sel[soa] & sel[val]])
                            rt_sd = numpy.std(data['RT'][sel[soa] & sel[val]])
                            rt_sem = rt_sd / numpy.sqrt(len(data['RT'][sel[soa] \
                            & sel[val]]))
                            acc_m = numpy.mean(data['correct'][sel[soa] \
                            & sel[val]])
                            # store the calculated values in descr
                            descr[soa][val]['rt_m'] = rt_m
                            descr[soa][val]['rt_sd'] = rt_sd
                            descr[soa][val]['rt_sem'] = rt_sem
                            descr[soa][val]['acc_m'] = acc_m

        # create a new figure with two subplots
        fig, (ax100, ax900) = pyplot.subplots(nrows=1, ncols=2, \
                sharey=True, figsize=(19.2, 10.8), dpi=100.0)

        # define the bar plot parameters
        width = 0.4
        intdist = 0.1
        # define the starting position (left edge) of the first bar
        barpos = 0.1

        # define the bar colours
        cols = {'valid':'#4e9a06', 'invalid':'#ce5c00'}

        for val in ['valid', 'invalid']:
                # draw the 100 ms SOA median reaction time
                ax100.bar(barpos, descr[100][val]['rt_m'], \
                        width=width, yerr=descr[100][val]['rt_sem'], \
                        color=cols[val], ecolor='black', label=val)
                # draw the 900 ms SOA median reaction time
                ax900.bar(barpos, descr[900][val]['rt_m'], \
                        width=width, yerr=descr[900][val]['rt_sem'], \
                        color=cols[val], ecolor='black', label=val)
                # update the bar position
                barpos += width + intdist

        # add y-axis label to the left plot
        ax100.set_ylabel('median reaction time (ms)')
        # add a legend to the right axis
        ax900.legend(loc='upper right')
        # hide x-axes
        ax100.get_xaxis().set_visible(False)
        ax900.get_xaxis().set_visible(False)
        # set x-axis limits
        ax100.set_xlim([0, barpos])
        ax900.set_xlim([0, barpos])
        # set y-axis limits
        ax100.set_ylim([100, 1000])
```

```
        ax900.set_ylim([100, 1000])
        # save the figure
        savefilename = os.path.join(IOUTDIR, \
            'reaction_times_%d.png' % (pnr))
        fig.savefig(savefilename)
        pyplot.close(fig)

        # store all median reaction times
        all_rt[0, 0, pnr] = descr[100]['valid']['rt_m']
        all_rt[1, 0, pnr] = descr[100]['invalid']['rt_m']
        all_rt[0, 1, pnr] = descr[900]['valid']['rt_m']
        all_rt[1, 1, pnr] = descr[900]['invalid']['rt_m']
        # store all proportion corrects
        all_acc[0, 0, pnr] = descr[100]['valid']['acc_m']
        all_acc[1, 0, pnr] = descr[100]['invalid']['acc_m']
        all_acc[0, 1, pnr] = descr[900]['valid']['acc_m']
        all_acc[1, 1, pnr] = descr[900]['invalid']['acc_m']

# create a new figure with a two subplots
fig, (rt_ax, acc_ax) = pyplot.subplots(nrows=2, \
    sharex=True, figsize=(19.2, 10.8), dpi=100.0)
# the x-axis will be the SOAs
x = [100, 900]
# the colours the valid and invalid conditions
cols = {'valid':'#4e9a06', 'invalid':'#ce5c00'}

# the y-axes will be the valid and invalid means
rt_valid = numpy.mean(all_rt[0, :, :], axis=1)
rt_invalid = numpy.mean(all_rt[1, :, :], axis=1)
# calculate the SEM (=SD/sqrt(N-1))
rt_valid_sem = numpy.std(all_rt[0,:,:], axis=1) \
    / numpy.sqrt(N - 1)
rt_invalid_sem = numpy.std(all_rt[1,:,:], axis=1) \
    / numpy.sqrt(N - 1)
# plot the means for valid and invalid as lines,
# including error bars for the standard error of the mean
rt_ax.errorbar(x, rt_valid, yerr=rt_valid_sem, \
    color=cols['valid'], ecolor='black', label='valid')
rt_ax.errorbar(x, rt_invalid, yerr=rt_invalid_sem, \
    color=cols['invalid'], ecolor='black', label='invalid')

# add y-axis label
rt_ax.set_ylabel('reaction time (ms)')
# add legend
rt_ax.legend(loc='upper right')

# calculate the accuracy means
acc_valid = numpy.mean(all_acc[0, :, :], axis=1)
acc_invalid = numpy.mean(all_acc[1, :, :], axis=1)
# calculate the SEM (=SD/sqrt(N-1))
acc_valid_sem = numpy.std(all_acc[0,:,:], axis=1) \
    / numpy.sqrt(N - 1)
```

```
acc_invalid_sem = numpy.std(all_acc[1,:,:], axis=1) \
     / numpy.sqrt(N - 1)
# plot the means for valid and invalid as lines,
# including error bars for the standard error of the mean
acc_ax.errorbar(x, acc_valid, yerr=acc_valid_sem, \
     color=cols['valid'], ecolor='black', label='valid')
acc_ax.errorbar(x, acc_invalid, yerr=acc_invalid_sem, \
     color=cols['invalid'], ecolor='black', label='invalid')

# add axis labels
acc_ax.set_xlabel('stimulus onset asynchrony (ms)')
acc_ax.set_ylabel('proportion correct')
# set x limits
acc_ax.set_xlim([0, 1000])
# save the figure as a PNG image
savefilename = os.path.join(OUTDIR, 'averages.png')
fig.savefig(savefilename)

# perform two related-samples t-test
t100, p100 = ttest_rel(all_rt[0,0,:], all_rt[1,0,:])
t900, p900 = ttest_rel(all_rt[0,1,:], all_rt[1,1,:])

print('\nstats report:')
print('SOA 100ms, valid vs invalid: t=%.2f, p=%.3f' % \
     (t100, p100))
print('SOA 900ms, valid vs invalid: t=%.2f, p=%.3f' % \
     (t900, p900))

t100, p100 = ttest_rel(all_acc[0,0,:], all_acc[1,0,:])
t900, p900 = ttest_rel(all_acc[0,1,:], all_acc[1,1,:])
print('SOA 100ms, valid vs invalid: t=%.2f, p=%.3f' % \
     (t100, p100))
print('SOA 900ms, valid vs invalid: t=%.2f, p=%.3f' % \
     (t900, p900))
```

Chapter 7: Analysing traces

Pygaze

analysis.py

```
import numpy
from matplotlib import pyplot
from scipy.stats import ttest_rel
from pygazeanalyser.edfreader import read_edf

# read data file
data = read_edf('ED_pupil.asc', 'PUPIL_TRIALSTART', \
     stop='pupdata_stop')

# create a new dict to contain traces
```

```python
traces = {'black':[], 'white':[]}

# loop through all trials
n_trials = len(data)
for i in range(n_trials):

    # check the trial type
    t0, msg = data[i]['events']['msg'][0]
    if 'black' in msg:
        trialtype = 'black'
    elif 'white' in msg:
        trialtype = 'white'

    # get the timestamps of baseline and monitor change
    t1, msg = data[i]['events']['msg'][1]
    t2, msg = data[i]['events']['msg'][2]
    # turn the timestamps into index numbers
    t1i = numpy.where(data[i]['trackertime'] == t1)[0]
    t2i = numpy.where(data[i]['trackertime'] == t2)[0]

    # get the baseline trace
    baseline = data[i]['size'][t1i:t2i]
    # get the pupil change trace (2000 samples)
    trace = data[i]['size'][t2i:t2i+2000]

    # divide the pupil trace by the baseline median
    trace = trace / numpy.median(baseline)

    # add the trace to the list for this trial type
    traces[trialtype].append(trace)

# convert lists to NumPy arrays
traces['black'] = numpy.array(traces['black'])
traces['white'] = numpy.array(traces['white'])

# create an empty dict to contain mean and SEM
avgs = {'black':{}, 'white':{}}
# loop through both conditions
for con in ['black', 'white']:
    # calculate the number of trials in this condition
    n_trials = len(traces[con])
    # calculate the average trace in this condition
    avgs[con]['M'] = numpy.mean(traces[con], axis=0)
    # calculate the standard deviation in this condition
    sd = numpy.std(traces[con], axis=0)
    # calculate the standard error in this condition
    avgs[con]['SEM'] = sd / numpy.sqrt(n_trials)

# do a t-test on every timepoint
t, p = ttest_rel(traces['black'], traces['white'], axis=0)

# Bonferroni-corrected alpha
```

```
alpha = 0.05 / len(t)

# define the plotting colours
cols = {'black':'#204a87', 'white':'#c4a000'}
# create a new figure with a single axis
fig, ax = pyplot.subplots(figsize=(19.2,10.8), dpi=100.0)

# loop through the conditions
for con in ['black', 'white']:
    # create x-values
    x = range(len(avgs[con]['M']))
    # plot the mean trace
    ax.plot(x, avgs[con]['M'], '-', color=cols[con], \
        label=con)
    # plot the standard error of the mean shading
    y1 = avgs[con]['M'] + avgs[con]['SEM']
    y2 = avgs[con]['M'] - avgs[con]['SEM']
    ax.fill_between(x, y1, y2, color=cols[con], alpha=0.3)

# create y arrays
y1 = numpy.zeros(len(x))
y2 = numpy.ones(len(x)) * 2
# shade significant difference between traces
ax.fill_between(x, y1, y2, where=p<alpha, \
    color='#babdb6', alpha=0.2)

# set axes limits
ax.set_xlim([0, 2000])
ax.set_ylim([0, 2])
# set axis labels
ax.set_xlabel('time (ms)')
ax.set_ylabel('proportional pupil size change')
# add legend
ax.legend(loc='upper left')

fig.savefig('pupil_traces.png')
```

Chapter 8: Eye-tracking experiment

Pygaze

constants.py

```
import os

# The DISPTYPE can be either 'pygame' or 'psychopy'
DISPTYPE = 'pygame'
# The DISPSIZE should match your monitor's resolution!
DISPSIZE = (1920, 1080)

# Set the TRACKERTYPE to the brand you use
```

```
TRACKERTYPE = 'eyelink'
# DUMMYMODE should be True if no tracker is attached
DUMMYMODE = True

# Foreground colour set to white
FGC = (255, 255, 255)
# Background colour set to black
BGC = (0, 0, 0)

# Fixation mark time (milliseconds)
FIXTIME = 2000
# Image time (milliseconds)
IMGTIME = 10000

# Get the path to the current folder
DIR = os.path.dirname(os.path.abspath(__file__))
# Get the path to the image folder
IMGDIR = os.path.join(DIR, 'images')
# Get a list of all image names
IMGNAMES = os.listdir(IMGDIR)
# Sort IMGNAMES in alphabetical order
IMGNAMES.sort()
```

experiment.py

```
import os
from constants import *
from pygaze.display import Display
from pygaze.screen import Screen
from pygaze.keyboard import Keyboard
from pygaze.eyetracker import EyeTracker
import pygaze.libtime as timer

# Initialise a Display to interact with the monitor
disp = Display()

# Initialise a Keyboard to collect key presses
kb = Keyboard(keylist=None, timeout=None)

# Create a Screen for the image task instructions
inscr = Screen()
inscr.draw_text(text='Please look at the images. \
     \n\n(Press any key to begin)', fontsize=24)

# Create a Screen with a central fixation cross
fixscr = Screen()
fixscr.draw_fixation(fixtype='cross', diameter=8)

# Create a Screen to draw images on later
imgscr = Screen()

# Initialise a new EyeTracker
```

```
tracker = EyeTracker(disp)

# Calibrate the eye tracker
tracker.calibrate()

# Feed the instructions to the Display
disp.fill(inscr)
# Show the instructions
disp.show()
# Wait until the participant presses any key
# (Allowing them to read the instructions at their own pace)
kb.get_key()

# Loop through all image names
for imgname in IMGNAMES:

     # Construct the path to the image
     imgpath = os.path.join(IMGDIR, imgname)

     # Draw the image on imgscr
     # (clear imgscr first, to be sure it's clean)
     imgscr.clear()
     imgscr.draw_image(imgpath)

     # Start recording gaze data
     tracker.start_recording()

     # Display a status message on the EyeLink computer
     # (EyeLink only; doesn't do anything for other brands)
     tracker.status_msg('Trial with %s image' % (imgname))

     # Log trial start
     tracker.log('TRIALSTART')

     # Feed the fixation Screen to the Display
     disp.fill(fixscr)
     # Update the monitor to show the fixation mark
     disp.show()
     # Log the fixation onset to the gaze data file
     tracker.log('fixation_onset')
     # Wait for the right duration
     timer.pause(FIXTIME)

     # Feed the image Screen to the Display
     disp.fill(imgscr)
     # Update the monitor to show the image
     disp.show()
     # Log the image onset to the gaze data file
     # Include the image name in the message!
     tracker.log('image_onset, imgname=%s' % (imgname))
     # Wait for the right duration
     timer.pause(IMGTIME)
```

```
    # Clear the Display
    disp.fill()
    # Update the monitor to show a blank screen
    disp.show()
    # Log the image offset
    tracker.log('image_offset')

    # Log the end of the trial
    tracker.log('TRIALEND')
    # Pause recording
    tracker.stop_recording()

# Clear the instructions Screen
inscr.clear()
# Write a new message
inscr.draw_text(text='All done!', fontsize=24)
# Feed the new message to the Display
disp.fill(inscr)
# Show the message
disp.show()
# Wait until the participant presses any key
# (Allowing them to read at their own pace)
kb.get_key()

# Close the connection to the eye tracker
# (This will also close the log file!)
tracker.close()

# Close the Display
disp.close()
```

Chapter 8: Eye-tracking analysis

Pygaze

constants.py

```
import os

# The DISPTYPE can be either 'pygame' or 'psychopy'
DISPTYPE = 'pygame'
# The DISPSIZE should match your monitor's resolution!
DISPSIZE = (1024, 768)

# Set the TRACKERTYPE to the brand you use
TRACKERTYPE = 'eyelink'
# DUMMYMODE should be True if no tracker is attached
DUMMYMODE = True

# Foreground colour set to white
FGC = (255, 255, 255)
```

```
# Background colour set to black
BGC = (0, 0, 0)

# Fixation mark time (milliseconds)
FIXTIME = 2000
# Image time (milliseconds)
IMGTIME = 10000

# Get the path to the current folder
DIR = os.path.dirname(os.path.abspath(__file__))
# Get the path to the image folder
IMGDIR = os.path.join(DIR, 'images')
# Get a list of all image names
IMGNAMES = os.listdir(IMGDIR)
# Sort IMGNAMES in alphabetical order
IMGNAMES.sort()
```

analysis.py

```
import os

from constants import *

from pygazeanalyser.edfreader import read_edf
from pygazeanalyser import gazeplotter

from matplotlib.pyplot import close

# Construct the name of the output directory
OUTPUTDIR = os.path.join(DIR, 'output')

# Check if the output directory exists yet
if not os.path.isdir(OUTPUTDIR):
␣␣␣␣ # If the output directory does not exist yet, make it
␣␣␣␣ os.mkdir(OUTPUTDIR)

# Read the data
data = read_edf('default.asc', 'image_onset', \
␣␣␣␣ stop='image_offset')

# Get the amount of trials in this dataset
ntrials = len(data)

# Loop through all trials
for trialnr in range(ntrials):

␣␣␣␣ # Get the image name
␣␣␣␣ imgname = IMGNAMES[trialnr]

␣␣␣␣ # Get the path to the image
```

```
     imgpath = os.path.join(IMGDIR, imgname)

     # Get the fixations in this trial
     fixations = data[trialnr]['events']['Efix']

     # Delete the first fixation
     fixations.pop(0)

     # Get the raw x and y gaze coordinates
     x = data[trialnr]['x']
     y = data[trialnr]['y']

     # Plot the fixations
     savename = 'fixations_%s' % imgname
     savepath = os.path.join(OUTPUTDIR, savename)
     fig = gazeplotter.draw_fixations(fixations, DISPSIZE, \
          durationsize=True, durationcolour=False, \
          imagefile=imgpath, savefilename=savepath)
     close(fig)

  # Plot a heatmap
     savename = 'heatmap_%s' % imgname
     savepath = os.path.join(OUTPUTDIR, savename)
     fig = gazeplotter.draw_heatmap(fixations, DISPSIZE, \
          imagefile=imgpath, savefilename=savepath)
     close(fig)
```

REFERENCES

Dalmaijer, E. S., Mathôt, S., & Van der Stigchel, S. (2014). PyGaze: An open-source, cross-platform toolbox for minimal-effort programming of eyetracking experiments. *Behavior Research Methods*, 46(4), 913–921. http://doi.org/10.3758/s13428-013-0422-2

Damian, M. F. (2010). Does variability in human performance outweigh imprecision in response devices such as computer keyboards? *Behavior Research Methods*, 42(1), 205–211. http://doi.org/10.3758/BRM.42.1.205

Hunter, J. D. (2007). Matplotlib: A 2D graphics environment. *Computing in Science & Engineering*, 9(3), 90–95. http://doi.org/10.1109/MCSE.2007.55

Mathôt, S., Dalmaijer, E., Grainger, J., & Van der Stigchel, S. (2014). The pupillary light response reflects exogenous attention and inhibition of return. *Journal of Vision*, 14(14), 1–9. http://doi.org/10.1167/14.14.7

Mathôt, S., Schreij, D., & Theeuwes, J. (2012). OpenSesame: An open-source, graphical experiment builder for the social sciences. *Behavior Research Methods*, 44(2), 314–324. http://doi.org/10.3758/s13428-011-0168-7

Oliphant, T. E. (2007). Python for scientific computing. *Computing in Science & Engineering*, 9(3), 10–20. http://doi.org/10.1109/MCSE.2007.58

Peirce, J. W. (2007). PsychoPy – Psychophysics software in Python. *Journal of Neuroscience Methods*, 162(1–2), 8–13. http://doi.org/10.1016/j.jneumeth.2006.11.017

Peirce, J. W. (2009). Generating stimuli for neuroscience using PsychoPy. *Frontiers in Neuroinformatics*, 2. http://doi.org/10.3389/neuro.11.010.2008

Posner, M. I. (1980). Orienting of attention. *Quarterly Journal of Experimental Psychology*, 32(1), 3–25. http://doi.org/10.1080/00335558008248231

Wallace, D. J., Greenberg, D. S., Sawinski, J., Rulla, S., Notaro, G., & Kerr, J. N. D. (2013). Rats maintain an overhead binocular field at the expense of constant fusion. *Nature*, 498(7452), 65–69. http://doi.org/10.1038/nature12153

INDEX

Taylor & Francis eBooks

Helping you to choose the right eBooks for your Library

Add Routledge titles to your library's digital collection today. Taylor and Francis ebooks contains over 50,000 titles in the Humanities, Social Sciences, Behavioural Sciences, Built Environment and Law.

Choose from a range of subject packages or create your own!

Benefits for you

» Free MARC records
» COUNTER-compliant usage statistics
» Flexible purchase and pricing options
» All titles DRM-free.

Benefits for your user

» Off-site, anytime access via Athens or referring URL
» Print or copy pages or chapters
» Full content search
» Bookmark, highlight and annotate text
» Access to thousands of pages of quality research at the click of a button.

REQUEST YOUR **FREE** INSTITUTIONAL TRIAL TODAY	**Free Trials Available** We offer free trials to qualifying academic, corporate and government customers.

eCollections – Choose from over 30 subject eCollections, including:

Archaeology	Language Learning
Architecture	Law
Asian Studies	Literature
Business & Management	Media & Communication
Classical Studies	Middle East Studies
Construction	Music
Creative & Media Arts	Philosophy
Criminology & Criminal Justice	Planning
Economics	Politics
Education	Psychology & Mental Health
Energy	Religion
Engineering	Security
English Language & Linguistics	Social Work
Environment & Sustainability	Sociology
Geography	Sport
Health Studies	Theatre & Performance
History	Tourism, Hospitality & Events

For more information, pricing enquiries or to order a free trial, please contact your local sales team: www.tandfebooks.com/page/sales